THINKING ABOUT F[

Peter van Inwagen, author of the classic book *An Essay on Free Will* (1983), has established himself over the last forty years as a leading figure in the philosophical debate about the problem of free will. This volume presents eleven influential essays from throughout his career, as well as two new and previously unpublished essays, "The Problem of Fr** W*ll" and "Ability." The essays include discussions of determinism, moral responsibility, "Frankfurt counterexamples," the meaning of "the ability to do otherwise," and the very definition of free will, as well as critiques of writings on the topic by Daniel Dennett and David Lewis. An introduction by the author discusses the history of his thinking about free will. The volume will be a valuable resource for those looking to engage with van Inwagen's significant contributions to this perennially important topic.

PETER VAN INWAGEN is the John Cardinal O'Hara Professor of Philosophy at the University of Notre Dame. He is the author of *An Essay on Free Will* (1983), and his numerous other publications include *Material Beings* (1990), *Ontology, Identity, and Modality: Essays in Metaphysics* (Cambridge 2002), *The Problem of Evil* (2006), and *Existence: Essays in Ontology* (Cambridge 2014).

THINKING ABOUT
FREE WILL

Peter van Inwagen

University of Notre Dame, Indiana

CAMBRIDGE
UNIVERSITY PRESS

CAMBRIDGE
UNIVERSITY PRESS

University Printing House, Cambridge CB2 8BS, United Kingdom

One Liberty Plaza, 20th Floor, New York, NY 10006, USA

477 Williamstown Road, Port Melbourne, VIC 3207, Australia

4843/24, 2nd Floor, Ansari Road, Daryaganj, Delhi - 110002, India

79 Anson Road, #06-04/06, Singapore 079906

Cambridge University Press is part of the University of Cambridge.

It furthers the University's mission by disseminating knowledge in the pursuit of education, learning, and research at the highest international levels of excellence.

www.cambridge.org
Information on this title: www.cambridge.org/9781107166509
10.1017/9781316711101

First published 2017

Printed in the United Kingdom by Clays, St Ives plc

A catalog record for this publication is available from the British Library

Library of Congress Cataloging in Publication Data

ISBN 978-1-107-16650-9 Hardback
ISBN 978-1-316-61765-6 Paperback

For Lisette

Contents

Preface

Essays I–II of this collection are those of my previously published papers on free will[1] that I consider worthy of being reprinted. The essays are numbered chronologically. I have not included essays that were published before *An Essay on Free Will*[2] and whose text was incorporated with little change into that book.[3] "Ability and Responsibility" (Essay 1) is the only essay in this collection that was published before *An Essay on Free Will.*

The unnumbered introductory essay, "Van Inwagen on Free Will," is a revised and updated version of an essay of the same title that was originally published in 2004.[4] It contains a history of my thinking about free will, and describes the place of the essays in the present volume in that history.

Essay 14 ("Ability") appears for the first time in this volume. Essay 13 ("The Problem of Fr** W*ll") may well appear for the first time in this volume. It is published more or less simultaneously here and in Hugh McCann, ed., *Free Will and Classical Theism*, published by or forthcoming from Oxford University Press. Essay 12 ("Preface to the French Translation of *An Essay on Free Will*") appears for the first time in English in this volume.

SOUTH BEND, INDIANA

---

1 I use the phrase "free will" because there is no other word or short phrase that can be used to describe, or even to indicate, the common theme of these essays. (And the phrase does appear in all but one of the essays, and in the titles of several of them.) I now regard this phrase as no longer having a clear sense, for reasons I set out in the essay that is Chapter 13.

2 Oxford: Clarendon Press, 1983.

3 Much of the content of Chapter 1 ("Ability and Responsibility") appeared in abbreviated form in *An Essay on Free Will* ([Oxford University Press, 1983], pp. 162–182). I thought, however, that it was worth reprinting "Ability and Responsibility." The treatment of "Frankfurt counterexamples" (Harry Frankfurt's famous counterexamples to "The Principle of Alternative Possibilities") in *An Essay on Free Will* has been largely ignored. It is my hope that the original paper's more detailed presentation of my way of treating Frankfurt counterexamples will call attention to it.

4 In J. K. Campbell, M. O'Rourke, and D. Shier (eds.), *Freedom and Determinism* (Cambridge, MA: MIT Press, 2004).

Introduction
Van Inwagen on Free Will

I can remember very clearly the first time van Inwagen encountered the problem of free will. In the autumn of 1965 he was talking with a fellow graduate student at the University of Rochester, one Myles Brand, and made some remark that presupposed the incompatibility of free will and determinism. Brand told him – second-year graduate student to first-year graduate student – that most philosophers believed that free will and determinism were compatible, and outlined some of the currently popular arguments for that position. As Athena from the head of Zeus, the argument that van Inwagen was to publish ten years later in "The Incompatibility of Free Will and Determinism"[1] sprang from his head pretty much full-grown – although it made its entrance into the world by way of his ever-active mouth and not by Athena's rather more unorthodox route.

The argument had it roots in the following reflections. If free will and determinism coexist, then someone is able to do something not contained in that one possible future that is consistent both with the past and the laws of nature. Suppose that Alice, an inhabitant of a deterministic world, is able to do something she is not in fact going to do; suppose, to be specific, that although she is going to remain a prisoner, she is able to escape from her prison. Her ability to escape can be looked upon as an ability to divert the river of coming events into a channel through which it is not in fact going to flow; to realize, that is, or to cause to be actual, a possible future that is not the future that lies before her, to cause to be actual one

---

This introductory essay is a revision of my "Van Inwagen on Free Will," a history of my thinking about free will that was published in 2004 (in *Freedom and Determinism*, ed. J. K. Campbell, M. O'Rourke, and D. Shier [Cambridge, MA: MIT Press, 2004], pp. 213–230). The revisions bring the history up to date.

[1] *Philosophical Studies* 27 (1975): 185–199. Reprinted in *Free Will*, ed. Gary Watson (Oxford University Press, 1983); in *Free Will*, ed. Derk Pereboom (Indianapolis, IN: Hackett, 1997); and in *Agency and Responsibility: Essays on the Metaphysics of Freedom*, ed. Laura Waddell Ekstrom (Boulder, CO: Westview Press, 2000).

of those possible futures in which she escapes. And what would these possible but non-actual futures be like? Let's say that the past *of* a possible but non-actual future is that possible past that would be the actual past if that future were the actual future. Any given future in which Alice escapes must either be a future whose past is the actual past and which is discontinuous with that past, or a future that is continuous with its past but whose past is not the actual past (a past different from the actual past all the way back to the Big Bang), or, finally, a future in which the world is governed by laws of nature that are not the actual laws. But Alice can bring about futures of none of these sorts. If it is insufficiently evident as it stands that she can bring about none of these futures, here is an argument. Let 'Clio' be a proper name for the actual past – thus, when I imagine, as I am about to, Alice using the name 'Clio' in another possible world, I imagine her referring to the past as it is in our world, not the past as it is in hers. Similarly, let 'Nomos' be a proper name for the actual laws of nature (which, remember, we are assuming to be deterministic). It would seem that if Alice is able to escape, she must be able in some sense to cause the actuality of or bring about or realize a future in which she could say, and in so saying speak truly, one of the following three things:

> There has been a causal break; the present state of affairs is not continuous with the past

> The present is continuous with the past, but that past is not Clio; it is some other past (a past different from Clio all the way back to the Big Bang)

> The laws of nature are not Nomos, but some other set of laws.

And, obviously, Alice is not able to get herself into a future in which she can say any of these things and be right.

When van Inwagen got round to writing down the argument that had occurred to him in his conversation with Brand – he first did this in a doctoral thesis he wrote under the supervision of Richard Taylor (*de jure*) and Keith Lehrer (*de facto*) – the argument he wrote down did not *look* much like the argument I have just set out. (It looked very much like the argument he would later publish in "The Incompatibility of Free Will and Determinism.") Nevertheless, the central idea of both arguments was the same, and they no doubt stand or fall together.

When van Inwagen had got his first academic job and was trying to publish this argument, he found it extraordinarily hard to do so. The reason was simple: the conclusion of the argument was known to be false. The unanimous position of the referees whose reports were enclosed with the rejection letters could have been expressed in the following words, which I take from an essay by Donald Davidson, words as well known as they are ungrammatical:

> I shall not be directly concerned with such arguments [*sc.* arguments for the incompatiblity of free will and determinism], since I know of none that is more than superficially plausible. Hobbes, Locke, Hume, Moore, Schlick, Ayer, Stevenson, and a host of others have done what can be done, or ought ever to have been needed, to remove the confusions that can make determinism seem to oppose freedom.[2]

It's not that no one was an incompatibilist in those days, of course. The same volume that contained the essay from which my quotation from Davidson is taken also contained David Wiggins's "Toward a Responsible Libertarianism." Roderick M. Chisholm was an incompatibilist, as were Richard Taylor, Carl Ginet, Elizabeth Anscombe, and Peter Geach. Still, it can hardly be denied that incompatibilists were thin on the ground in the sixties and early seventies.

Eventually, however, van Inwagen was able to publish two papers in which he argued for the incompatibility of free will and determinism. (He has always suspected that "The Incompatibility of Free Will and Determinism," which had been rejected by many journals, was accepted by *Philosophical Studies* only because Sellars chose Keith Lehrer as its referee, but he has never known whether this suspicion was correct.) His other paper on the subject, "A Formal Approach to the Problem of Free Will and Determinism,"[3] had, in respect of publication, the advantage of making use of the then new and exciting apparatus of possible worlds. (This paper was strongly influenced by Montague's "Deterministic Theories";[4] the impetus for writing it was a suggestion of Rolf Eberle's.)

Van Inwagen summed up his thought on free will on his 1983 book *An Essay on Free Will*,[5] and has pretty much avoided learning anything about the problem since – other than by sitting about and thinking it over. (The publication of this book by Oxford University Press was due to the good offices of Tony Kenny and Derek Parfit, neither of whom could have had any sympathy whatever with its content, and van Inwagen has always

---

[2] "Freedom to Act," in Ted Honderich (ed.), *Essays on Freedom of Action* (London: Routledge & Kegan Paul, 1973), pp. 137–156. The quoted passage occurs in the opening paragraph of the essay.
[3] *Theoria* 40 (1974): Part 1, 9–22.
[4] Richmond H. Thomason (ed.), *Formal Philosophy: Selected Papers of Richard Montague* (New Haven, CT: Yale University Press, 1974), pp. 303–359.
[5] Oxford: Clarendon Press, 1983.

been grateful to them for their generosity and has tried to imitate it. He has done his best to learn from them the hard lesson that a philosophical book that he regards as thoroughly wrong-headed can nevertheless be a good book.) Van Inwagen likes to think that this book bears a significant share of the responsibility for the fact that incompatibilists are now much more common than they were thirty or forty years ago. In a paper that he read at a conference in the early nineties, van Inwagen made a remark to the effect that compatibilism was the standard view among philosophers. Michael Slote, who was in the audience, said that he thought that, on the contrary, incompatibilism had become the standard view, or at least the majority view. A few years later, van Inwagen asked Ted Warfield whether he thought that was right. Warfield, who comes as close as is humanly possible to knowing what every analytical philosopher thinks about anything, replied that he thought that the majority of analytical philosophers who had actually worked on the free-will problem were incompatibilists, and that the majority of analytical philosophers (full stop) were compatibilists.[6]

There was one passage in *An Essay on Free Will* that, after the publication of the book, van Inwagen became more and more worried about

---

[6] According to the PhilPapers Survey (conducted online in late 2009; see David Bourget and David J. Chalmers, "What Do Philosophers Believe?," *Philosophical Studies* 170 [2014]: 465–500), the philosophers who responded to the survey responded in the following proportions with respect to four options regarding the problem of free will and determinism:

> Compatibilism: Accept (34.8 %), Lean toward (24.3 %)
>
> Libertarianism: Accept (7.7 %), Lean toward (6.0 %)
>
> No free will: Lean toward (6.6 %), Accept (5.7 %)
>
> Other: Agnostic/undecided (4.1 %), The question is too unclear to answer (2.8%)

I would make the following points: (i) By 2009, philosophers no longer used the terms 'free will', 'compatibilism' and 'libertarianism' consistently. For example, by 2009, many philosophers had come to use 'compatibilism' as a name for the thesis that *moral responsibility* is compatible with determinism, and had come to use 'free will' for the thesis that human agents have access to "whatever kinds of alternative possibilities are required for moral responsibility." In the thesis advanced in the text I meant this by 'free will': agents have free will if they are sometimes able to act otherwise than they do, and by 'compatiblism' I mean the thesis that free will in that sense is compatible with determinism. A great many philosophers who would now call themselves 'compatibilists' do not reject what I call 'incompatibilism'; these philosophers would say that the question whether free will in the "able to act otherwise sense" is compatible with determinism is no longer thought to be an interesting question, owing to the fact (they suppose it to be a fact) that we now know that free will in *that* sense is not required for moral responsibility. (ii) There is no way to know what proportion of the respondents to the PhilPapers Survey "actually work on" (i.e., devote a significant proportion of their published work to) the problem of free will. This would, of course, be a rather small proportion of philosophers, and, very likely, a rather small proportion of the respondents. Even if all the respondents who said that they accepted or leaned toward compatibilism meant 'compatibilism' in *my* sense (and I suspect that a large proportion of them did not), I do not find the result "accept or lean towards compatibilism: 59.1%" surprising or in tension with the thesis I advanced in the text.

as time passed.[7] (His worries were aggravated by pointed questions from Alex Rosenberg, and also, curiously enough, by a science-fiction novel by Larry Niven called *Protector* – a novel about which van Inwagen is ready to tell you considerably more than you want to know.) Van Inwagen had said in that passage that although no one was able to render a *physical* law false, it seemed that if there were *psychological* laws, and if we had free will, we had to be able to render *these* laws false. But that raises the question: If one has it within one's power to render some proposition false, in what sense can that proposition be a law? As a sort of schematic example of a psychological law, van Inwagen proposed, 'No one who has received moral training of type A in early childhood ever spreads lying rumors about his professional colleagues in order to advance his career'. He imagined someone asking, "Why does the pattern of behavior described in this statement occur if people don't *have* to conform to it?" He answered this question as follows: 'Perhaps it is just the people who have received moral training of type A in early childhood who *see the point* in not spreading lying rumors about their colleagues'.

He gradually came to see, or to think he saw, that this response to the difficulty was facile, and that the difficulty he had his finger on was broader and deeper than the original puzzle about psychological laws. He gradually came to the conclusion that if one was faced with the necessity of doing either A or B, and that if one saw every reason to do A and no reason whatever to do B, then one would simply not be able to do B. From this conclusion it was no great leap to the slightly stronger conclusion that, if one was faced with a choice between A and B, and one was aware of considerations that could be brought in support of both alternatives, and if the considerations that supported A seemed to one clearly and decisively to outweigh the considerations that supported B, then one would simply not be able to do B. Van Inwagen defended, in "When Is the Will Free?,"[8] the thesis that the general principles about ability that lead philosophers to incompatibilism should lead anyone who accepts them to accept these conclusions as well. And he went on to argue that, since occasions that call for serious deliberation – occasions, that is, on which one is choosing between alternatives and it does not seem to one that (once all the purely factual questions have been settled) that the reasons that favor either alternative are clearly the stronger – at best only a small proportion of the occasions on which we make a choice are occasions on which we make a *free* choice. ("At best" because there may be no free will at all; perhaps determinism is

---

[7] See pp. 63–64.   [8] Chapter 5 of the present volume.

true, or perhaps – as Broad believed – free action is incompatible both with determinism and indeterminism and is therefore a self-contradictory idea.) Van Inwagen concluded that no action is free unless it is the outcome of deliberation in which one considers reasons that support that act, reasons that support various alternative acts, and in the course of which one finds no obvious answer to the question, "Which set of reasons should prevail?" To take one example among many different sorts of possible example of the consequences of this position, if you answer the telephone "automatically," if you answer the telephone without so much as considering the question whether you should answer it, your act is not a free act: you could not have done otherwise than answer the telephone; you were not *able* to let it ring till it fell silent; it was *not within your power* not to raise the receiver.

After presenting arguments for this thesis, van Inwagen went on to attempt to show that it does not, or does not obviously, have a certain untoward consequence that it might be thought to have. He contended that from the premise that at best a very small proportion of our acts are free acts, the conclusion does not follow that (at best) only a very small proportion of our ascriptions of moral responsibility are correct. For, he maintained, although there is an inseverable connection between free will and moral responsibility, this connection, inseverable though it be, can be stretched exceeding fine. An example will illustrate his point. Suppose a man is driving drunk and that a pedestrian suddenly looms before him. He attempts to swerve, but too late: he hits and kills the pedestrian because his reflexes are impaired by alcohol. Compare his case with the case of a sober, able, and alert driver whose car strikes and kills a pedestrian in cir-cumstances in which swerving in time to avoid the pedestrian would have required a reaction time smaller than that allowed by the speed of prop-agation of human neural impulses. In neither case was the driver able to avoid hitting the pedestrian who suddenly loomed before him, but when we consider the former case, we hold the driver morally responsible for the pedestrian's death, and when we consider the latter case we do not.

The relevant difference, of course, is that the man whose reflexes were impaired by drink, was, so to speak, *able* to avoid being unable to avoid hitting the pedestrian, and the sober and alert driver was *unable* to avoid being unable to avoid hitting the pedestrian. At the moment he first saw the pedestrian, the drunk driver was unable to avoid hitting him, but he had earlier been able, or so we should suppose if we were judge or jury, to avoid driving with the impaired reflexes that were the cause of his fatal inability at the time of the accident. Van Inwagen suggested that this sort of case could serve as a model for the relation between ability and responsibility.

Here is a second case, a case in which the inseverable connection between ability and responsibility, though it remains unsevered, as inseverable connections do, is stretched considerably further than it is in most philosophical examples concerning moral responsibility and the ability to do otherwise. Consider a man who is, in middle age, a corrupt politician and is, owing to his corrupted nature, unable to refuse bribes when he believes there is no significant likelihood of the bribery coming to light. That is how he is, but how did he get that way? Suppose the answer is this: As a young man, he made a certain series of free choices, choices preceded by genuine deliberation, which collectively had the effect of establishing him in settled and unbreakable habits of venality. Van Inwagen argued – guided, I suppose, by Aristotle – that this politician can properly be held morally responsible for the baleful effects on the public welfare of the informal services he renders to his political cronies in return for money. And this despite the fact that he is unable, in middle age, to reject the bribes he is offered. He can properly be held responsible for, say, the deaths of the four children in the fire in the building that wasn't up to code, because he could, as a young man, have avoided becoming the sort of man who would be unable to resist the bribe offered by the slumlord who owned the building.

Several philosophers have disputed van Inwagen's conclusion that the principles that lead philosophers to incompatibilism entail that free acts, if they exist at all, are extremely rare, but van Inwagen has never been able to see any force in their arguments. Although he has published answers to them,[9] he is of the opinion that no answers were needed; that his original arguments were untouched by the arguments of his critics. One philosopher, who generally disagrees with van Inwagen about free will, Dan Dennett, agrees with van Inwagen that these arguments are unanswerable. As Dan put it, referring to "When Is the Will Free?," "Thank you, Peter, for the lovely *reductio* of incompatibilism."

Now van Inwagen's arguments for this conclusion, whether they are good or bad, presuppose that there is an inseverable connection between moral responsibility and the power to do otherwise, however flexible this connection may be. The inseverable connection is this: If one is morally responsible for anything, it follows logically that one has had a free choice about something. But Harry Frankfurt has presented a famous argument that some have taken to refute this thesis.[10] A significant proportion of

[9] "When the Will Is Not Free," *Philosophical Studies* 75 (1994): 95–113.
[10] See his classic essay "The Principle of Alternate Possibilities," *Journal of Philosophy* 66 (1969): 829–839.

van Inwagen's work on free will has been devoted to Frankfurt's argument. And Frankfurt's argument is important. If it is indeed true that one might be morally responsible for various things, despite one's *never* having been able to do otherwise than one has done, then the problem of free will loses much of its interest – for the simple reason that most people would find the thesis that we lack free will much less unappealing if this thesis could be shown not to entail that we can never be held to moral account for anything.

I have said that Frankfurt's argument has been taken by some to show that it is possible for one to be morally responsible for something even though one has never been able to do otherwise. The actual conclusion of Frankfurt's argument, however, is this: The so-called Principle of Alternative Possibilities is false, or at least not a necessary truth. (I'll call it the Principle of *Alternative* Possibilities. Frankfurt has recently presented an ill-advised defense of his use of the adjective 'alternate' in his name for the principle. It is, I concede, uncharitable of me to mention this. I'll attempt to atone for my lapse by very charitably saying nothing further about it.) This is the Principle of Alternative Possibilities:

A person is morally responsible for what he has done only if he could have done otherwise.

Van Inwagen has always thought that Frankfurt's argument – which, of course, consists in the presentation of a certain sort of counterexample to the Principle of Alternative Possibilities – has a great deal of force and has never been shown conclusively to be mistaken. His position has never been that Frankfurt's proposed counterexamples to the Principle of Alternative Possibilities fail; his position has been rather that even if these counterexamples succeed, even if the Principle of Alternative Possibilities is false, the existence of moral responsibility nonetheless requires the existence of free will.

I have used the qualified phrases "has a great deal of force" and "has never been shown conclusively to be mistaken" because, although van Inwagen is inclined to think that Frankfurt's counterexamples show that the Principle of Alternative Possibilities is false if it is meaningful at all, he's also inclined to think that it's meaningless. I'll briefly say something about why he's inclined to think it's meaningless. If the Principle of Alternative Possibilities is meaningful, the following must be one of the particular statements the general principle endorses:

Bill is morally responsible for lying under oath only if he could have done otherwise.

Van Inwagen has never been able to convince himself that he understands sentences like 'Bill is morally responsible for lying under oath'. It has always seemed reasonably plain to him that what one is morally responsible for is not one's acts but the *consequences* of one's acts, or, more exactly, *certain* of the consequences of one's acts – for no one would suppose that one could be responsible for *all* the consequences of one's acts. (When I say 'it has always seemed plain to him', I mean that it has seemed plain to him since he first encountered the idea that what a person is morally responsible for is the consequences of his acts and not the acts themselves.)[11] And the consequences of one's acts, it would seem, are members of the same ontological category or categories as the consequences of anything that takes place within the causal and temporal order; whatever ontological category one thinks the consequences of a person's acts should be assigned to, one should assign them to the same category or categories as the consequences of an earthquake or a scientific discovery or a rise in the prime lending rate. There would seem to be two serious candidates for this categorial office: "concrete event" (for example, Caesar's death), on the one hand, and something proposition-like on the other, "fact," perhaps, or "state of affairs" (for example, the fact that Caesar disregarded the soothsayer's warning, or Caesar's having chosen to believe that Brutus' strong republican sentiments would never overcome his friendship with and personal loyalty to Caesar).

Now if what one is responsible for is certain of the consequences of one's acts (and if, for example, one's telling a lie and the fact that one has lied do not count as "consequences" of themselves), then it is doubtful whether 'Bill is responsible for lying under oath' makes sense, and it is therefore doubtful whether the Principle of Alternative Possibilities makes sense, doubtful whether the sentence that formulates it means anything. Van Inwagen, as I have said, has long doubted whether the Principle of Alternative Possibilities does make sense. But he has also been fairly sure that if he's wrong about this and the sentence 'A person is morally responsible for what he has done only if he could have done otherwise' does express some proposition, the proposition it expresses is false, and that Frankfurt's counterexamples show this.

To recapitulate, van Inwagen thinks that (a) the Principle of Alternative Possibilities is either nonsensical or false, and that (b) moral responsibility

---

[11] He first encountered it when he read P. H. Nowell-Smith's essay "Action and Responsibility," in Myles Brand and Douglas Walton (eds.), *Action Theory* (Dordrecht: Reidel, 1976), pp. 311–322. (See especially p. 315.)

nevertheless requires free will – that if anyone is morally responsible for anything, there must be something that person had a free choice about.

He has defended the latter thesis by presenting other principles than the Principle of Alternative Possibilities that have the consequence that moral responsibility requires free will, and presenting arguments designed to show that these other principles seem to be true and cannot be refuted by counterexamples in the style of Frankfurt's counterexamples to the Principle of Alternative Possibilities.[12] One of these principles is

> A person is morally responsible for a certain state of affairs only if that state of affairs obtains and he could have prevented it from obtaining.

(Or this was van Inwagen's original formulation of one of these principles. He later came to think that the principle needed to be revised. The revised principle would look something like this:

> A person is morally responsible for a certain state of affairs only if that state of affairs obtains and there was a time at which he could so have acted that that state of affairs not obtain.)

The states of affairs quantified over in this principle are "proposition-like": the state of affairs "Caesar's having been murdered" obtains because certain conspirators stabbed Caesar to death in Rome in 44 BC; but it, that very same state of affairs, could have obtained because Cleopatra poisoned him in Alexandria in 48 – just as the proposition that Caesar was murdered is true because certain conspirators stabbed Caesar to death in Rome in 44 BC and could have been true because Cleopatra poisoned him in Alexandria in 48. This state of affairs may thus be contrasted with the concrete event *the murder of Caesar*, which would not have occurred if Cleopatra had poisoned Caesar in Alexandria in 48, although, in that event, there would have been a concrete event, which does not in fact exist, that would have been denoted by the words 'the murder of Caesar'. (He has also endorsed a principle about concrete events that corresponds to or parallels the above principle about states of affairs.)

Van Inwagen has never seen any need to rethink the position he took concerning this principle when he first formulated it in the late seventies (with this minor qualification: as I have said, he has come to prefer a revised version of the principle), to wit that it is extremely plausible, that it entails that moral responsibility requires free will, and that it cannot be refuted by any adaptation of the counterexamples Frankfurt brought against the Principle of Alternative Possibilities. This last point has been disputed, but van

---

[12] See Chapters 1 and 6 of the present volume.

Inwagen has never been able to see any merit in the arguments by means of which the point has been disputed. He has responded to them,[13] but, as far as he is concerned, his original arguments for this position are the only answer to these counterarguments that was really needed.

This brings us to somewhere around the turn of the century. (Or it does if we ignore two minor essays of the middle eighties. In one of these essays,[14] Van Inwagen defended the position that the "conditional-analysis" argument for the compatibility of free will and determinism, and what he has dubbed the *Mind* Argument for the incompatiblity of free will and indeterminism – the latter argument is named for the journal, not for the human intellectual faculty – are inconsistent; inconsistent in this sense: from the soundness of either, the unsoundness of the other follows. In the other essay,[15] he proposed a conditional-analysis argument for the compatibility of free will and *in*determinism; this argument was, admittedly, a rather absurd argument; his point was that the unbiased inquirer should see that the conditional analysis argument for the compatibility of free will and determinism was equally absurd, and absurd for an exactly parallel reason.) Between 1985 and 2000, van Inwagen devoted very little thought to the problem of free will, but his occasional thoughts on the problem in that period caused him to change his mind on one important point and to become increasingly insistent on another.[16]

The point on which he has changed his mind is this: he came to see that Rule β, as he presented it in *An Essay on Free Will* and other places, is invalid. This rule of inference was stated as follows:

p and no one has, or ever had, any choice about that

If p then q, and no one has, or ever had, any choice about that

   hence,

q and no one has, or ever had, any choice about that.

Van Inwagen had thought that this rule was obviously valid, had made use of it in formulating one version of his argument for the incompatibility of free will and determinism (his favorite version, the version inspired by Carl Ginet's "Might We Have No Choice?"),[17] had said that, despite its seeming obviousness, it was nevertheless the weakest link in the chain of reasoning

---

[13] See Chapter 6 of the present volume and van Inwagen's critical notice of John Martin Fischer's *The Metaphysics of Free Will* in *Philosophical Quarterly* 47 (1997): 373–381.

[14] Chapter 2 of the present volume.   [15] Chapter 3 of the present volume.

[16] See Chapter 7 of the present volume.

[17] In Keith Lehrer (ed.), *Freedom and Determinism* (New York: Random House, 1966), pp. 87–104.

that led from the assumption of determinism to the conclusion that no one is ever able to do otherwise. And, although this principle is used in only one of the three formal versions of the argument he has presented, van Inwagen is on record as saying that, in his opinion, if Rule β should turn out to be invalid, it would almost certainly be the case that the two versions of the argument that do not involve the concept "having a choice" would also turn out to be invalid.[18]

Imagine, then, his embarrassment when Thomas McKay and David Johnson presented a counterexample to Rule β – a "beta blocker," to use the term that John Martin Fischer coined for counterexamples to Rule β.[19] (Actually, McKay and Johnson presented a counterexample to a different rule of inference, but since the invalidity of that other rule implies the invalidity of β, they have in effect presented a counterexample to β.)[20]

Van Inwagen has presented a revised rule of inference that is immune to McKay–Johnson-style counterexamples.[21] Finch and Warfield have proposed a different sort of revision that is also immune to these counterexamples,[22] and McKay and Johnson themselves suggested some revisions that are, I think, workable. Unfortunately, these revised rules, although they are far from implausible, lack the "luminous evidence" that was a striking, albeit illusory, property of the original Rule β. And this fact can very properly prompt the compatibilist to ask a pointed question along the following lines: "If the apparent intuitive obviousness of the original Rule β turned out to be an illusion – since the rule has in fact turned out to be

---

[18] At any rate, he is on record as saying things that commit him to this position. In *An Essay on Free Will*, he said (p. 57), "I am quite sure that any specific and detailed objection to one of the arguments can be fairly easily translated into specific and detailed objections to the others; and I think that any objection to one of the arguments will be a good objection to *that* argument if and only if the corresponding objections to the others are good objections to *them*." One of the arguments referred to as "the arguments" in this quotation is the argument that explicitly appeals to Rule β; and he has said ("When Is the Will Free?," p. 66 in this volume) that if that argument is unsound, its unsoundness must be due to the invalidity of Rule β. And he has said ("When the Will Is Not Free," p. 95), "My position is that all (logically adequate) arguments for incompatibilism must make some sort of implicit or hidden or covert appeal to [Rule β]."

[19] Thomas McKay and David Johnson, "A Reconsideration of an Argument against Compatibilism," *Philosophical Topics* 24 (1996): 113–122.

[20] See Chapter 7, "Free Will Remains a Mystery," pp. 93–94.

[21] Ibid., pp. 98–101. But see Lynne Rudder Baker, "The Irrelevance of the Consequence Argument," *Analysis* 68.1 (2008): 13–22, for an argument that purports to show that the revised version fails. Even if is Baker is right, however, her argument against the version of β presented in "Free Will Remains a Mystery" does not apply to the version van Inwagen has proposed in "The Consequence Argument," in P. van Inwagen and D. Zimmerman, *Metaphysics, The Big Questions*, 2nd edn. (Oxford: Basil Blackwell, 2008), pp. 450–456. This version of β is briefly stated in note 34 to Chapter 14 of the present volume.

[22] Alicia Finch and Ted A. Warfield, "The *Mind* Argument and Libertarianism," *Mind* 107 (1998): 516–528.

invalid – how much confidence should we have in the revised versions? Nemesis, in the form of a counterexample, was all along lying in wait for Rule β; why should we not take very seriously the epistemic possibility that in some dark corner of logical space, cousins of this Nemesis patiently await their appointments with the revised rules?" This pointed question is pointed indeed. Van Inwagen admits that he has no good answer to this question, and that, in consequence, although he *accepts* the revised rule, he assigns its validity a rather lower subjective probability than the near certainty he once so confidently assigned to the validity of the original β. He does, however, withdraw his assent to a thesis I mentioned a moment ago, the thesis that if Rule β should turn out to be invalid, this would mean that there was almost certainly something wrong with the other arguments he has given for the incompatibility of free will and determinism. He withdraws his assent because the counterexamples that have shown the invalidity of Rule β, the McKay–Johnson counterexamples, depend on some unexpected properties of an English phrase – 'has a choice about' – that played a key role in his formulation of the original principle. He is inclined to think that the "general idea" behind Rule β was sound, and that its invalidity stemmed from the fact that certain features of the English phrase unfit it for the task he assigned to it. When he made the statement from which he has now withdrawn his assent, he was assuming that if Rule β were shown to be invalid, this would be because someone had shown that the general idea behind the principle was fundamentally defective. But the revised versions of the rule appeal to this same general idea; they are merely (it is hoped) adequate implementations of this idea, implementations from which a technical defect has been removed.

I have said that in recent times, van Inwagen has changed his mind about one point and has become increasingly insistent on another. I have discussed the point on which he has changed his mind. The point on which he has become increasing insistent is this: Free will is a mystery, a ground-floor, first-water, Colin McGinn-style philosophical mystery. Free will is a mystery because, although it obviously exists – of *course* we sometimes confront a choice between A and B and are, while we are trying to decide whether to do A or to do B, able to do A and able to do B – it seems to be incompatible with both determinism and indeterminism, and thus seems to be impossible. When he says that free will seems to be incompatible both with determinism and indeterminism, van Inwagen means that there are good arguments for the incompatibility of free will and determinism and good arguments for incompatibility of free will and indeterminism, and that no one has ever identified a very plausible candidate for the flaw in any of the arguments in either class. Van Inwagen, of course, believes that the arguments he has given for the incompatibility of free will and determinism contain *no* flaws – or, at the worst, contain minor, technical flaws that could be repaired without altering their essential points – and that there is some flaw, or are some flaws, in the familiar arguments for the incompatibility of free will and indeterminism. But as to the latter class of arguments – well, he's damned if he knows what the flaws in them might be. He simply hasn't a clue. If you ask him how free will is possible, he can say only, "That's a mystery." This is, of course, a situation that a philosopher must regard as unsatisfactory, but van Inwagen has two consolations. First, he thinks that if he believed that an undetermined act could not be a free act, he'd be forced to believe something even more mysterious than what he now believes. He'd be forced to believe that at least one of the following three propositions was false:

Free will is incompatible with determinism

Moral responsibility does not require free will

People are sometimes morally responsible for various things.

And the falsity of any of these propositions would be, in his view, an even greater mystery than the falsity of the proposition that free will is compatible with indeterminism. Secondly, there are *lots* of philosophical mysteries, most of which have nothing to do with free will. I might cite one or more of the great philosophical mysteries, such as "temporal passage" or human consciousness. But I will mention instead two minor mysteries that are no less mysterious for being minor. I will mention two mysteries that carry much less emotional weight than the mystery of free will, or are, as one might say, unconnected with anything we care deeply about – unlike free will and time and consciousness, which are connected with many things that we care deeply about: the mystery of vagueness and the mystery of the Liar. It is obviously true that a currently living American male who is seven feet four inches tall is tall without qualification (i.e., is not simply tall to degree 0.99972 or something like that). It is obviously true that the president-elect, falsely believing herself to have lost the election, might address an audience and say, bitterly and sincerely, "Everything the president-elect tells anyone today is false." I do not think that either of these obvious truths is free from apparent paradox – although, of course, no paradox can be more than apparent, for no truth can *really* imply a self-contradictory statement or even a false statement. And yet there are very good arguments for the conclusion that each of these obvious truths entails various statements that are self-contradictory or at least obviously false. And neither van Inwagen nor I (he and I hold more or less the same philosophical opinions) can find any flaw in these arguments, though, of course, there must *be* flaws in them. Van Inwagen's expectation is that some premise (or more than one) in the several arguments for the incompatibility of free will and indeterminism is false but seems to us to be an obvious truth – as was once the case with the proposition that there are twice as many natural numbers as there are even numbers, the Galilean Law of the Addition of Velocities, the argument that, since space is unbounded, it must be infinite, and the unrestricted comprehension principle in set theory. But if van Inwagen is wrong about this, the following is *certainly* the case: *Some* proposition (or maybe there is more than one) about matters relating to free will, determinism, and moral responsibility that seems to us to be obviously true is false. Perhaps we shall one day discover what proposition this is, or what propositions these are, and it, or they, will come to have no more appeal to philosophers than the proposition that there are twice as many natural numbers as there are even numbers (which Galileo thought evident, despite his awareness that the two classes of numbers could be put into one–one correspondence) has for philosophers today. Or perhaps, as Chomsky and McGinn have suggested,[23] some evolutionarily contingent feature of the design of the human intellect renders it biologically impossible for us to think our way through the free-will problem to a satisfactory conclusion. I will remark, because it makes a nice link with my next topic, that van Inwagen has strong, I might almost say fraternal, feelings for Chomsky when he considers Chomsky's position on free will and determinism. Chomsky thinks that free will must be compatible with determinism, and that, nevertheless, it is a mystery how this could be. Van Inwagen thinks that free will must be compatible with indeterminism, and that, nevertheless, it is a mystery how this could be. Van Inwagen's feeling is that Chomsky, although he is mistaken about a particular point (an important point, to be sure), appreciates the depth and difficulty of the free will problem, while the majority of van Inwagen's fellow incompatibilists, although they are right on a particular point (and a very important point it is), do not really appreciate the depth and difficulty of the problem.

---

[23] Noam Chomksy, *Language and Problems of Knowledge* (Cambridge, MA: MIT Press, 1988), pp. 151–152. Colin McGinn, *Problems in Philosophy: The Limits of Inquiry* (Oxford: Blackwell, 1993).

I want now to explain why van Inwagen thinks one important group of incompatibilists, those who appeal to what is called agent causation, do not appreciate the depth and difficulty of the problem of free will. Many philosophers would agree with this judgment for the simple reason that they think that the concept of agent causation is incoherent, or think that agent causation is metaphysically impossible. Van Inwagen is inclined to agree with them (although he has no firm opinion on this question), but he has lately stressed a different point. It is this: Suppose there is nothing conceptually or metaphysically impossible about agent causation; suppose in fact that agent causation is a real phenomenon and that an episode of agent causation figures among the antecedents of every voluntary movement of a human hand or limb or vocal apparatus. Van Inwagen's position is that even if this is so, and even if (as some have argued) we understand the concept of agent causation at least as well as we understand the concept of event-causation, all this does nothing to diminish the mystery of free will. I will try to explain why van Inwagen thinks this by considering a particular human action.[24] Suppose Marie wants to vote in favor of the proposal before the meeting, and that, for this reason, she raises her right hand when the chair says, "All in favor…?" Suppose that one of the causal antecedents of her hand's rising was a certain event in her brain that was undetermined by past events, that the state of her body and her immediate environment at the moment this brain-event occurred were causally sufficient for her hand's rising, that if this event had not occurred, her hand would not have risen, and that *she*, Marie, a particular member of the metaphysical category "substance" or "continuant," was the cause – that is to say, the agent-cause – of that crucial brain-event. The friends of agent causation, if van Inwagen understands them, believe that these suppositions are sufficient for her having freely raised her hand. If that is so, these suppositions must entail the following proposition: At some moment shortly before Marie raised her hand, she was able to raise her hand and she was able not to raise her hand. But van Inwagen doesn't see why this entailment should be supposed to hold. In fact, he thinks he sees a good argument for the conclusion that it was not up to her whether her hand rose. Suppose God were miraculously to return the world to precisely the state it was in, say, one minute before Marie raised her hand, and that he then allowed affairs once more to proceed, without any further miracles. What would happen? What would Marie do? Well, if her raising her hand was a free act, and if free will is incompatible with determinism,

---

[24] For a more detailed presentation of this argument, see Chapter 7 of the present volume.

then we can't say. We can say only that she might have raised her hand and might not have raised her hand. If God were to cause this episode to be thus "replayed" a very large number of times, it might turn out that she raised her hand in thirty percent of the replays and refrained from raising it in seventy percent of the replays. This much is a simple consequence of incompatibilism, and it brings one of the main reason philosophers become compatibilists into stark relief. It seems to lead us inescapably to the conclusion that on each particular replay, what Marie does on *that* occasion is a mere matter of chance. And if there are no replays, if there is only one occasion on which Marie is in this situation, it seems to lead us just as inescapably to the conclusion that on that one occasion what Marie does is a mere matter of chance. And if it is a mere matter of chance whether Marie raised her hand, then it cannot have been true beforehand that Marie was both able to raise her hand and able to refrain from raising her hand, for to have both these abilities would be to be able to determine the outcome of a process whose outcome is due to chance. It is true that we have, by stipulation, inserted into this process, this process whose outcome is due to chance, an episode of agent causation. But, if I may so express myself, so what? That doesn't change the fact that the outcome of that process was due to chance. If God caused Marie's decision to be replayed a very large number of times, sometimes (in thirty percent of the replays, let us say) Marie would have agent-caused the crucial brain event and sometimes (in seventy percent of the replays, let us say) she would not have. Surely, then, whether she agent-caused the brain-event was a mere matter of chance? Whether her deliberations were followed by her agent-causing the brain event was, it would seem, a matter of chance; Marie, therefore, cannot have been both able to agent-cause the brain-event and able to refrain from agent-causing the brain-event, for to have both these abilities would be to be able to determine the outcome of a process whose outcome was due to chance – an impossible ability. I conclude that even if an episode of agent causation is among the causal antecedents of every voluntary human action, these episodes do nothing to undermine the *prima facie* impossibility of an undetermined free act. Postulating agent causation, therefore, does nothing to diminish the mystery of free will. Van Inwagen's conclusion is that incompatibilists had better abandon the concept of agent causation, and seek a resolution of the mystery of free will elsewhere – if, indeed, there *is* an "elsewhere."

During the first fifteen years of the new century, van Inwagen's thoughts turned more frequently to the free-will problem than they had during the previous fifteen years. Chapters 8 through 14 of the present volume were written during this period. Chapter 8, although its topic certainly falls under the general heading "the problem of free will," is on a topic almost entirely unrelated to his other work on free will. In Chapter 9, van Inwagen finally replied to David Lewis's 1981 paper, "Are We Free to Break the Laws?"[25] – Lewis's important criticism of van Inwagen's "Consequence Argument" for incompatibilism. (Chapter 9 is largely concerned with questions of philosophical method. The reply to the argument of "Are We Free to Break the Laws?" serves as an illustration of some points about philosophical method.)

Chapter 11 is an attempt at a corrected version of an invalid argument presented in Chapter 7 – an argument for the conclusion that if an agent is trying to decide whether to do A or B, and if it is undetermined which of those alternatives the agent will choose, then it cannot be either that the agent is able to choose A or able to choose B. (The argument is thus a version of the *Mind* argument.) But if an agent has chosen one of A and B, then what it is for the agent's choice to have been a *free* choice is precisely for the agent to have been able, before the choice was made, to choose A and able, before the choice was made, to choose B. But, one may ask, in what sense of 'ability' must a free choice between A and B rest on a prior ability to have chosen A and a prior ability to have chosen B? – for 'ability' has many senses. Chapter 14, which appears for the first time in this volume, is van Inwagen's attempt to clarify the sense of 'ability' that should figure in discussions of the free-will problem.

If in the period 1985–2000, van Inwagen became "increasingly insistent" on a certain point (that free will is a philosophical mystery), in the years 2000–2015 he became increasingly insistent on another point: that philosophers working on the problem of free will after about 1985 were guilty of ill-advised departures from the traditional vocabulary of and traditional understanding of the free-will problem. Chapters 10, 12, and 13 (and, to a certain extent, Chapter 14) record his growing impatience with various tendencies on display in recent (that is, post-1985) work on free will, determinism, and moral responsibility. The most radical of these chapters is Chapter 13, in which van Inwagen contends that much recent work on the problem of free will, determinism, and moral responsibility is infected by what he calls *verbal essentialism* – by which he means that much of this work essentially involves the *phrase* 'free will' and is insufficiently attentive

---

[25] *Philosophical Papers, Volume II* (Oxford University Press, 1987), pp. 291–298. "Are We Free to Break the Laws?" was originally published in *Theoria* 47 (1981): 113–121. It is available online at www .andrewmbailey.com/dkl/Free_to_Break_the_Laws.pdf

to the fact that this phrase is a mere technical term. 'Free will', he maintains, is not a phrase like such philosophically important phrases as 'knows that' and 'is the cause of' and 'there exists', phrases that have some sort of grounding in ordinary, everyday usage. The so-called problem of free will (or the problem of free will, determinism, and moral responsibility) could therefore (he contends) be stated and discussed without using the phrase 'free will' at all – or any such related word or phrase as 'freedom', 'acts freely', 'free choice' … In Chapter 13 he shows how to do this: he presents a detailed statement of a philosophical problem to which he gives the arbitrary name 'the Culpability Problem' (a problem essentially the same as the problem *he* has always called 'the problem of free will'), and he presents this problem without using any of the traditional vocabulary of the free-will problem other than 'determinism'. He defends the conclusion that all work on "the problem of free will" in which the phrase 'free will' occurs essentially is by that very fact irrelevant to the Culpability Problem, for the phrase 'free will' is nowhere to be found in the statement of that problem (nor does the statement contain any of the words 'free', 'freely', and 'freedom').

CHAPTER I

Ability and Responsibility

I

There was a time when philosophers would debate the relative merits of the doctrines of "liberty" and "necessity," or, as we should say today, debate whether it is more reasonable to believe in free will or in universal causal determinism. As everyone knows, the parties to this debate shared a premise: that free will and universal causal determinism are incompatible. And, as everyone knows, there arose a philosophical tradition – represented by Hobbes, Hume, Jonathan Edwards, Mill, and Moritz Schlick – in which just this premise is denied. Thus the debate between the libertarians and necessitarians was undercut, and most of the debates about free will today are, as they have been for a long time, essentially debates about whether free will and determinism are compatible or incompatible.

But why should anyone care whether we have free will or whether determinism is true? The first part of this question is perhaps easier to answer than the second: We care about free will because we care about moral responsibility, and we are persuaded that we cannot make ascriptions of moral responsibility to agents who lack free will. Recently, however, Harry Frankfurt has denied just this principle, or, at least, a principle that sounds very much like it, which he calls the Principle of Alternate Possibilities.[1] His formulation of the Principle of Alternate Possibilities is

PAP   A person is morally responsible for what he has done only if he could have done otherwise.

If Frankfurt has made out a good case for the falsity of PAP (and I think he has), then it would seem that he has undercut the debate between the

I should like to thank the editors of the *Philosophical Review* for their careful comments on earlier versions of this paper, which have led to many improvements. I am especially grateful to them for pointing out to me that an argument I employed was invalid.
[1] "Alternate Possibilities and Moral Responsibility," *Journal of Philosophy* 66 (1969): 829–839; the formulation is at p. 829.

"compatibilists" and the "incompatibilists" (to use the current jargon) in a way very similar to the way in which Hobbes and others undercut the debate between the libertarians and the necessitarians.

Frankfurt supports his contention that PAP is false by means of a certain style of counterexample; I shall call counterexamples in this style "Frankfurt counterexamples."[2] The following Frankfurt counterexample is due to David Blumenfeld.[3] It is worked out with rather more concrete detail than any of Frankfurt's own counterexamples:

> Suppose that the presence of a certain atmospheric reaction always causes Smith to decide to attack the person nearest to him and to actually do so. Suppose also that he always flushes a deep red when he considers and decides *against* performing an act of violence and that under certain circumstances the atmospheric reaction is triggered by the appearance of just this shade of red. Now imagine that on a day on which circumstances are favorable to the triggering of the reaction, Smith considers whether or not to strike a person with whom he is conversing, decides in favor of it, and forthwith does so.

The general idea behind Frankfurt counterexamples is this. An agent S is in the process of deciding which of n alternative acts $A_1, ..., A_k, ..., A_n$ to perform. He believes (correctly) that he cannot avoid performing some one of these acts. He decides to perform, and, acting on this decision, does perform A_k. But, unknown to him, there were various factors that *would have* prevented him from performing (and perhaps even from deciding to perform) any of $A_1, ..., A_k, ..., A_n$ *except* A_k. These factors would have "come into play" if he had shown any tendency towards performing (perhaps even towards deciding to perform) any of $A_1, ..., A_k, ..., A_n$ except A_k. But since he in fact showed no such tendency, these factors remained mere unactualized dispositions of the objects constituting his environment: they played no role whatever in his deciding to perform or in his performing A_k.

According to Frankfurt, it is evident that in such cases we should say (i) that S had no alternative to performing A_k, couldn't have done otherwise than perform A_k, and (ii) S is nonetheless responsible for having performed A_k (or, at least, if he is *not* responsible for having performed A_k, this must be due to some factor other than his inability to perform any act other than A_k for the reason described).

---

[2] Or perhaps they should be called "Frankfurt–Nozick" counterexamples. See note 2 (p. 835) to Frankfurt's article.

[3] David Blumenfeld, "The Principle of Alternate Possibilities," *Journal of Philosophy* 68 (1971): 339–345, n. 3 (p. 341).

Now if Frankfurt has indeed shown that PAP is false, this may be of no great consequence. For it may well be that some trivial modification of PAP is immune to Frankfurt counterexamples and that this modified version of PAP entails that if universal causal determinism and incompatibilism are both true, then all our ascriptions of moral responsibility are false. Frankfurt argues that this is not the case, however, and that what one might call the "correct version" of PAP (that is, the correct principle governing excuse from responsibility in cases in which alternative possibilities for action are absent) cannot be used to show that determinism and moral responsibility are in conflict.[4] I shall not in this paper try to determine whether Frankfurt's proposed principle is true or false, or discuss whether it in fact plays a role in our deliberations about moral responsibility. I shall instead exhibit three principles, which, if they are not "versions" of PAP, are at least principles very similar to PAP, and which *do* play a role in our deliberations about responsibility. I shall argue that these principles are immune to Frankfurt-style counterexamples. (I shall call counterexamples that are directed against principles similar to but distinct from PAP, and which are as strategically similar to Frankfurt counterexamples as is possible, Frankfurt-*style* counterexamples. I shall reserve the term "Frankfurt counterexample" for counterexamples directed just against PAP itself.)

PAP, as Frankfurt formulates it, is a principle about performed acts (things we have done). In Part II, I shall consider a principle about *unperformed* acts (things we have left undone). In Part III, I shall consider two principles about the *consequences* of what we have done (or left undone). In Part IV, I shall argue that if these three principles are true and if a version of incompatibilism appropriate to each is true, then determinism and moral responsibility are in conflict, even given that PAP is false.

II

Consider the following principle (the Principle of Possible Action):

PPA   A person is morally responsible for failing to perform a given act only if he could have performed that act.

This principle is intuitively very plausible. But the same might have been said about PAP. Can we show that PPA is false by constructing a

---

[4] The "correct version" of PAP is: "A person is not morally responsible for what he has done if he did it only because he could not have done otherwise" (p. 838).

counterexample to it that is like Frankfurt's counterexamples to PAP? An adaptation to the case of unperformed acts of Frankfurt's general strategy would, I think, look something like this: An agent is in the process of deciding whether to perform a certain act *A*. He decides not to perform *A*, and, owing to this decision, refrains from performing *A*.[5] But, unknown to him, there were various factors that *would have* prevented him from performing (and perhaps even from deciding to perform) *A*. These factors would have come into play if he had shown any tendency towards performing (perhaps even towards deciding to perform) *A*. But since he in fact showed no such tendency, these factors remained mere unactualized dispositions of the objects constituting his environment: they played no role whatever in his deciding not to perform or his failure to perform *A*.

Putative counterexamples to PPA prepared according to this recipe produce, in me at least, no inclination to reject this principle. Let us look at one.

Suppose I look out the window of my house and see a man being robbed and beaten by several powerful-looking assailants. It occurs to me that perhaps I had better call the police. I reach for the telephone and then stop. It crosses my mind that if I do call the police, the robbers might hear of it and wreak their vengeance on me. And, in any case, the police would probably want me to make a statement and perhaps even to go to the police station and identify someone in a lineup or look through endless books of photographs of thugs. And it's after eleven already, and I have to get up early tomorrow. So I decide "not to get involved," return to my chair, and put the matter firmly out of my mind. Now suppose also that, quite unknown to me, there has been some sort of disaster at the telephone exchange, and that every telephone in the city is out of order and will be for several hours.

Am I responsible for failing to call the police? Of course not. I couldn't have called them. I may be responsible for failing to *try* to call the police (that much I *could* have done), or for refraining from calling the police, or for having let myself, over the years, become the sort of man who doesn't (try to) call the police under such circumstances. I may be responsible for being selfish and cowardly. But I am simply not responsible for failing to call the police. This "counterexample," therefore, is not a counterexample at all: PPA is unscathed.

---

[5] This schema and the instance of it that follows involve the agent's intentionally refraining from performing a given act. Of course, not every case in which we might want to consider holding an agent responsible for failing to perform some act is a case in which the agent intentionally refrains from performing that act: he may never even have considered performing that act. This distinction between two ways of failing to perform a given act is of no importance for our present purposes. The points made in the text would be equally valid if we had chosen to examine a case in which the agent failed even to think of performing the act whose non-performance we are considering holding him responsible for.

It is, of course, proverbially hard to prove a universal negative proposition. Perhaps there are Frankfurt-style counterexamples to PPA. But I don't see how to construct one. I conclude that Frankfurt's style of argument cannot be used to refute PPA.

III

Both PAP and PPA are principles about acts, performed or unperformed. But, in fact, when we make ascriptions of moral responsibility, we do not normally say things like "You are responsible for killing Jones" or "He is responsible for failing to water the marigolds." We are much more likely to say, "You are responsible for Jones's death," or "He is responsible for the shocking state the marigolds are in." That is, we normally hold people responsible not for their acts or failures to act (at least explicitly), but for the results or consequences of these acts and failures. What, ontologically speaking, are results or consequences of action and inaction? What sorts of thing are Jones's death and the shocking state the marigolds are in? The general terms "event" and "state of affairs" seem appropriate ones to apply to these items. But what are events and states of affairs? This question, like all interesting philosophical questions I know of, has no generally accepted answer. Philosophers do not seem even to be able to agree about whether events and states of affairs are particulars or universals. In order to avoid taking sides in the debate about this, I shall adopt the following strategy. I shall state a certain principle about excuse from responsibility that seems to me to be a plausible one, provided the events or states of affairs we hold people responsible for are particulars. *And* I shall state a similar principle that seems to me to be plausible, provided the events or states of affairs we hold people responsible for are universals. For each of these principles, I shall argue that it cannot be refuted by Frankfurt-style counterexamples. The first of these principles (which I shall call principles of possible prevention) is:

PPP1   A person is morally responsible for a certain event (particular)
        only if he could have prevented it.

This principle is about events; but if we were to examine a principle, otherwise similar, about "state-of-affairs particulars" (for example, the way secondary education is organized in Switzerland)[6] we could employ arguments that differ from the following arguments only in verbal detail.

---

[6] Perhaps it is debatable whether this phrase designates a particular.

What are events if they are particulars? They are items that can be witnessed (at least if they consist in visible changes in visible particulars), remembered, and reported.[7] They are typically denoted by phrases like "the fall of the Alamo," "the death of Caesar," "the death of Caesar in 44 BC," and "what Bill saw happen in the garden."[8] How shall we identify and individuate event-particulars (hereinafter, "events")? Individuating particulars, whether events, tables, or human beings, is always a tricky business. (Consider the Ship of Theseus.) As Davidson says, "Before we enthusiastically embrace an ontology of events we will want to think long and hard about the criteria for individuating them. I am inclined to think we can do as well for events generally as we can for physical objects (which is not very well)."[9] In a paper later than the one this quotation is taken from, Davidson tries to "do as well." He tells us that finding a satisfactory criterion of individuation for events will consist in providing "a satisfactory filling for the blank in:

If x and y are events, then $x = y$ if and only if ____.[10]

The "filling" he suggests for this blank is (roughly) "x and y have the same causes and effects." The biconditional so obtained, is, I have no doubt, true. But this biconditional will not be "satisfactory" for our purpose, which is the evaluation of PPP1. What we want to be able to do is to tell whether some event that *would* happen if what we earlier called "unactualized dispositions of the objects constituting the agent's environment" were to come into play, is the same as some event (the event responsibility for which we are enquiring about) that actually *has* happened; that is, we want to know how to tell of some given event whether *it*, that very same event, would (nevertheless) have

---

[7] I doubt, however, whether they can be anticipated. The objects of anticipation and other "future-directed" attitudes are, I think, universals.

[8] Perhaps the last of these phrases could also be used to name an event-universal. We seem to be using it this way if we say, "What Bill saw happen in the garden happens all too frequently." But, I think, we use it to name a particular when we say, "What Bill saw happen in the garden last night will live in infamy," or "could have been prevented with a little foresight." The phrases "the fall of the Alamo" and "the death of Caesar," however, seem to be suited only for denoting particulars: even if the Alamo had fallen twice, even if Caesar (like Lazarus) had died twice, we could not say, "The fall of the Alamo has happened twice" or "The death of Caesar has happened twice." (This is not due, or not due *solely*, to the presence of the definite article in these phrases, for we can say, "The thing Bill fears most has happened twice.")

[9] From Davidson's contribution to a symposium on events and event-descriptions in *Fact and Existence*, ed. J. Margolis (Oxford: Blackwell, 1969), p. 84.

[10] "The Individuation of Events," in N. Rescher (ed.), *Essays in Honor of Carl G. Hempel* (Dordrecht: Kluwer, 1969), p. 225.

happened if things had been different in certain specified ways. (For when we ask whether an agent could have *prevented* a certain event *E* by doing, say, *X*, we shall have to be able to answer the question whether *E* would *nonetheless* have happened if the agent had done *X*.) To see why Davidson's criterion cannot be used to answer our sort of question about event-identity, consider the following formally similar criterion of individuation for persons: "*x* and *y* are the same person if and only if *x* and *y* have the same blood relatives (including siblings)." This criterion, while *true*, does not help us if we are interested in counterfactual questions about persons. For, obviously, any given man might have had different relatives from those he in fact has (he might have had an additional brother, for example). Davidson's proposed criterion is of no help to us for what is essentially the same reason: Any given event might have had different effects from the effects it has in fact had. For example, if an historian writes, "Even if the murder of Caesar had not resulted in a civil war, it would nevertheless have led to widespread bloodshed," he does not convict himself of conceptual confusion. But he is certainly presupposing that the very event we call "the murder of Caesar" might have had different effects.

The above considerations are not offered in criticism of Davidson's criterion, which is, after all, *true*, and may be a very useful criterion to employ (say) when we are asking whether a given brain-event and a given mental event are one event or two. But Davidson's criterion is not the *sort* of criterion we need. We need a criterion that stands to Davidson's criterion as "*x* and *y* are the same human being if and only if *x* and *y* have the same causal genesis" stands to the above criterion of personal identity. (I use "causal genesis" with deliberate vagueness. A *necessary* condition for *x* and *y* having the same causal genesis is "their" having developed from the same sperm and egg.[11] But this is not sufficient, or "identical" – monozygotic – twins would be *numerically* identical.) This criterion can be used to make sense of talk about what some particular person would have been like if things had gone very differently for him.[12] Can we devise a criterion for counterfactual talk about events that is at least no *worse* than our criterion for persons? I would suggest that we simply truncate Davidson's criterion: *x* is the same event as *y* if and only if *x* and *y* have the same causes. (Note the similarity of this criterion to the causal-genesis criterion of personal

---

[11] Or so it seems to me. Of course, a Cartesian (for example) will have a different view of the matter.

[12] Cf. Saul Kripke, "Naming and Necessity," in D. Davidson and G. Harman (eds.), *Semantics of Natural Language* (Dordrecht: Kluwer, 1972), pp. 312–314.

identity.) I do not know how to justify my intuition that this criterion is correct, any more than I know how to justify my belief in the causal-genesis criterion. But, of course, arguments must come to an end some-where. I can only suggest that since substances (like human beings and tables) should be individuated by their causal origins, and since we are talking about events that, like substances, are particulars, the present pro-posal is plausible. Moreover, I am aware that this proposed criterion is vague. It is not clear in every case of, say, a story about the events leading up to Caesar's murder, whether it would be correct to say that the murder had "the same causes" in the story that it had in reality. But I think the notion of *same event* is clear just insofar as the notion of *same causes* is clear. And this latter notion is surely not hopelessly unclear: If Cleopatra had poisoned Caesar in 48, then, clearly, there would have happened an event that has not in fact happened, an event that it would have been correct to call "Caesar's death," and which would have had different causes from the event that *is* called "Caesar's death." And, just as clearly, we cannot say of the event we in fact call "Caesar's death," "Suppose *it* had been caused four years earlier by Cleopatra's poisoning Caesar in Alexandria." Moreover, it is hardly to be supposed that we should be able to devise a criterion that will resolve all "puzzle cases," since we are unable to devise such a criterion for people, mountains, or tables.[13]

Let us now return to PPP1. Can we devise a Frankfurt-style counter-example to this principle? Let us try.

---

[13] A theory of event-particulars that is inconsistent with the view presented in this paper is held by R. M. Martin and Jaegwon Kim. (See Martin's contribution to the symposium referred to in note 9, and, for Kim's latest published views on events, "Causation, Nomic Subsumption, and the Con-cept of Event," *Journal of Philosophy* 70 [1973]: 217–236). If we abstract from the particular twists that each of these authors gives to his own account of events, we may say that, on the "Kim–Mar-tin" theory, the class of events is the class of substance-property-time triples. For example, Caesar's death is the triple ⟨Caesar, being dead, 15 March 44 BC⟩. (Strictly speaking, the term "15 March 44 BC" in the preceding sentence should be replaced with a term designating the precise instant at which Caesar died.) A "Kim–Martin" event *happens* just in the case that its first term acquires its second term at its third term. However useful Kim–Martin events may be in certain contexts of discussion, I do not think it is correct to think of them as particulars. They are, rather, highly specified universals, just as the property *being the tallest man* is a highly specified (in fact, "definite") universal (cf. note 20). This property, though only one man can have it, is nonetheless such that it *could have* been possessed by someone other than the man who in fact has it. Similarly, any Kim–Martin event that happens *could have* been caused by quite different antecedent events from those that in fact caused it. To suppose that event-particulars have this feature is to violate my intuitions (at any rate) about particulars. An additional problem: every Kim–Martin event is such that there is some particular moment (its third term) such that the event *must* happen just at that moment if it happens at all. But surely Caesar's death might have happened at least a few moments earlier or later than it in fact did, just as a given man might have been born (or even conceived) at least a few moments earlier or later than he in fact was.

Gunnar shoots and kills Ridley (intentionally), thereby bringing about Ridley's death, a certain event. But there is some factor, F, which (i) played no causal role in Ridley's death, and (ii) would have caused Ridley's death *if* Gunnar had not shot him (or, since factor F might have caused Ridley's death *by* causing Gunnar to shoot him, perhaps we should say, "if Gunnar had decided not to shoot him"), and (iii) is such that Gunnar could not have prevented it from causing Ridley's death except by killing (or by deciding to kill) Ridley himself. So it would seem that Gunnar is responsible for Ridley's death, though he could not have prevented Ridley's death.

It is easy to see that this story is simply inconsistent. What is in fact denoted by "Ridley's death" is not, according to the story, caused by factor F. Therefore, if Gunnar had not shot Ridley, and, as a result, factor F had caused Ridley to die, then there *would have been* an event denoted by "Ridley's death" which had factor F as (one of) its cause(s). But then this event would have been an event other than the event *in fact* denoted by "Ridley's death"; the event in fact denoted by "Ridley's death" would not have happened at all. But if this story is inconsistent, it is not a counterexample to PPP1. And I am unable to see how to construct a putative Frankfurt-style counterexample to PPP1 that cannot be shown to be inconsistent by an argument of this sort.

Let us now turn to a principle about universals:

PPP2   A person is morally responsible for a certain state of affairs only if (that state of affairs obtains and) he could have prevented it from obtaining.[14]

The states of affairs "quantified over" in this principle are universals in the way propositions are universals. Just as there are many different ways the concrete particulars that make up our surroundings could be arranged that would be sufficient for the truth of a given proposition, so there are many different ways they could be arranged that would be sufficient for the *obtaining* of a given state of affairs. Consider, for example, the state of affairs that consists in Caesar's being murdered. This state of affairs obtains *because* certain conspirators stabbed Caesar at Rome in 44 BC, but (since it is a universal), *it*, that very same state of affairs, *might have* obtained because (say) Cleopatra had poisoned him at Alexandria in 48.

---

[14] Nothing in PPP1 corresponds to the parenthetical qualification "that state of affairs obtains and" in this principle. So far as I can see, to say of a given event-particular that it "happens" is equivalent to saying that it exists. And, of course, there exist no events that do not exist. Thus there exist no events that do not happen. But states of affairs may exist without obtaining, just as propositions may exist without being true or properties without being instantiated.

But this is a bit vague. In order the better to talk about "states of affairs," let us introduce "canonical" names for them. Such names will consist in the result of prefixing "its being the case that" (hereinafter, "C") to "eternal" sentences.[15] Thus, a canonical name for the state of affairs referred to above would be "C (Caesar is murdered)." And let us say that the result of flanking the identity-sign with canonical names of states of affairs expresses a truth just in the case that the eternal sentences embedded in these names express equivalent propositions, where propositions are *equivalent* if they are true in just the same possible worlds. (Hereinafter, I shall assume that every proposition is equivalent to and *only* to itself. This assumption could be dispensed with at the cost of complicating the syntax of the sequel.) A state of affairs will be said to *obtain* if the proposition associated with it – that is, the proposition expressed by the sentence embedded in any of its canonical names – is true.[16] Thus C(Caesar is murdered), C(Caesar is stabbed), and C(Caesar is poisoned) are three distinct states of affairs, the first two of which obtain and the last of which does not. To *prevent* a state of affairs from obtaining is to prevent its associated proposition from being true (or to *see to it that* or *ensure that* that proposition is not true).

Let us now, so armed, return to PPP2. Can we show that PPP2 is false by constructing Frankfurt-style counterexamples to it? What would an attempt at such a counterexample look like? Like this, I think.

Gunnar shoots Ridley (intentionally), an action sufficient for the obtaining of Ridley's being dead, a certain state of affairs. But there is some factor, F, which (i) played no causal role in Ridley's death, and (ii) would have caused Ridley's death *if* Gunnar had not shot him (or had decided not to shoot him), and (iii) is such that Gunnar could not have prevented it from causing Ridley's death except by killing (or by deciding to kill)

---

[15] The choice of eternal sentences as the arguments to which the operator "C" attaches is made largely for the sake of convenience. If we had chosen, in addition to eternal sentences, non-eternal sentences, sentences that can change their truth-values as time passes, for this purpose, then we should have canonical names for states of affairs that can obtain at one time and fail to obtain at other times. If we were to work out a comprehensive and consistent theory of these entities, we should end up with a theory rather like the theory of "states of affairs" R. M. Chisholm presents in "Events and Propositions," *Noûs* 4 (1970): 15–24. We might, in fact, say that what *we* are calling "states of affairs" are just that subclass of Chisholm's "states of affairs" that he calls *propositions*. If we were to interpret PPP2 as involving quantification over *all* those things Chisholm calls "states of affairs," then (I claim without argument) we could nevertheless defend it against Frankfurt-style counterexamples by arguments essentially the same as those we shall present in the text, but these arguments would be considerably more complicated. For a discussion of the propriety of applying the term "universal" to "states of affairs," see note 20.

[16] In Chisholm's view (see note 15) the proposition "associated with" a given state of affairs just *is* that state of affairs.

Ridley himself. So it would seem that Gunnar is responsible for Ridley's being dead though he could not have prevented this state of affairs from obtaining.

This case *seems* to show that PPP2 is false. But in fact it does not. Let us remember that if this case is to be a counterexample to PPP2 and not to some other principle, some principle involving particulars, we must take the words "Ridley's being dead" that occur in it as denoting a universal. What universal? Presumably, C(Ridley dies). But while it is indeed true that Gunnar could not have prevented C(Ridley dies) from obtaining, I do not think it is true that Gunnar is responsible for C(Ridley dies). Why should anyone think he is? Well, Gunnar did something (shooting Ridley) that was *sufficient* for C(Ridley dies). What is more, he performed this act intentionally, knowing that it was sufficient for this state of affairs. This argument, however, is invalid. For consider the state of affairs C(Ridley is mortal). When Gunnar shot Ridley, he performed an act sufficient for (the obtaining of) this state of affairs. But it would be absurd to say that Gunnar is *responsible* for C(Ridley is mortal). God, or Adam and Eve jointly, or perhaps no one at all, might be held accountable for Ridley's mortality; certainly not his murderer. (Unless, of course, Ridley would have lived forever if he hadn't been murdered; let's assume that is not the case.)

In fact, it is a defensible position that C(Ridley dies) is the very same state of affairs as C(Ridley is mortal). Given our principle of identity for states of affairs, these "two" states of affairs are one if the two eternal sentences "Ridley dies" and "Ridley is mortal" express the same proposition. And what proposition *could* either of them express but the proposition also expressed by "Ridley does not live forever" and "Ridley dies at some time or other"? So, it should seem, Gunnar is not responsible for C(Ridley dies), and the attempted counterexample to PPP2 fails.

Nor do matters go differently if (somewhat implausibly) we think of "Ridley's being dead" as denoting some more "specific" state of affairs, such as C(Ridley is killed). If Gunnar is indeed responsible for C(Ridley is killed), we shall nevertheless have a counterexample to PPP2 only if Gunnar could not have prevented this state of affairs from obtaining. Let us flesh out "factor F" with some detail to insure that this is the case: Suppose there is a third party, Pistol, who would have killed Ridley if Gunnar had not; and suppose Gunnar was able to prevent Pistol's killing Ridley only by killing Ridley himself. By these stipulations, we insure that Gunnar could not have prevented C(Ridley is killed). But do we, in making these stipulations, absolve Gunnar from responsibility for this state of affairs, or is his being responsible for it at least consistent with our stipulations?

I think we absolve him, and that we can show this by an argument of the same sort as the one we used in connection with C(Ridley dies). Let us first note that we cannot show that Gunnar is responsible for C(Ridley is killed) by pointing out that he did something logically or causally sufficient for that state of affairs; for, by the same argument, we could show that he is responsible for C(Ridley is mortal). Now consider the state of affairs – call it "D" – C(either Pistol or Gunnar kills Ridley). Is Gunnar responsible for D? Note that D would have obtained no matter what Gunnar had done, just as C(Ridley is mortal), C(either 2 + 2 = 4 or Gunnar kills Ridley), and C(grass is green or Gunnar kills Ridley) would have. These latter states of affairs are obviously not ones Gunnar is responsible for. Is there some important difference between them and D in virtue of which Gunnar is responsible for D? There is only one non-trivial difference I can see: There is *no* possible world in which Gunnar is responsible for C(either 2 +2 = 4 or Gunnar kills Ridley); and while there are doubtless possible worlds in which Gunnar is responsible for C(Ridley is mortal) and others in which he is responsible for C(either grass is green or Gunnar kills Ridley), these worlds are exceedingly "remote" from actuality.[17] But some worlds in which Gunnar is responsible for D are much "closer" to actuality than any of these: For example, "close" worlds in which the counterfactual propositions about Pistol that were built into our example are false and Ridley would not have been killed if Gunnar had not shot him. But a miss is as good as a mile; I am contending only that Gunnar is not *in fact* responsible for D.

Now if Gunnar is not responsible for D, then he is not responsible for C(either Pistol or Gunnar or someone else kills Ridley). And *this* state of affairs and C(Ridley is killed) are one and the same, since the proposition that either Pistol or Gunnar or someone else kills Ridley is equivalent to the proposition that Ridley is killed.[18]

In this example, "factor F" involved a second agent who would have shot Ridley if Gunnar had not. But it would have made no real difference if we had imagined factor F being such that it would have caused Ridley's death by "working through" Gunnar. (See Blumenfeld's counterexample

[17] Worlds (say) in which Ridley would have lived forever if Gunnar had not shot him, and worlds in which the color of grass is up to Gunnar.

[18] The editors of the *Philosophical Review* have called my attention to the fact that the validity of this argument appears to depend on the doubtful assumption that "Gunnar is responsible for *x*" is an

to PAP, quoted in Part I.) Suppose, for example, that Gunnar decides to kill Ridley and does so. Suppose that if he had decided *not* to kill Ridley he would have flushed red (which he couldn't help) and that this red flush together with the prevailing atmospheric conditions would have caused him to decide to kill and, as a result of this decision, to kill, Ridley. Suppose the presence of these atmospheric conditions and the effect on him of their copresence with his flushing red are things he has no choice about. It follows from these suppositions that Gunnar could not have prevented C(Ridley is killed). But we can show by an argument essentially the same as the argument we employed in the "Pistol" case that Gunnar is not responsible for this state of affairs. We proceed by showing first that Gunnar is not responsible for

K   C(Ridley is killed by someone who is caused to kill him by factor F [red flush, atmospheric conditions, and so on] or else Ridley is killed by someone who is not caused to kill him by factor F).

This state of affairs plays the role played by C(either Pistol or Gunnar or someone else kills Ridley) in our demonstration that, in the "Pistol" case, Gunnar is not responsible for C(Ridley is killed). We cannot say of K what we said of D, and what we could have said of C(either Pistol or Gunnar or someone else kills Ridley), that it would have obtained no matter what Gunnar had done, for it would not have obtained if Gunnar had not shot Ridley. But we can say of K that it would have obtained no matter what *choices* or *decisions* Gunnar had made, and this seems to me to entail that

---

extensional context. But it need not depend on this assumption. Let us say that in each of the following pairs of sentences the second sentence is a *disjunctive elaboration* of the first.

All grass is green.

All grass in London or elsewhere is green.

Ridley is killed.

Ridley is killed by something or other at some time or other at some place or other.

There is a stack of plates on the table.

There is a stack of plates on the table that contains twelve plates or else some other number of plates.

Then, I think, a defender of the argument presented in the text need appeal to no principle stronger than: From 'S is not responsible for C(p)', derive 'S is not responsible for C(q)', provided p is a disjunctive elaboration of q. For example, from "Henry is not responsible for C(there is a stack of plates on the table that contains twelve plates or else some other number of plates)" we derive "Henry is not responsible for C(there is a stack of plates on the table)." This inference seems to me to be plainly valid, even if we suppose Henry to be unable to count beyond three and to be ignorant of the logical principle of Addition.

Gunnar is not responsible for it. (I owe this point to the editors of the *Philosophical Review*.) The remaining step in the demonstration consists simply in observing that the proposition associated with K is equivalent to the proposition that Ridley is killed and, therefore that K and C(Ridley is killed) are one and the same state of affairs, from which fact we infer that Gunnar is not responsible for C(Ridley is killed). (Or, if this inference be thought dubious, we can say that the remaining step consists in observing that the sentence embedded in the displayed name of K is a "disjunctive elaboration" of "Ridley is killed," together with an application of the rule stated in note 18.) If we had chosen to examine instead of C(Ridley is killed) some even more "specific" state of affairs, such as C(Ridley is shot to death at 3:43 p.m., January 12, 1949, in Chicago), this would have made no difference to our argument, which in no way depended on the degree of specificity of C(Ridley is killed). An argument of the same sort could be applied to *any* attempt at a Frankfurt-style counterexample to PPP2: the putative counterexample will not be a counterexample *unless* it entails that the agent whose responsibility is in question could not have prevented some given state of affairs; but if the "counterexample" does indeed have this feature, then (I claim) we can always find an argument (sound, I claim), constructed along the lines of the above models, for the conclusion that the agent is not responsible for that state of affairs.

The intuitive plausibility of this conclusion can be shown if we think in terms of the following rather fanciful picture. We are imagining cases in which an agent "gets to" a certain state of affairs by following a particular "causal road," a road intentionally chosen by him in order to "get to" that state of affairs. But, because this state of affairs is a universal, it can be reached by *various* causal roads, some of them differing radically from the road that *is* taken. And, in the cases we imagine, *all* the causal roads that the agent *could* take, all that are *open* to him, lead to this same state of affairs. Perhaps the point of this fanciful talk about "roads" will be clearer if we look at the case of an agent who is unable to prevent a certain state of affairs from obtaining, where this case involves roads in a literal sense. Suppose Ryder's horse, Dobbin, has run away with him. Ryder can't get Dobbin to slow down, but Dobbin will respond to a left or right tug on the bridle: whenever Ryder and Dobbin come to a fork in the road or a crossroads, it is up to Ryder which way they go. Ryder and Dobbin are approaching a certain crossroads, and Ryder recognizes one of the roads leading away from it as a road to Rome. Ryder has conceived a dislike for Romans and so (having nothing better to do) he steers Dobbin on to the road he knows leads to Rome, motivated by the hope that the passage of a runaway horse through the streets of Rome will result in the injury of some of her detested citizens. Unknown to Ryder, however, *all* roads lead to Rome: Dobbin's career would have led him and Ryder to Rome by *some* route no matter what Ryder had done. That is, Ryder could not have prevented C(Ryder passes through Rome on a runaway horse). Is Ryder responsible for this state of affairs? It is obvious that he is not. And it seems obvious that he is not responsible for this state of affairs *just because* he could not have prevented it. I conclude that Frankfurt-style counterexamples cannot be used to show that PPP2 is false. The universals that PPP2 is "about" are states of affairs; but if we had examined a principle, otherwise similar, about "event-universals" (for example, "its coming to pass that Caesar dies"), we could have employed arguments that differed from the above arguments only in verbal detail.

It has been suggested to me[19] that these arguments appear less plausible if one reflects on the fact that essentially similar arguments could be used to show, for example, that Gunnar did not *bring about* C(Ridley is killed) or that Gunnar's pulling the trigger did not *cause* this state of affairs. It is certainly true that if the above arguments are sound, then similar arguments can be used to show that Gunnar did not bring about C(Ridley is killed) and that his bodily movements did not cause this state of affairs to obtain. But these conclusions appear to me to be simply *true*. Let us concentrate on

(1) Gunnar did not bring about C(Ridley is killed).

Why should anyone think (1) is false? It would be clearly invalid to argue that (1) is false since Gunnar did something logically or causally sufficient for C(Ridley is killed), for by the same argument we could establish the falsity of the (true) proposition that Gunnar did not bring about C(Ridley is mortal). Or consider the case of Ryder and Dobbin. In turning down a certain road, Ryder did something causally sufficient for passing through Rome on a runaway horse, but would anyone want to say that Ryder brought about the (for him inevitable) state of affairs C(Ryder passes through Rome on a runaway horse)?

The states of affairs we have been considering are *universals*. There are *many* ways the concrete particulars that make up the world could be arranged that would be sufficient for their obtaining. What Gunnar and Ryder can bring about is *which* of these possible arrangements of particulars (which murderer, which road) the universals will be "realized in"; that

---

[19] By the editors of the *Philosophical Review*.

some arrangement or other of the particulars will realize these universals is something totally outside their control; it is not something they bring about. Here is an analogy involving another sort of universal, properties. Chisel is a sculptor and sculpts the heaviest statue that ever was or will be, *The Dying Whale.* Thus Chisel brings it about that a certain particular, *The Dying Whale*, exemplifies the property of being the heaviest statue.[20] But he does not bring it about that this property is exemplified, since, no matter what he had done, this property would "automatically" have been exemplified by something or other: he causes something to exemplify this property, but he does not cause this property to be exemplified.

In affirming (1), I do not mean to affirm the falsehood

(2) Gunnar did not bring about Ridley's death,

where "Ridley's death" denotes an *event-particular* (individuated from other particulars in virtue of having different causal antecedents), one

---

[20] Perhaps some philosophers would be disinclined to call the property of being the heaviest statue there ever was or will be a *universal*, on the ground that a universal must be "sharable," must be capable of being exemplified by more than one object. And, for similar reasons, it might be held that what I have called "states of affairs" are not true universals, since each of them either obtains or fails to obtain without further qualification, whereas a state of affairs that was truly a universal should be capable (say) of obtaining in 1943 but not in 1956 (cf. note 15), or of obtaining in both Britain and the United States but not in France. Well, let us say that our "states of affairs" and properties like being the heaviest statue are, if not "true" universals, at least *cross-world universals.* A property or other abstract object is a cross-world universal if there are worlds W1 and W2 such that x falls under it in W1 and y falls under it in W2 and $x \neq y$. (I use the words "fall under" with deliberate vagueness; what "falls under" a property is whatever has it; what "falls under" a state of affairs is whatever arrangement of particulars realizes it.) If this usage is an extension of traditional philosophical usage, it is a very natural one; I call, e.g., C(Gunnar kills Ridley) a "universal" because it is not "tied to" any given arrangement of particulars. I do not pretend that these remarks are very precise. Certainly the notion of an "arrangement of particulars" could do with some clarification. For example, it is not clear what should be said about states of affairs that, unlike those discussed above, involve only a single particular. (Let us say that a state of affairs *involves* a particular if that particular is such that its existence is entailed by the obtaining of that state of affairs.) Consider, for example, C(there is such a building as the Taj Mahal). Are there many "arrangements of particulars" in which this state of affairs could be realized? Tentatively, I should say Yes. I should think that "the arrangement of particulars that realizes a given state of affairs" should in general be taken to be an arrangement of a broader class of particulars than those it "involves." For example, C(there are human beings) does not in the strict sense defined above *involve* you or me (in fact, *no* contingent being is such that this state of affairs involves it), but you and I are, in a very intuitive sense, among those particulars the arrangement of which realizes it. Similarly, though no block of marble is such that C(there is such a building as the Taj Mahal) involves it – at least on the assumption that mereological essentialism is false – many blocks of marble would seem to be among those particulars the arrangement of which realizes it. Or even if we do not consider *parts* of the Taj Mahal, we must admit that the state of affairs we are considering would obtain if the Taj Mahal were differently placed or differently oriented; and it seems intuitively correct to say that if the place or orientation of the Taj Mahal were different from what it in fact is, then C(there is such a building as the Taj Mahal) would be realized in a different arrangement of particulars.

that is also perhaps denoted by "Ridley's death on Thursday," "the only death Gunnar ever caused," and so on. Anyone who feels inclined to reject (1) should make sure that this inclination does not arise from a failure to distinguish between (1) and (2). To revert to the sculpture example, (1) and (2) stand to each other roughly as

> Chisel did not cause the property of being the heaviest statue to be exemplified,

and

> Chisel did not cause (the particular thing that is) the heaviest statue to exist

stand to each other. The former is, as I argued above, true, and the latter false.[21]

So, it would seem, we are unable to devise a Frankfurt-style counter-example either to PPP1 or to PPP2. If our attempts at counterexamples looked initially plausible, this, I think, was due to a confusion. When we hear the Gunnar–Ridley story, it *seems* correct to say that it follows from the story that Gunnar is responsible for Ridley's death *and* that Gunnar could not have prevented Ridley's death. But "Ridley's death" is ambiguous. If we are using this phrase to denote a universal, then we may say that Gunnar could not have prevented Ridley's death, but not that he was responsible for Ridley's death. If we are using this phrase to denote a particular, then we may say that Gunnar was responsible for Ridley's death, but not that he could not have prevented it.

This result might lead us to wonder whether Frankfurt's counterexamples to PAP rest on a similar confusion. Suppose we were to split PAP into two principles, one about "act-particulars" (event-particulars that are voluntary movements of human bodies) and one about "act-universals" (that is, things that could be done by distinct agents, such as murder, prayer, or killing Jones at noon on Christmas Day 1953). Should we then see that Frankfurt's alleged counterexamples to PAP depend for their plausibility on treating one and the same act as a particular at one point in the argument, and a universal at another?

I do not think that Frankfurt is guilty of any such confusion. The "acts" that figure in his counterexamples seem to me to be treated consistently

---

[21] I do not mean to give the impression that one never brings about any state of affairs. For example, (granting the correctness of the Warren Commission Report), Lee Harvey Oswald brought about C(Kennedy dies on November 22, 1963). But it is *not* true that Oswald brought about C(Kennedy dies). That state of affairs was brought about by God or by Adam and Eve or by no one at all. Moreover, it *is* true that Oswald brought about the event-particular, Kennedy's death.

as universals. If this is the case, it raises two questions. Let us split PAP into two principles as was suggested in the preceding paragraph: PAP1 (about particulars) and PAP2 (about universals). The first question: If indeed Frankfurt's "acts" are universals, he is arguing against PAP2; can his argument be met by considerations like those we raised in defense of PPP2? The answer seems to me to be No, but I am not at all sure about this. The considerations raised in defense of PPP2 depended on our having at our disposal a fairly precise notion of "state-of-affairs universal," and I am not at present able to devise an equally precise notion of "act-universal" that I find satisfactory.[22] The second question: What about PAP1? I do not find this question interesting, since I do not think that "event-particulars that are voluntary movements of human bodies" are what we hold people responsible for. I shall not, however, defend this view here. An adequate defense of it would be fairly complex, and I do not think my reasons for thinking what I do on this matter are worth developing merely to establish a negative conclusion.

IV

We have shown that three principles relating ability and responsibility cannot be refuted by Frankfurt-style counterexamples:

PPA   A person is morally responsible for failing to perform a given act only if he could have performed that act.

PPP1   A person is morally responsible for a certain event only if he could have prevented it.

PPP2   A person is morally responsible for a certain state of affairs only if (that state of affairs obtains and) he could have prevented it from obtaining.

---

[22] An adequate construction of such a notion would require the introduction of a canonical language for act-universals. I am unable to devise a language for this purpose that comes close to satisfying me. Even without having such a language at my disposal, however, I think I see a serious obstacle to any attempt to refute Frankfurt's arguments against PAP2 by raising considerations like those used to defend PPP2 in the text. Let us suppose that "the act of killing Ridley" denotes a certain act-universal, an act such that *it*, that very act, could be the act of any among a number of agents and be performed under a great variety of conditions. Consider the following Frankfurt counterexample to PAP2: Gunnar performs the act of killing Ridley; moreover, if he had decided not to perform it, some third party, Cosser, would have caused him to perform it. If we were to try to refute this counterexample by arguments parallel to those we used in defense of PPP2, we should have to find an act-denoting phrase that stands to "the act of killing Ridley" roughly as "C(either Pistol or Gunnar

Now consider three versions of incompatibilism:

> If determinism is true, then if a given person failed to perform a given act, that person could not have performed that act.

> If determinism is true, then no event is such that anyone could have prevented it.

> If determinism is true, then if a given state of affairs obtains, then no one could have prevented that state of affairs from obtaining.[23]

Obviously, if these three theses are true, then (since PPA, PPP1, and PPP2 are true) it follows that determinism entails that no one has ever been or could ever be responsible for any event, state of affairs, or unperformed act. Moreover if the following schema

R   If S is responsible for Φing, then there is some event or state of affairs for which S is responsible

(here "Φing" is to be replaced by any grammatically appropriate action phrase) is valid, then determinism is (assuming incompatibilism) incompatible not only with our being responsible for the consequences of our acts but for our acts themselves. And this schema is extremely plausible. I cannot myself conceive of a case in which an agent is responsible for having performed some act but is responsible for *none* of the results or consequences (either universal or particular) of this act.[24]

---

or someone else kills Ridley)"stands to "C(Ridley is killed)." I am not sure what such a phrase would look like, but I think something like this:

> The act of killing Ridley, either without having been caused to kill Ridley by anyone, or as a result of having been caused to kill Ridley by Cosser or someone else.

I am very doubtful whether this phrase makes any sense. To take a simpler case, given that there is such an act as eating forbidden fruit, an act one might perform as a result of one's having been given bad advice, is there such an act as the act of eating forbidden fruit as a result of having been given bad advice? I find the notion of such an act difficult to grasp. But if no coherent act-universal-name can be found to play the formal role played by "C(either Pistol or Gunnar or someone else kills Ridley)" in our defense of PPP2, then no parallel argument in defense of PAP2 can be constructed.

These considerations, of course, do not show that Frankfurt's attack on PAP is successful. They do, however, raise serious doubts about the possibility of defending PAP against this attack by constructing an argument formally parallel to our argument in defense of PPP2.

[23] I think I am justified in calling these three theses "versions" of a single doctrine, since, *if* there were a good argument for any of them, then, I should think, it could be easily modified to yield a good argument for either of the others. I have presented arguments for what is essentially the first of these three versions of incompatibilism in "A Formal Approach to the Problem of Free Will and Determinism," *Theoria* 40 (1974): Part 1, pp. 9–22, and "The Incompatibility of Free Will and Determinism," *Philosophical Studies* 27 (1975): 185–199.

[24] An obvious argument for the validity of R is this: If someone Φs and is responsible for so acting, then, whatever other events or states of affairs he may be responsible for, he is at least responsible for its being the case that he Φs. But this argument is unsound. Consider the case (pp. 31–32 above)

Thus, if all three versions of incompatibilism are true, and if determinism is true, then there is simply no such thing as moral responsibility. There is such a thing as moral responsibility only if someone is responsible for something he has done, or for something he has left undone, or for the results or consequences of what he has done or left undone. And the principles for which I have argued (PPA, PPP1, PPP2, and the validity of schema R) entail that if incompatibilism is true, then determinism is incompatible with anyone's being responsible for anything whatever.

Therefore, even if PAP is false,[25] and even if Frankfurt's "correct version" of PAP (see note 4) cannot be used to show that determinism and moral responsibility are incompatible, it is *nonetheless* true that unless free will and determinism are compatible, determinism and moral responsibility are incompatible. Thus, Frankfurt's arguments do not, even if they are sound, rob the compatibilist–incompatibilist debate of its central place in the old controversy about determinism and moral responsibility.

---

involving the counterfactual propensities of atmospheric conditions to cause Gunnar to decide to kill, and to kill, Ridley. I argued that in that case Gunnar is not responsible for C(Ridley is killed). A similar argument could be used to show that in that case Gunnar is not responsible for C(Gunnar kills Ridley). But it does not follow that Gunnar is not responsible for killing Ridley. For Gunnar might have freely decided to kill Ridley and have killed him as a result of this free decision (and thus be responsible for killing Ridley); nevertheless, *if* he had (freely) decided *not* to kill Ridley, external factors outside his control would *then* have "come into play" and caused him (unfreely, of course) to kill Ridley. Therefore, while Gunnar is responsible for killing Ridley, he is not responsible for C(Gunnar kills Ridley freely or Gunnar kills Ridley unfreely) and hence is not responsible for C(Gunnar kills Ridley). Thus our "obvious" argument for the validity of R is fallacious.

Nonetheless, R seems to me to be valid. Certainly the case we have just considered is not a counterexample to its validity. For, in this case, while Gunnar is not responsible for C(Gunnar kills Ridley), he *is* responsible for C(Gunnar kills Ridley without having been caused to do so by atmospheric conditions). Moreover, he is responsible for the event-particular, Ridley's death.

[25] Of course, if the above arguments are correct, and if determinism and incompatibilism are both true, then PAP *is* true: it is vacuously true because no one, in that case, is responsible for anything he does. Frankfurt, of course, does not mean to deny that PAP might be, as a matter of contingent fact, vacuously true.

CHAPTER 2

On Two Arguments for Compatibilism

The two most popular arguments for the compatibility of free will and determinism are probably the following:

The Ethics Argument
Analysis shows that statements of ability are disguised conditionals. More exactly, the correct analysis of 'X could have done A' is 'If X had decided (chosen, willed ...) to do A, X would have done A'. Therefore, having acted freely – having been able to act otherwise than one in fact did – is compatible with determinism (with the causal determination of one's acts).

The Mind Argument
If one's acts were undetermined, they would be "bolts from the blue"; they would no more be *free* acts than they would if they had been caused by the manipulations of one's nervous system by a freakish demon. Therefore, free action is not merely *compatible* with determinism; it *entails* determinism.

(I call the first of these the *Ethics* Argument because two classic statements of it are to be found in books of that title. See G. E. Moore, *Ethics* (London: Home University Library, 1912), chapter 6; P. H. Nowell-Smith, *Ethics* (London: Penguin Books, 1954), chapters 19 and 20. I call the second the *Mind* Argument because it has appeared so often in the pages of that journal. See R. E. Hobart, 'Free Will as Involving Determination and Inconceivable Without It' (*Mind* 1934); P. H. Nowell-Smith, 'Free Will and Moral Responsibility' (*Mind* 1948); J. J. C. Smart, 'Free Will, Praise and Blame' (*Mind* 1961). A. J. Ayer's 'Freedom and Necessity', *Philosophical Essays* (London: Macmillan, 1954), did not appear in *Mind*. I am at a loss to account for this.) My statements of these two arguments are not intended to be complete or adequate. They are intended only to jog the reader's memory. For complete and adequate statements of the two arguments, the reader is referred to the places cited above.

I wish to thank Mark Brown for suggesting an improvement in the structure of the argument, and Jonathan Bennett for the point about motivation in the second to last paragraph.

I do not believe that it has been noticed that these two arguments are incompatible. That is: If either argument is sound (if its conclusion follows from its premises and if those premises are true), then the other is unsound.

To show this, we must first show that if the premise of the *Ethics* Argument is true, then free will is compatible not only with determinism but with *indeterminism* as well. To show this we need only tell a story having these three features: (1) in the story, an agent acts, and his act is causally undetermined; (2) in the story, his act is free; and (3) if statements of ability are disguised conditionals, then that story is internally consistent.

A story having these features is easy to construct. Suppose that Miss X has been deliberating about whether to tell the truth or to lie. Suppose that she has decided to tell the truth (and that, acting on this decision, she *has* told the truth). Suppose that this event – her having come to a decision to tell the truth – was not determined by earlier events or states: If God created a perfect duplicate of her as she was a moment before she made her decision to tell the truth, and if God placed that duplicate in circumstances identical with her circumstances at that moment, the duplicate might very well decide to lie. Suppose further that if X *had* chosen to lie, she would have lied. It is evident that (i) this story is consistent, and (ii) if 'X could have lied' is equivalent to 'if X had decided to lie, X would have lied', then the story entails the following three propositions:

X told the truth

X could have lied

X's telling the truth was causally undetermined.

(I take the first two of these propositions jointly to entail 'X told the truth freely'.) It would seem that we have told a story with the required features, and have therefore demonstrated that if statements of ability are disguised conditionals, then free will is compatible with indeterminism. (It may be objected that there are available more sophisticated analyses of ability-statements as conditionals than the one that figures in the above argument. This is true, but I do not think that the argument would fail if it were reconstructed so as to involve any of these more sophisticated conditional analyses of ability. Of course, one could always offer *this* analysis: 'X could have done A' means 'If X had decided to do A, X would have done A, and either X's decision to do A or the non-occurrence of a decision by X to do A – whichever of the two in fact occurred – was causally determined'. But no one *has* ever offered any such analysis, and I can see no motivation for doing so, other than a desire to devise a version of the *Ethics* argument that is compatible with the *Mind* argument. But what might move anyone to devise a version of the *Ethics* argument with *that* particular feature? A desire to have available as many arguments for compatibilism as possible?)

The promised conclusion is now easy to demonstrate. If the *Ethics* Argument is sound, then 'X could have done A' means 'If X had decided to do A, X would have done A'. If 'X could have done A' means 'If X had decided to do A, X would have done A', then (as we have seen) free will is compatible with indeterminism. If the *Mind* Argument is sound, then free will entails determinism. If free will entails determinism, then free will is not compatible with indeterminism. Therefore, if either argument is sound, the other is unsound.

CHAPTER 3

Compatibilistic Reflections

There are four possible positions one might take about the logical relations that obtain among free will, determinism, and indeterminism. (1) Free will is compatible with determinism and incompatible with indeterminism (*sc.* of human actions); (2) Free will is incompatible with determinism and compatible with indeterminism; (3) Free will is incompatible with determinism and incompatible with indeterminism; (4) Free will is compatible with determinism and compatible with indeterminism.

Positions (1) and (2) are the historically important ones. Position (3) has, to my knowledge, been taken only by C. D. Broad.[1] Position (4) has, to my knowledge, been taken by no one.[2]

The adherents of positions (1) and (2) spend a good deal of time accusing each other of confusion and lack of insight. While I should not want to deny that one of these positions is a repository of confusion and lack of insight, I think that positions (1) and (2) are a lot more similar than is usually supposed. Each is, in a way I hope to make evident, a sort of mirror image of the other. In the present paper, I will lay out what seems to me to be a deep symmetry between what adherents of position (1) have often said in defense of the thesis 'Free will is compatible with determinism' and something that adherents of position (2) might with equal justification say in defense of the thesis 'Free will is compatible with indeterminism' – though, to their credit, none of them ever *has* said it.

The words of Section I are spoken by an imaginary defender of position (1). (But he is typical, for all he is imaginary.) The words of Section II are spoken by a wholly imaginary defender of position (2).

---

[1] *Determinism, Indeterminism and Libertarianism* (Cambridge University Press, 1934). (Note that the present essay was originally published in 1985.)

[2] (Note added in 2015.) In "Are We Free to Break the Laws?," David Lewis says, "I am a compatibilist but no determinist ..." Since Lewis certainly believed that we sometimes act freely, he must have accepted (4). See *Philosophical Papers, Volume II* (Oxford University Press, 1987), p. 291.

I

Free will is compatible with determinism Many philosophers have denied this (among writers in the twentieth century, one might cite C. D. Broad, A. C. Campbell, Roderick M. Chisholm, and Richard Taylor), but we may prove them wrong as follows. Free will is the ability to act otherwise than one in fact does. That the possession of this ability is consistent with determinism may be seen from the following analysis of 'can':

Analysis I   X can do A = $_{df}$ If X decided to do A, X would do A.

It is evident that even if it is determined by past events and the laws of nature that X is not going to do A, the conditional 'If X decided to do A, X would do A' may very well be true.

II

Free will is compatible with indeterminism. Many philosophers have denied this (among writers in the twentieth century, one might cite C. D. Broad, R. E. Hobart, A. J. Ayer, and J. J. C. Smart), but we may prove them wrong as follows. Free will is the ability to act otherwise than one in fact does. That the possession of this ability is consistent with indeterminism may be seen from the following analysis of 'can':

Analysis II   X can do A = $_{df}$ If X decided to do A, X might do A.[3]

It is evident that even if it is not determined by past events and the laws of nature whether X is going to do A, the conditional 'If X decided to do A, X might do A' may very well be true.

III

It might be objected that the symmetry I allege to hold between the argument of Section I and the argument of Section II is contrived and merely verbal, owing to the fact that 'X can do A' is *not* equivalent to 'If X decided to do A, X might do A'. These statements are not equivalent

---

[3] Note that the 'would' counterfactual of Analysis I and the 'might' counterfactual of Analysis II are intimately connected. As David Lewis has observed (*Counterfactuals* [Cambridge, MA: Harvard University Press, 1973], p. 2), 'would' and 'might' counterfactuals are interdefinable:

If it were the case that A, it might be the case that B = $_{df}$ (if it were the case that A, it would be the case that ~B)

If it were the case that A, it would be the case that B = $_{df}$ ~ (if it were the case that A, it might be the case that ~B).

(it will be said) because the conditional could be true even if it were a *mere matter of chance* whether a decision by X to do A would be followed by X's actually doing A; but (the argument continues) if it were a mere matter of chance whether a decision by X to do A would be followed by his actually doing A, then 'X can do A' would be false, since it would not be up to X whether a decision of his to do A would actually issue in his doing A.

I will concede that this argument shows that Analysis II is incorrect. This concession does not entail that the symmetry I have alleged is merely verbal, however, since Analysis I is also incorrect. This is well known: to suppose that X *decides* to do A may well be to suppose him to be endowed with powers in respect of doing A that he does not in fact possess,[4] and this possibility generates a rather diverse class of counterexamples to Analysis I. Analysis I, for example, entails that a man who is in a coma – but who is otherwise unimpaired as regards rising and walking – *can* rise and walk: if he decided to rise and walk he would. (To imagine him deciding to arise and walk is to imagine him as having emerged from his coma, and is therefore to imagine him as endowed with powers he does not in fact possess.)

Let us take this line of thought a step further. Those who think that Analysis I is on the right track, even if it is wrong as it stands, often propose adding to its analysans a conjunct saying that X can decide to do A:

Analysis Ia   X can do A = $_{df}$ If X decided to do A, X would do A, and X can decide to do A.

The 'can' in the analysans is normally treated as having a different sense from the 'can' in the analysandum (Analysis Ia could hardly be called an analysis if this were not so), and its presence in the analysans is held to constitute a promissory note: when the sense of *that* 'can' has been spelled out, the analysis of 'can' in the primary sense will be complete.

But if there were any philosophers who thought that Analysis II was on the right track, even if it was wrong as it stood, why couldn't they likewise add a conjunct and issue a note? What would be wrong with their proposing the following revision of Analysis II?

Analysis IIa   X can do A = $_{df}$ If X decided to do A, X might do A, and X can act on a decision to do A.

---

[4] Cf. Keith Lehrer, "'Can' in Theory and Practice: A Possible Worlds Approach," in M. Brand and D. Walton (eds.), *Action Theory* (Dordrecht: Reidel, 1976).

IV

Objection

The added conjunct in Analysis IIa is equivalent to 'X can do A' – that is, to the analysandum itself, while the added clause in Analysis Ia is not equivalent to 'X can do A'.

Reply

It is not true that 'X can act on a decision to do A' is equivalent to 'X can do A'. For it might be that X lacks the power to do A, though he *would* have the power to do A *if* he decided to do A. In other words, it might be that it is not within X's power to decide to do A, though it is within X's power to act on a decision to do A. We have considered just such a case in Section III: the case of the comatose man.

Objection

If human acts are undetermined, then it is not *only* true that if X decided to do A, X might do A; it is also true that if X decided to do A, X might not do A. And these two conditionals together are inconsistent with 'X can act on a decision to do A'. Thus, the analysans of Analysis IIa could not be true if human acts were undetermined.

Reply

Perhaps. That depends on whether 'can' in the analysans of Analysis IIa is being used in a sense that entails that 'X can act on a decision to do A' is inconsistent with the proposition that there would be only an indeterministic connection between a decision by X to do A and his subsequent action (his doing or not doing A, as the case may be).

Compare this exchange with the following exchange:

If human decisions to act are determined, and if X does not decide to do A, then it is determined that X not decide to do A. But the proposition that it is determined that X not decide to do A is inconsistent with 'X can decide to do A'. Therefore, the analysans of Analysis Ia could not be true if human decisions to act were determined and X did not decide to do A.

Perhaps. That depends on whether 'can' in the analysans of Analysis Ia is being used in a sense that entails that 'X can decide to do A' is inconsistent with the proposition that it is determined that X not decide to do A.

V

There have been various attempts to spell out 'X can decide to do A' in a way that entails that this proposition is compatible with its being determined that X not decide to do A. (And which are not themselves conditionals; a conditional analysis of 'can decide' would presumably invite its critics to raise the question whether the truth of the antecedent of the conditional mightn't augment X's powers in respect of *deciding* to do A, and the advocates of the analysis would find themselves with the problem of analysis not solved but postponed.) For example, here is an adaptation of a proposal by Wilfrid Sellars:

X can (at t) decide to do A = $_{df}$ There obtains at t no state of affairs that is incompossible with X's deciding at t to do A.[5]

But what is sauce for Analysis Ia is sauce for Analysis IIa:

X can (at t) act on a decision = $_{df}$ There obtains at t no state of affairs
to do A   that in conjunction with X's deciding at t to do A would determine that X not do A.

Note that if this analysis is correct, then 'X can act on a decision to do A' is compatible with its being the case that a decision by X to do A would have no determinate connection with his subsequent action (with his doing or his not doing A, as the case may be).

VI

In sections I through V of this paper, two lines of argument are presented. One of them is an argument for the compatibility of free will and determinism. The other is an argument for the compatibility of free will and

---

[5] "Fatalism and Determinism," in K. Lehrer (ed.), *Freedom and Determinism* (New York: Random House, 1966). This, of course, is a very sketchy adaptation of Sellars's proposal. It is meant merely to provide an example and is not supposed to be an accurate representation of what Sellars actually says. It is perhaps worth noting (a) that 'incompossible' refers to physical, as opposed to logical, incompossibility, and (b) that Sellars's actual proposal involves not decisions but "volitions" in a certain technical sense.

indeterminism. The former seems to be regarded by many philosophers as an adequate defense of the thesis that free will is compatible with determinism. The latter is regarded by no one as an adequate defense of the thesis that free will is compatible with indeterminism, for I have made it up and it certainly does not strike *me* as an adequate defense of that thesis. Though I in fact do think that free will is compatible with indeterminism, the argument for that conclusion that I have presented in this paper has, in my judgment, no merit whatever. What I should like to know is: Why does anyone suppose that the other argument is any better?

CHAPTER 4

Critical Study of Dennett's Elbow Room

The announced purpose of this book[1] is to dispel the confusions and anxieties by means of which philosophers persuade one another that there is such a thing as "the problem of free will." For that is what they do: if they didn't, everyone would long ago have turned his attention to more profitable areas of philosophical inquiry. Despite the fact that a "compatibilist" treatment of the so-called problem is obviously correct (Dennett maintains), philosophers are still arguing about it; the arguments, therefore, are evidently a mere facade. Behind the facade lurk fears – the fear of naturalism; the fear that one is a mere automaton; the fear that one is not really a *self* – fears begotten by conceptual confusion or the desire to have something to write articles about.[2] These misbegotten fears are not viable, but they are kept alive by extraordinary measures: continual transfusions of plausibility from really fearsome things by misapplied "intuition pumps." My impression is that Dennett regards even the traditional compatibilist as prey to the fears that collectively make up the free-will problem: if the compatibilist weren't prey to these fears, he wouldn't bother arguing with the incompatibilist. (Dennett does not say much about other compatibilists, and he certainly does not acknowledge the predominance of the doctrine among contemporary writers on free will. Why Dennett does not tell his readers that the *content* of his views on free will – as opposed to his views on the etiology of the free-will debate – is the prevailing orthodoxy, I'm not quite sure. I *am* sure that a reader of *Elbow Room* who was not familiar with the history of philosophy in the English-speaking countries would not learn from it that most analytical philosophers are compatibilists. Because Dennett says so little about his fellow compatibilists, my description of his attitude

---

[1] Daniel C. Dennett, *Elbow Room: The Varieties of Free Will Worth Wanting* (Cambridge, MA: MIT Press, 1984).

[2] Or perhaps on a humanistic hatred of science. The immediate ancestry of the fears is not consistently described, but there is certainly bad blood in the family.

toward them is largely guesswork. My impression is that he regards them with the sort of condescension that Marxist and Freudian atheists reserve for old-fashioned Enlightenment atheists like Holbach and Russell: such people don't understand the real sources of the superstition they fulminate against and are therefore at best imperfectly free of it themselves.) Like many cultural diagnosticians, Dennett sees symptoms everywhere. (I am put in mind of a Freudian analysis of science fiction I once read, in which a spaceship was a phallus if it was longer than it was wide, and a womb otherwise.) An incompatibilist can't so much as mention a man locked in a room without Dennett's accusing him of insidiously suggesting that if determinism were true, it would be just as if we were all in jail.[3] Dennett also has an annoying trick of asking rhetorical questions of the *What do you suppose it is that makes him beat his wife so much?* type. What is it, he wonders rhetorically, that people find so horrible about determinism? (See, e.g., p. 15. But the idea that philosophical rejections of determinism are based on fear is one of the central ideas of the book, and it surfaces repeatedly.) Having raised the question, he proceeds to answer it. He does not raise the question whether anyone actually does find determinism horrible (as opposed to false, ill-supported, or in conflict with some thesis that seems antecedently more probable than determinism). As long as we are speculating about people's hidden motives, I will speculate that philosophers (other than myself) who speculate about the hidden motives of other philosophers do so because it is easier to speculate about the invisible and unverifiable than to address arguments. (And, of course, it is very pleasant to represent oneself as someone who is in a position to expose the hidden motives of others. *I'm* certainly enjoying it.) Is this fair to Dennett? Let's say that it is as fair as speculation about hidden motives ever is.

Despite all this diagnostic nonsense – *I* think it's nonsense, anyway – this is a rather good book. A lot of confusions that some people are doubtless prey to are nicely straightened out.[4] (I particularly commend the beautiful exposure in Chapter Three of certain widespread confusions about control and self-control), and a wealth of fascinating empirical information

---

[3] I once needed to make the point that someone can *make* a choice without *having* a choice; I remarked that a man who is locked in a room without knowing it can make a choice about leaving without having a choice about leaving. Dennett (p. 105) cites this harmless piece of conceptual analysis as an instance of "the well-worn intuition pump, the Invisible Jail." Dennett's rule, apparently, is that any incompatibilist who uses a story involving a locked room for any conceptual purpose whatever is subliminally suggesting that a deterministic world would be like a prison.

[4] In the original version of this review, I cited a then recently published book that I said "might have been written to prove that there are people who are prey to these confusions." I see no point in identifying the book in this reprinting.

finds its way into the examples. But I don't think the book does much to advance our understanding of the traditional problem of free will. In the sequel, I will explain my reservations.

Dennett's discussion of what *I* would call "the problem of free will and determinism" occurs in Chapter Six, the chapter called "Could Have Done Otherwise." I have had a *very* hard time deciding what the argument of this chapter is. I will present my own rational reconstruction of parts of the argument. Doubtless it is no more accurate than most rational reconstructions.

As I read Dennett, Chapter Six is mainly an attack on the principle

CU   An agent is morally responsible for an act only if that act was causally undetermined.

But this is a controversial interpretation. Dennett's *announced* target is stated in more or less the following words (he gives no "official" statement of it):

CDO   An agent is morally responsible for an act only if that agent could have done otherwise.[5]

What Dennett *means* by 'X did A and could have done otherwise', however, seems to be something like 'X's doing A was causally undetermined'. At any rate, I try to show that this is what he has to mean by this phrase if his argument against CDO is even to be relevant to its conclusion (much less *valid*). It might be objected that I must be wrong about this, since, according to Dennett, he proposes to attack a "widely accepted" principle – and CU, far from being widely accepted, is an object of popular derision. I answer that Dennett *thinks* he is attacking a widely accepted principle and he is wrong.

Dennett's mistake is a complicated one. In broad outline, it is this. Consider the principle

WA   An agent is morally responsible for an act only if that agent was able to do otherwise.

The principle CDO is ambiguous: it might mean either CU or WA. WA is widely accepted. But it is to CU that Dennett's argument applies.

Dennett's argument, or an important part of it, is something like this. When philosophers employ the principle CDO, they mean that the agent in question is morally responsible only if he could have done otherwise

---

[5] I.e., could have done otherwise than perform that act – PvI.

in exactly the same circumstances. But it is in practice impossible to find out whether someone could have done otherwise than he did in *exactly* the same circumstances, for 'circumstances' in this context refers (in defiance of its etymology) not only to *external* circumstances but also to the state of the agent's body and brain. If CDO were correct, therefore, we could never know whether an agent was responsible for anything. If a concept is such that we can never, in practice if not in principle, know whether it applies, then that concept, however interesting it may be to philosophers, is not a concept that would be of any use in everyday life. Therefore, if there is *any* concept that goes by the name "moral responsibility" and which satisfies the demands of CDO, it is not the concept that goes by that name in everyday life.

I shall presently criticize this argument. But first I will show that it must be read as an attack on the disreputable principle CU and not on the respectable principle WA.

It is well known to students of the free-will problem that 'could have' is ambiguous: these words can mean either 'might have' or 'was able to'. This ambiguity can be especially acute when 'could have' occurs in the consequent of a conditional. Consider the sentences, 'If you'd startled Alice, she could have fallen' and 'If you'd distracted the guard, Alice could have escaped'. On the most natural ways of reading them, these sentences mean, respectively,

You startled Alice $\Diamond\!\!\rightarrow$ she fell

You distracted the guard $\Box\!\!\rightarrow$ Alice was able to escape.

In the former sentence, 'could have' is absorbed into the conditional-mood connective; in the latter, into the indicative-mood consequent. The following two cases (adapted from Austin) provide a second example of this ambiguity. In each case, one financier addresses another. *Case One* (could have = were able to): "You could have ruined me this morning, but you didn't. I owe you one." *Case Two* (could have = might have): "You could have ruined me this morning. *Warn* me the next time you're going to pull a stunt like that one." It is important to remember that the proposition that X was able to do otherwise does not, uncontroversially, entail the proposition that X might have done otherwise in exactly the same circumstances. Those who say that this entailment holds are called *incompatibilists*. Those who deny that it holds are called *compatibilists*.

Now recall Dennett's argument. According to Dennett, what the proponents of CDO really mean by their thesis is more completely expressed in these words:

ESC   An agent is morally responsible for an act only if that agent could
have done otherwise in exactly the same circumstances.

Consider the consequent of this conditional (call the agent 'X'):

X could have done otherwise in exactly the same circumstances.

Do the words 'could have done' in this sentence mean 'was able to do'
or 'might have done'? They must mean 'might have done'; they cannot
mean 'was able to'. Or, at any rate, charity forbids the latter interpretation.
For suppose 'could have done' did mean 'was able to'. Then this sentence
would read

X was in exactly the circumstances X was actually in $\square \rightarrow$X was able to
do otherwise.

But the antecedent of this conditional is "automatically" true, so what is
the point of it? What is the point of saying, e.g., "If the election had turned
out exactly the way it did, Reagan would have been elected"? Why not say
simply, "Reagan was elected"? What is the point of saying, "If he had been
at *t* exactly as he then was, he would (at *t*) have been able to do something
other than what he in fact proceeded to do"? Why not simply say, "He
was (at *t*) able to do something other than what he in fact proceeded to
do"?[6] (But it makes perfect sense to say, "(Even) if he had been at *t* exactly
as he then was, he might have done something other than what he in fact
proceeded to do.") Charity dictates that we assume that people do not add
pointless qualifications to what they say – especially when they insist on
the importance of those qualifications. Charity dictates, therefore, that we
take ESC to mean

An agent is morally responsible for an act only if that agent might
have done otherwise in exactly the same circumstances.

To say that an agent might have done otherwise in exactly the same circumstances is to say that if the agent and his environment were returned
to *exactly* the state they were in just before he acted, then he might well
act differently the "second time round." And to assert that conditional is
to say that what the agent did in actuality was causally undetermined. For
if what he did in actuality was causally *determined* by his inner state and
the state of his environment at *t*, then returning him and his environment

---

[6] Or put the point like this: to say that someone was (at *t*) able to raise his hand is simply to say that at
t he possessed a certain property: being able to raise one's hand. It makes no more sense to say, "He
was (at *t*) able to raise his hand in exactly the same circumstances" than it does to say "He was (at *t*)
bald in exactly the same circumstances."

to *exactly* their condition at *t* would have to produce the *same* result the second time round.

Therefore, the real target of Dennett's argument is not the respectable principle WA (or any other widely accepted principle), but CU, a principle most philosophers reject. Is his argument against this unpopular principle cogent? In order the better to answer this question, let us recast it as an argument that is explicitly directed against CU:

Since we can never in practice return an agent's body, brain, and environment to exactly the conditions they were in at some previous time – since, in fact, we cannot even trace in any detail the workings of the brain – it is in practice impossible to find out whether an agent's act was causally undetermined. If CU were correct, therefore, we could never know whether an agent was responsible for anything. If a concept is such that we can never, in practice if not in principle, know whether it applies, then that concept, however interesting it may be to philosophers, is not a concept that would be of any use in everyday life. Therefore, if there is *any* concept that goes by the name "moral responsibility" and which satisfies the demands of CU, it is not the concept that goes by that name in everyday life.

(We may note that anyone who accepts this argument should reject the contention of Broad, Hobart, Ayer, Nowell-Smith, Smart, and many others, that an agent can be morally responsible for an act only if that act was determined.[7] For it is exactly as hard to find out whether a given act is determined as it is to find out whether that act is undetermined.)

This argument seems to me to be invalid. Take any concept that we are perfectly sure we do employ in everyday life. The concept of a dog, say. That there are dogs entails the truth of Goldbach's Conjecture, or else entails the falsity of Goldbach's Conjecture. It is, in practice if not in principle, impossible for me (and you, too) to find out whether Goldbach's Conjecture is true or false. But it hardly follows from these facts that the concept of a dog is of no interest to the working veterinarian or burglar.

Now it might be held that this reply works by exploiting the "paradoxes of strict implication" or some other defect in the orthodox philosophical understanding of entailment. This rejoinder, however, is directed at a merely accidental feature of the above criticism of Dennett's argument. Consider "rogs." Rogs are robotic "dogs" – creatures of the philosophically invaluable Martians – which we cannot (in practice) tell from standard,

[7] And Dennett does reject this contention. See "On Giving Libertarians What They Say They Want," which is chapter 15 of *Brainstorms: Philosophical Essays on Mind and Psychology* (Cambridge, MA: MIT Press/Bradford Books, 1978).

protein dogs. Let DR be the principle, 'A thing is a dog only if it is not a rog'. We argue:·

It is in practice impossible to find out whether a (superficially doggish) thing is a rog or a dog. If DR were correct, therefore, we could never know whether a (doggish) thing was a dog … Therefore, if there is *any* concept that goes by the name "dog" and which satisfies the demands of DR, it is not the concept that goes by that name in everyday life.

The conclusion of this argument is false, since a thing that looked like a dog but which was really a clever robot would *not* be a dog. The argument is therefore defective. What is wrong with it? It is important to keep in mind that this is not a *skeptical* argument. Its conclusion is not the (false) proposition that we never know whether anything is a dog; it is, rather, the (false) proposition that the everyday concept "dog" is compatible with "robot." Nevertheless, the argument shares certain premises with the standard "wild hypothesis" arguments for skepticism. It shares, for example, the premise that if p entails q, then one cannot come to know that p unless one first (or, at least, simultaneously) finds out whether q. This principle has come in for a good deal of deserved abuse. Dennett's argument against CU – or CDO or whatever its target is – would appear also to have this principle as a premise. I would suggest that *whatever* the defect in the rog/dog argument is, Dennett's argument shares that defect.

It may be suggested that the two arguments are not really parallel, owing to the fact that, while the thesis that our acts are causally determined is not absurd, not something we are justified in assigning an infinitesimal subjective probability to (some even find it highly plausible), the thesis that there are rogs at large in our environment is absurd. I accept these two judgments. But I would point out that neither the thesis that human acts are causally determined nor its denial had occurred to anyone during the formative years of the concept of moral responsibility. Therefore, *no* fact about this thesis (whether it be the fact that it does not seem to twentieth-century, middle-class, naturalistically inclined professors of philosophy to be absurd, or any other fact about it) had any opportunity to play a causal role in the development of the concept of moral responsibility. If, in the future, some amazing revelation transpired that made us think that there might well be rogs abroad in the land, this prodigy would not change the fact that the rog/dog argument is a bad argument for a false conclusion.

Dennett has a second argument against CU – or at least it is most charitably interpreted as an argument against CU. He imagines a robot that has performed badly in some unanticipated way in a certain situation. He imagines its designers thereupon asking one another, "Could it have done otherwise?" (He *says* that they use those words. It's his case; but it doesn't seem to me that people in those circumstances would be likely to say that.) What the designers would be asking, Dennett suggests, is whether the robot would behave in the same undesirable way in circumstances that were *for all practical purposes* the same: if it would have behaved in the same undesirable way in relevantly similar circumstances, then it "couldn't have done otherwise." (The designers would grant – if they thought about it – that the robot would behave in the same way in *exactly* the same circumstances; but since the chance of an *exact* duplication of the robot's original situation is infinitesimal, it will probably not occur to them even to formulate this thesis.) If the robot "couldn't have done otherwise," the designers have a good reason to modify or reprogram the robot or its successors. Dennett's point, apparently, is that this case is analogous to cases in which we ask the question 'Could he have done otherwise?' about a human being, and he strongly suggests that what we really want to know when we ask whether a human being could have done otherwise is this: Should we modify him (or his successors) in such a way that in relevantly similar circumstances he (or they) will do better? – or, if we are not in a position to effect such modifications, should he be kept out of relevantly similar circumstances in the future? We are *not* raising the question whether we should modify him to deal with (or should keep him out of) a recurrence of *identical* circumstances, since the probability of a recurrence of identical circumstances is effectively zero. Therefore (finally), the answer, whatever it may be, to the philosophical question, 'Would X have done otherwise in exactly the same circumstances?', has no bearing on the everyday question 'Could X have done otherwise?'

Sometimes something like Dennett's account of the everyday use of 'Could he have done otherwise?' may be right. We send a spy into Ruritania, having given him certain training and instructions, and he is immediately captured. "Could he have done better?" we ask, meaning, 'Should the training and instructions given to his successors be different?' And we might indeed use these words, though it seems to me to be far more probable that we'd say something along the lines of, "Was that sheer bad luck, or do we need to review our training procedures?" But remember that our general topic is the responsibility of the *agent* (no pun intended). And if we ask, concerning the spy, "Could he have done better?" in Dennett's sense, we are not even raising the question whether *he* was responsible for the failure to his mission – though we may proceed to raise the question whether the Director of Espionage Training was. Contrast this use of 'could have done better' with its use in the following exchange. M says, "I'm inclined not to blame our preparations, but 007 himself. It's his fault. He could have done better." A friend of 007's defends him: "Really, M. The pilot dropped him in the middle of a KGB battalion. There was nothing he could have done." The friend is saying that, since 007 did not have it within his power to do better, he cannot be blamed.[8] And this returns us to the question of incompatibilism: Does the everyday use of 'could have done [= was able to do] otherwise' entail 'might have done otherwise in exactly the same circumstances'? There are arguments for incompatibilism. Perhaps they are defective, but, if so, the reader will not find out about their defects (or their content or their existence) from Dennett's book.

I have tried to show that Dennett's arguments against CDO must, since they contain the qualification "in exactly the same circumstances," be understood as arguments against CU and not against WA; and that, considered as arguments against CU, they are unconvincing.

What about WA? Has Dennett any arguments that show, or which could be modified to show, that WA is false? It is clear that he thinks he has such an argument. As I have said, he thinks that his target is widely accepted; and at one point (p. 132) he identifies his target with the principle that Harry Frankfurt has attacked under the name "the Principle of Alternate Possibilities."[9] Dennett's belief that, in the arguments discussed above, he is attacking a widely accepted principle is a result of his failure to make appropriate distinctions among the similar-sounding principles WA, CDO, ESC, and CU. But Frankfurt's "Principle of Alternate Possibilities" is just WA. Since Dennett gives an accurate transcription of Frankfurt's argument against WA, and – while not disputing the cogency of Frankfurt's argument – promises a more radical attack on the same principle, I think he does mean to attack WA "under that description."

Dennett has only one argument that does not involve the fatal qualification 'in exactly the same circumstances' and which is, therefore, not automatically inapplicable to WA. Dennett asks us to consider Martin Luther, who – according to popular, if not to academic, history – said, "Here I stand. I can do no other." Several people have told me that they find Dennett's interpretation of Luther's words puzzling. Surely, they protest, what Luther meant (or what someone in Luther's position would mean if he in fact said those words) is this: This is the only morally permissible course of

---

[8] Here, of course, I am insidiously suggesting that living in a deterministic world would be like being at the mercy of a hostile armed force.

[9] "The Principle of Alternate Possibilities," *Journal of Philosophy* 66 (1969): 829–839.

action open to me. Surely – their protest continues – these words cannot be taken to mean, 'I am, literally, *unable* to do otherwise'. It is certainly true that when someone says "I can't," he often means "I can't without …," where the content of the ellipsis is supplied by context. Luther (might have) meant "I can't do it without acting wrongly." The bank officer who tells you that he can't approve your request for a loan does not mean that it isn't within his power so to arrange matters that your request is approved; he means that it isn't within his power to do this without violating the bank's rules (and thereby putting his job in jeopardy). I think that there is probably something to this reaction to Dennett's reading of Luther's words, but it would be a mistake to press the point, since other cases could be found that would serve Dennett's purposes. Cato the Elder and George Washington are both supposed to have been unable to lie. (Mark Twain: "I am morally superior to George Washington. He couldn't tell a lie. I can and I don't.") Suppose Washington refused to tell a lie on a certain occasion. Don't we admire him, even if we believe he wasn't able to lie? Don't we regard his telling the truth (in the face of a severe spanking for chopping down the cherry tree) as an act for which he was morally responsible? I despair of trying to answer these questions adequately in a few sentences. There are too many things that would have to be discussed first. I will briefly mention a few of them. First, I doubt whether we ever do, in ordinary moral discourse, "hold people responsible for their acts." We hold them responsible for the *results* or *consequences* of their acts (or failures to act). 'Just look at what you've done' means 'Just look at what you've caused'.[10] Secondly, talk of moral responsibility is much more closely tied to expressions of blame than to expressions of gratitude. (People often talk as if 'praise' were the opposite of 'blame'. It is not: you can praise Einstein's genius, but you can't blame a moron for being one. 'Blame' has no real opposite. 'Gratitude' is a better candidate than 'praise', but it is not satisfactory, since, although there is impersonal, disinterested blame, there is no such thing as disinterested gratitude.)[11] Thirdly, I believe that the staunchest proponents of WA admit that this principle is loosely stated, and that it should be elaborated to take account of "drunk driver" cases: cases in which a person's present inability to do otherwise is due to past misbehavior. (He was unable to swerve fast enough to avoid hitting the taxi at *t*, but we still hold him responsible for the accident, since there

---

[10] Cf. P. H. Nowell-Smith, "Action and Responsibility," in Myles Brand and Douglas Walton (eds.), *Action Theory* (Dordrecht: Reidel, 1976), pp. 311–322. See especially p. 315.

[11] "We give thanks to Thee for Thy great glory," says the *Gloria in Excelsis*. Perhaps this is poetic license.

was a time at which he could have so arranged matters that his reflexes were unimpaired at t – or that he was not at t in a situation that called for unimpaired reflexes.)

One who takes these three points seriously (as I do) may well want to say (as I do) that WA *is* false, but that it nevertheless expresses an important moral insight, one that is better expressed as follows:

> No event (or state of affairs) can be X's fault, or even partly X's fault, unless there was a time at which X was able so to arrange matters that that event (or state of affairs) not occur (or obtain).

Now this principle, too, can be disputed on various grounds.[12] (A philosopher is someone who thinks otherwise.) But I think it is a quite reasonable principle, and that it seems no less reasonable after I have examined its consequences for the cases of Luther, Cato, and Washington. I think, moreover, that it can do all the philosophical work that anyone has ever expected WA to do.

I conclude that, despite its considerable merits, *Elbow Room* has nothing to tell us about whether the thesis that we are sometimes morally accountable for the consequences of our acts is compatible with the thesis that those acts and their consequences are jointly necessitated by the laws of nature and certain propositions about the remote past.

---

[12] The most troublesome involve "overcausation": X and Y, acting independently, perform acts either of which would be sufficient for the death of Z ...

CHAPTER 5

When Is the Will Free?

There is, it seems to me, something that might be called an "orthodox" or "classical" tradition in the history of thinking about the problem of free will and determinism. This tradition, as I see it, descends from Hobbes through Locke and Hume and Mill to the present day. I say "it seems to me" and "as I see it" because I am no historian and I freely grant that what appears to my untutored mind to be "the classical tradition" in the debate about free will and determinism may be an artifact of certain historians – or even of the editors of certain anthologies. (And, of course, in identifying this tradition as "classical," I exhibit the Anglo-Saxon bias that my education was designed to inculcate: Bergson, Heidegger, and Sartre are not going to appear in my list of the members of anything called "the classical tradition.")

However this may be, I speak as a member of this tradition, and I want to begin by describing its presuppositions – *my* presuppositions.

According to "the classical tradition," the history of the problem of free will and determinism is, primarily, the story of a debate between two schools of philosophers, the "compatibilists" and the "incompatibilists"; that is between those who hold that free will is compatible with determinism and those who hold that free will is incompatible with determinism. Now I am going to have almost nothing to say about determinism in this paper. In fact, I am not going to talk about the problem of free will and determinism – or not directly about it. I begin with a brief characterization of the history of this problem because, while the paper is not about the problem of free will and determinism, it presupposes the correctness of a

This paper was read at a conference on "Freedom and Mind" at McGill University in September 1986, and as an invited paper at the 1987 meeting of the Central Division of the American Philosophical Association. On the latter occasion, the commentator was Robert Kane. The paper was also read to the Philosophy Department at Virginia Polytechnic Institute and State University. The audiences on these occasions are thanked for their useful comments, as are those who have been kind enough to correspond with me about the topics discussed herein. Special thanks are due to Daniel Dennett, Robert Kane, and Lawrence H. Davis.

certain way of looking at that problem. I do not propose to defend that way of looking at the problem – the way adherence to which defines membership in what I am pleased to call "the classical tradition" – but I do want to make it clear what that way of looking at the problem is, and that it is my way. Since I shall have almost nothing to say about determinism, I shall not attempt to give any very careful explanation of this important idea. I will say only this. Determinism is the thesis that the past and the laws of nature together *determine* a unique future, that only one future is consistent with the past and the laws of nature. I am, however, going to have a great deal to say about free will and I will lay out in some detail the concept that the classical or orthodox tradition associates with the words 'free will'.

The term 'free will' is a philosophical term of art. (It is true that this term occurs in ordinary English, but its occurrence is pretty much restricted to the phrase 'of his own free will' – which means, more or less, 'uncoerced'. If someone uses the words 'free will' and does not use them within this phrase, he is almost certainly a participant in a philosophical discussion.) The first thing to realize about the use of the words 'free will' by philosophers belonging to the classical tradition is that, *now* at least, these words are a mere label for a certain feature, or alleged feature, of human beings and other rational agents, a label whose sense is not determined by the meanings of the individual words 'free' and 'will'. In particular, the ascription of "free will" to an agent by a current representative of the classical tradition does not imply that the agent has a "faculty" called 'the will'. It was not always so. Once upon a time, to say that X "had free will" was to imply that X had something called a 'will' and that this will was not only unimpeded by external circumstances (in which case the agent X *himself* was called 'free'), but that X's internal constitution left him "free" to "will" in various alternative ways. (The title of this paper is a relic of those times.) A tradition, however, is a changing thing, and the classical tradition has abandoned these implications of the words "free will." When a *current* representative of the classical tradition says of, e.g., Mrs. Thatcher, that she "has free will," he means that she is at least sometimes in the following situation: She is contemplating incompatible courses of action A and B (lecturing the Queen and holding her tongue, say), and she *can* pursue the course of action A and *can also* pursue the course of action B.

Now the word 'can' is one of the trickiest of all the little philosophically interesting Anglo-Saxon words. It is not only ambiguous; it is ambiguous in a rather complicated way. Accordingly, representatives of the classical tradition, when they are explaining the sense of their term of art 'free will', generally prefer to use some other words, in addition to 'can', to get their point across, rather as if they were trying to convey what someone looked like by displaying a photograph and a painted portrait and a pen-and-ink caricature. They say not only 'can do A and can also do B', but 'is able to do A and is also able to do B', and 'has it within his power to do A and has it within his power to do B', and 'has a choice about whether to do A or to do B'. They may also use language that is not ordinary English at all, but which seems somehow useful in conveying the sense they intend. They may, for example, talk of a sheaf of alternative possible futures that confront the agent, and say that he has free will just in the case that more than one of these futures is "open" to him or "accessible" to him.

Compatibilists, then, say that "free will" in this sense can exist in a deterministic world, and incompatibilists say that it cannot. The classical tradition sees the problem of free will and determinism as centered round the debate between the compatibilists and the incompatibilists. But what is at stake in this debate? Why should anyone care whether we have free will (in this special sense)? The answer is this: We care about morality, or many of us do, and, according to the classical tradition, there is an intimate connection between "free will" and morality. The connection is complicated, and various representatives of the classical tradition would describe it differently. But the following statement would, I think, be accepted by everyone within the classical tradition. Most within the tradition would want to say more; some much more. But this "highest common factor" by itself explains why many people care about whether we have free will.

> Some states of affairs are bad. They ought not to exist. And among these bad states of affairs are some that *are the fault of* certain human beings. These human beings *are to be blamed* for those states of affairs. The Nazis, for example, are *to be blamed* for the death camps: the existence of those camps is *their fault*. The Kennedy and Johnson and Nixon administrations are to be blamed for the US involvement and actions in Vietnam. They (and perhaps others, but they at least) can be *held to account* for that involvement and many of its consequences. On a more homely and personal level, our profession is to blame for the fact that many young men and women are being graduated from universities who cannot compose an English sentence or tell you who Galileo was. And, doubtless, each reader of this paper knows of bad states of affairs that are his fault and his alone. But if there were no free will – if no one were able to act otherwise – then no state of affairs would be anyone's fault. No one would ever be morally accountable for anything.

The actions of some people might indeed be among the causes of various bad states of affairs, but those things they caused would never be their fault. For example, suppose a father has raped his nine-year-old daughter and, as a result, she has suffered immediate physical pain and terror and has experienced lifelong psychological and emotional disorders. Unless the father had at least some measure of free will, the pain and terror and the rest are not his fault. He cannot be blamed for them. They are not something for which he can be held to account

I have not argued for this position. I am only reminding you of what the classical tradition says about the relationship between being able to do otherwise than one does and moral accountability. It is because, rightly or wrongly, the members of the classical tradition believe in this relationship that they think it is an important question whether we have free will. Almost all of the members of the classical tradition have in fact believed in free will, although there are exceptions. Baron d'Holbach believed that determinism was true and that free will was incompatible with determinism and that there was thus no free will. C. D. Broad believed that free will was incompatible with both determinism and indeterminism, and was thus impossible. But Holbach and Broad were exceptions. Almost all of the members of the classical tradition believe in free will. What they differ about is what free will is compatible with. Most incompatibilists, at least among trained philosophers, believe in free will. All compatibilists I am aware of believe in free will; there's not much point in being a compatibilist and not believing in free will.

Before going further, I want to point out what seems to me to be a blunder made by some writers on the problem of free will and determinism. Some writers speak of an "incompatibilist sense of 'can do otherwise'" – and a "compatibilist sense of 'can do otherwise'." But when English-speaking compatibilists and incompatibilists argue about whether people could act otherwise in a deterministic world, they are using the words 'could act otherwise' in exactly the same sense. Otherwise they wouldn't be disagreeing about anything, would they? Each of them, being a speaker of English, knows what 'could have', 'was able to', and so on, mean when they are used in everyday life, and each means to be, and is, using these words in that everyday sense. Their case may be compared with the case of the dualist and the materialist in the philosophy of mind. Each uses phrases like 'feels pain' and 'is thinking about Vienna' in the same *sense* – the sense provided by the English language – though the two of them have radically opposed opinions as to the nature of the events and processes to which these terms apply.

Similarly with the compatibilist and the incompatibilist: the two of them use phrases like 'could have acted otherwise' in just the same sense – the sense provided by the English language – and disagree about whether that one sense expresses something that could obtain in a deterministic world. Now it may be that a particular compatibilist or incompatibilist has a mistaken *theory* about what 'could act otherwise' means. But, in such a case, that philosopher does not *himself* mean by 'could act otherwise' what his mistaken theory says these words mean. For example, suppose that a certain compatibilist has published an essay the burden of which is that '*x* could act otherwise' means '*x* would act otherwise if he chose to'. And suppose that this is wrong: suppose that this is not a correct account of the meaning of the English phrase 'could act otherwise'. Then that compatibilist is not only wrong about what others mean by 'could act otherwise'; he is also wrong about what *he* means by these words. (Compare this case: If I mistakenly think that 'knowledge' means 'justified true belief', it does not follow that that is what I mean by 'knowledge'.) If philosophers always used words to mean what their theories said those words meant, no philosopher would ever revise a definition because of a counterexample. But this occasionally happens. Now if all anyone means by talk of an "incompatibilist sense" or a "compatibilist sense" of the central terms in the free-will debate is that philosophers have sometimes proposed theories about the meanings of these terms, theories that support compatibilism (or, it may be, incompatibilism), I have no objection. But then we must remember that it remains an open question whether compatibilists use these terms in a "compatibilist sense" and whether incompatibilists use these terms in an "incompatibilist sense."

Finally, it is this single sense of 'can do otherwise', the sense provided by ordinary English, that compatibilists and incompatibilists contend is so intimately connected with the possibility of moral accountability. This is the classical tradition.

Let me now turn to my title. My question is, just how often is it that we are able to do otherwise? A belief in one's free will is the belief that one can sometimes do otherwise. But then it is consistent to say of X that he has free will despite the fact that he can almost never do otherwise. The central thesis of this paper is that while it is open to the compatibilist to say that human beings are very often – hundreds of times every day – able to do otherwise, the incompatibilist must hold that being able to do otherwise is a comparatively rare condition, even a *very* rare condition.

It is almost self-evident that compatiblism entails that being able to do otherwise is as common as pins. Or, at any rate, it is evident that typical versions of compatibilism entail this. Typical versions of compatibilism entail that being able to do otherwise is some sort of conditional causal power. For example, one primitive version of compatibilism – a version pretty generally agreed to be unsatisfactory – holds that for one to have been able to act differently is for one to have been such that one would have acted differently if one had chosen to act differently. (More generally, for one to be able to do A is for one to be such that one would do A if one chose to.) And who could deny that at most moments each of us is such that he would then be acting differently if he had chosen to act differently?

The case is otherwise with incompatibilism. To see why this is so, let us remind ourselves of why people become incompatibilists. They become incompatibilists because they are convinced by a certain sort of argument. My favorite version of it – which I reproduce from my book *An Essay on Free Will*[1] – turns on the notion of "having a choice about." Let us use the operator 'N' in this way: 'Np' stands for 'p and no one[2] has, or ever had, any choice about whether p'. The validity of the argument turns on the validity of two rules of deduction involving 'N':

Rule Alpha: From $\Box p$ deduce Np. ($\Box$ represents "standard necessity": truth in all possible circumstances.)

Rule Beta: From Np and N $(p \supset q)$ deduce Nq.

Now let 'P' represent any true proposition whatever.[3] Let 'L' represent the conjunction into a single proposition of all laws of nature. Let 'P$_0$' represent a proposition that gives a complete and correct description of the whole world at some instant in the remote past – before there were any human beings. If determinism is true, then $\Box (P_0 \ \& \ L. \supset P)$. We argue from this consequence of determinism as follows.

1. $\Box (P_0 \ \& \ L. \supset P)$
2. $\Box (P_0 \supset (L \supset P))$ 1; modal and sentential logic
3. $N(P_0 \supset (L \supset P))$ 2; Rule Alpha
4. NP_0 Premise
5. $N(L \supset P)$ 3, 4; Rule Beta
6. NL   Premise
7. NP   5, 6; Rule Beta

---

[1] Oxford: Clarendon Press, 1983. See pp. 93–105.
[2] That is, no human being. We shall not take into account the powers of God or angels or Martians.
[3] For the sake of concision, I am going to be more liberal about expositionally useful confusions of use and mention than I usually am.

If this argument is sound, then determinism entails that no one has or ever had any choice about anything. Since one part of "anything" is what any given person does, this amounts to saying that determinism entails that no one could ever have done otherwise. No one, I think, could dispute the two premises or Rule Alpha. The question of the soundness of the argument thus comes down to the question whether Rule Beta is valid. It is not my purpose in this paper to defend Beta. I reproduce this argument only to point out the central role that Beta (or something equivalent to it) plays in the incompatibilist's reasons for accepting his theory. I will go so far as to say that, in my view, one could have no reason for being an incompatibilist if one did not accept Beta. If one accepts Beta, one should be an incompatibilist, and if one is an incompatibilist, one should accept Beta.

What I propose to show in the sequel is this: Anyone who accepts Beta should concede that one has precious little free will, that rarely, if ever, is anyone able to do otherwise than he in fact does. I shall argue for this position as follows. I shall first show that if Rule Beta is valid, then no one is able to perform an act he considers morally reprehensible. I shall then extend this argument; by a similar sort of reasoning, I shall show that, given Rule Beta, no one is able to do anything if he wants very much *not* to do that thing and has no countervailing desire to do it. Finally, by more or less the same reasoning, I shall show that the validity of Rule Beta entails that if we regard an act as the one obvious thing or the only sensible thing to do, we cannot do anything but that thing.

In *Elbow Room*,[4] Daniel Dennett has argued eloquently that he is simply unable to do anything he regards as morally reprehensible. Compatibilists may feel a bit uneasy about agreeing with Dennett about this. Really simple-minded and primitive compatibilists, those who hold that one can do something just in the case that one would do it if one chose to, must disagree with Dennett. Take Dennett's primary example, the torture of an innocent victim in return for a small sum. Dennett will concede, I am sure, that we can easily imagine situations in which he, being more or less as he is now, would succeed in carrying out such torture *if he chose to*. His point is that, being as he is, he would never choose to. *I* think that this is a perfectly good point, but, of course, it is a point that must be disallowed by the primitive compatibilist who identifies the ability to perform an act with the absence of environmental impediments to performing that act. Leaving aside the question of what more sophisticated compatibilists might say

---

[4] Daniel C. Dennett, *Elbow Room: The Varieties of Free Will Worth Wanting* (Cambridge, MA: MIT Press/Bradford Books, 1984). See p. 133ff.

about such cases, let us turn to the incompatibilists. They, I maintain, must agree with Dennett. Dennett uses himself as an example. I will use myself. Let us consider some act I regard as reprehensible. I might, like Dennett, use torture as an example, but my acquaintance with torture is purely literary, and I should like to try to avoid that dreamlike sense of unreality that is so common in philosophical writing about morality. I will pick an example that touches my own experience. Recently, a member of my university, speaking on the floor of a college meeting, deliberately misrepresented the content of the scholarly work of a philosopher (who was not present), in an attempt to turn the audience against him. Suppose such a course of action were proposed to me. Suppose someone were to say to me, "Look, you don't want Smith to be appointed chairman of the Tenure Committee, so tell everyone that he said in print that all sociologists are academic charlatans. (I've got a quotation you can use that seems to say that if you take it out of context.) Then the sociologists will block the appointment." Call the act that is proposed A. I regard lying about someone's scholarly work as reprehensible. And, while I should prefer not to see Smith appointed, I certainly wouldn't think of blocking his appointment by any such means. In short, I regard the proposed act A as being indefensible. (I mean in the actual circumstances: I might lie about the content of someone's scholarly work to prevent World War III, but the start of World War III is not in fact what hangs on my performing or not performing A.) I may even say that I regard doing A as being "indefensible, given the totality of information available to me." And, of course, I do not so regard not doing A: there's nothing much to be said against that. We may also suppose that I am unable (as things stand) to search out any further relevant information – the vote will come in a moment, and I must speak at once if my speaking is to affect it. Now consider the following conditional:

C   If X regards A as an indefensible act, given the totality of relevant
    information available to him, and if he has no way of getting further
    relevant information, and if he lacks any positive desire to do A, and
    if he sees no objection to *not* doing A (again, given the totality of
    relevant information available to him), *then* X is not going to do A.

What is the modal status of C? It seems to me to be something very like a necessary truth. What would be a conceivable circumstance in which its antecedent is true and its consequent false (i.e., X proceeds to do A)? If X changes his mind about the indefensibility of A (perhaps because of the intervention of some "outside" agent or force, or because of an access of new information, or because he suddenly sees some unanticipated implication of the information available to him)? If X just goes berserk? If so, build the non-occurrence of these things into the antecedent of C: he is not going to change his mind about the indefensibility of A and he is not going to go berserk.

It seems to me that there is no possible world in which C is false. What would it be *like* for *C* to be false? Imagine that X does do A. We ask him, "Why did you do A? I thought you said a moment ago that doing A would be reprehensible." He replies:

> Yes. I did think that. I still think it. I thought that at every moment up to the time at which I performed A; I thought that while I was performing A; I thought it immediately afterward. I never wavered in my conviction that A was an irremediably reprehensible act. I never thought there was the least excuse for doing A. And don't misunderstand me: I am not reporting a conflict between duty and inclination. I didn't *want* to do A. I never had the least desire to do A. And don't understand me as saying that my limbs and vocal cords suddenly began to obey some will other than my own. It was my will that they obeyed. It is true without qualification that *I* did A, and it is true without qualification that I *did* A.

This strikes me as absolutely impossible. It's not, of course, impossible for someone to say these words – just as it's not impossible for someone to say, "I've just drawn a round square." But it is impossible for someone to say these words and thereby say something true.

Now consider the proposition that I consider the act A to be indefensible. I think it's pretty clear that I have – right now – no choice about how I feel about A. Like most of my beliefs and attitudes, it's something I just find myself with. (Which is not to say that I don't think that this attitude is well grounded, appropriate to its object, and so on.) If you offered me a large sum of money, or if you promised – and I believed you could deliver – the abolition of war, if only I were to change my attitude toward A, I should not be able to take you up on this offer, however much I might want to. It is barely conceivable that I have the ability to change my attitude toward A over some considerable stretch of time, but we're not talking about some considerable stretch of time; we're talking about right now.

Let us now examine a certain Beta-like rule of inference, which I shall call Beta-prime:

From Nx, p and Nx, $(p \supset q)$ deduce Nx, q.

Here 'N' is a two-place operator, and 'N x, p' abbreviates 'p and x now has no choice about whether p'. The one-place operator 'N' served my purposes in *An Essay on Free Will*, because there the premises of my argument concerned only propositions that were related in just the same way to all human beings, past, present, and future: laws of nature and propositions about the state of the world before there were any human beings. It is clear, I think, that whatever relation any given human being bears to such a proposition, any other given human being bears that relation, too. Since I was interested only in such propositions, I employed the impersonal and timeless one-place 'N'; it was simpler to do so. The arguments I wish to consider in the present paper, however, involve propositions about particular human beings and what they do at particular times and their attitudes toward what they do at those times. For that reason, I need to use the person- and time-relative rule Beta-prime, and I must forego the convenience of Beta. And Beta-prime seems hardly less evident than Beta. The same intuitive considerations that support Beta seem to support Beta-prime, and it is hard to imagine a philosopher who accepts Beta but rejects Beta-prime.

Consider the following instance of Beta-prime:

N I, I regard A as indefensible

N I, (I regard A as indefensible $\supset$ I am not going to do A)

hence, N I, I am not going to do A.

In this argument, 'I regard A as indefensible' is short for 'I regard A as an indefensible act, given the totality of relevant information available to me, and I have no way of getting further relevant information, and I lack any positive desire to do A, and I see no objection to not doing A, given the totality of relevant information available to me.' (Compare the antecedent of the conditional C, above.) The conclusion of this argument, written out in full, is 'I am not going to do A and I now have no choice about whether I am not going to do A'. Now the second conjunct of this sentence is a bit puzzling. But we may note that the sentences 'I have a [or *no*] choice about whether *p*' and 'I have a [or *no*] choice about whether not-*p*' would seem to be equivalent. Therefore, we may read the conclusion of the argument as 'I am not going to do A and I now have no choice about whether I am going to do A'. (The reason the original version of the conclusion seems puzzling is this: the mind looks for a function for that final 'not' to perform and finds none.)

The first premise of this argument is true, because, as we have seen, I (right now, at any rate) have no choice about whether I regard A as indefensible. The second premise is true because, as we have seen, the conditional 'I regard A as indefensible $\supset$ I am not going to do A' is a necessary truth, and no one has any choice about the truth-value of a necessary truth.

The general lesson is: If I regard a certain act as indefensible, then it follows not only that I *shall not* perform that act but that I *can't* perform it. (Presumably, 'I am not going to do A and I have no choice about whether I am going to do A' is equivalent to 'I can't do A'.)

This conclusion is not intuitively implausible. To say that you can do A (are able to do A, have it within your power to do A) is to say something like this: there is a sheaf of alternative futures spread out before you; in some of those futures you do A; and some at least of those futures in which you do A are "open" to you or "accessible" to you. Now if this picture makes sense (as a picture; it's only a picture), it would seem to make sense to ask what these futures are like. You say you can do A; well, what would it be like if you did? You say that a future in which you do A is "open" to you or "accessible" to you; well, in what circumstances would you find yourself if you "got into" or "gained access to" such a future? If you can't give a coherent answer to this question, that, surely, would cast considerable doubt on your claim to be able to do A.

And suppose I do regard doing A as indefensible (for me, here, now). Then, I think, I cannot give a coherent description of a future (one coherently connected with the present) in which I proceed to do A. I have already considered what such an attempt would sound like ("Yes. I did think that …") and have rejected it – rightly – as incoherent.

We must conclude, therefore, that (given the validity of Beta-prime) I cannot perform an act I regard as indefensible, and that this is a perfectly intuitive thesis. Its connection with incompatibilism is displayed in the following argument.

(1) If the rule Beta-prime is valid, I cannot perform an act I regard as indefensible.

(2) If the rule Beta is valid, the rule Beta-prime is valid.

(3) Free will is incompatible with determinism only if Beta is valid.

hence,

(4) If free will is incompatible with determinism, then I cannot perform an act I regard as indefensible.

Throughout this little argument, 'I cannot perform an act I regard as indefensible' is to be understood in a *de re*, not a *de dicto* sense. It does not mean, 'Not possible: I perform an act I regard as indefensible'; it means, 'For any act *x*, if I regard x as indefensible, then I do not have it within my power to perform *x*'. (I don't mean to deny the *de dicto* statement; it is in fact true, but it doesn't figure in the argument.)

The defense of premise (1) of this argument has been the main task of the paragraphs preceding the argument.

Premise (2) seems undeniable because, as I have said, the intuitions that support Beta also support Beta-prime.

Premise (3) can be defended on this ground: the only reason known for accepting incompatibilism is that it follows from Beta. This, of course, does not prove that (3) is true. But it is unlikely that anyone would accept incompatibilism and reject Beta.

Let us now leave the topic of indefensibility and turn to desire – to cases of simple, personal desire having no moral dimension whatever.

Suppose that someone has an (occurrent) desire to perform some act. Suppose that this desire is very, very strong, and that he has no countervailing desire of any sort. (We have considered the case in which duty is unopposed by inclination. We now turn to the case in which inclination is unopposed by inclination.) Consider the case of poor Nightingale in C. P. Snow's novel *The Masters*. Nightingale wants to be a Fellow of the Royal Society – in the idiom of the 1980s, he wants this distinction so badly he can taste it. Every year, on the Royal Society's election day, Nightingale strides out to the porter's lodge of his Cambridge college and leaves *strictest* instructions that, if a telegram arrives for him, he is to be notified *immediately*. (He threatens the porter with summary dismissal if there is the slightest delay.) Now suppose that poor Nightingale, on the day of the election, is sitting in his rooms biting his nails and daydreaming about being able to call himself 'F.R.S.'. The telephone rings. He snatches the handset from its cradle and bawls, "Nightingale here," doubtless deafening his caller.

What I want to know is: *Could* he have refrained from answering the telephone? Was he able not to touch it? Did he have it within his power to let it ring till it fell silent? If what we have said above (in connection with indefensibility) is correct, he could have refrained from answering the telephone only if we can tell a coherent story (identical with the story we *have* told up to the point at which the telephone rings) in which he *does* refrain from answering the telephone. Can we? Well, we might tell a story in which, just as the telephone rings, Nightingale undergoes a sudden religious conversion, like Saul on the road to Damascus: All in a moment, his most fundamental values are transformed and he suddenly sees the Fellows of the Royal Society as cocks crowing on a dunghill. Or we might imagine that Nightingale's mind snaps at the moment the telephone rings and he begins to scream and break up furniture and eventually has to be put away. But, remember, neither of these things *did* happen. Let's suppose that they did not even come close to happening. Let's suppose that there was at the moment we are considering no disposition in the mind of God or in Nightingale's psyche (or wherever the impetus to religious conversion is lodged) toward a sudden change in Nightingale's most fundamental values. Let's suppose also that the moment at which the telephone rang was the only moment at which there was no possibility of Nightingale's mind snapping – it was a moment of sudden, intense hope, after all. Build these suppositions into our story of how it was with Nightingale up till the moment at which the telephone rang. Build into it also the proposition that no bullet or lightning bolt or heart attack is about to strike Nightingale. Call this story the Telephone Story. I am inclined to think that there is no possible world in which the Telephone Story is true and in which Nightingale does not proceed to answer the telephone. We have the following instance of the rule Beta-prime (imagine that the present moment is the moment at which the telephone rings):

> N Nightingale, the Telephone Story is true.
>
> N Nightingale, (the Telephone Story is true ⊃ Nightingale is going to answer the telephone)
>
> *hence,* N Nightingale, Nightingale is going to answer the telephone.

The conclusion may be paraphrased, 'Nightingale is going to answer the telephone, and he has no choice about whether to answer the telephone'. And the premises seem undeniably true.

The lesson would seem to be: If the rule Beta-prime is valid, then if a person has done A, and if he wanted very much to do A, and if he had no desires whatever that inclined him towards not doing A, then he was unable not to do A; not doing A was simply not within his power. An argument similar to the one given above shows that the incompatibilist ought to accept this consequence of Beta-prime.

Let us, finally, turn to a third kind of case. On many occasions in life, with little or no deliberation or reflection, we simply do things. We are not, on those occasions, in the grip of some powerful desire, like poor Nightingale. The things just seem – or would seem if we reflected on them at all – to be the obvious things to do in the circumstances. I suppose that on almost all occasions when I have answered the telephone, I have been in more or less this condition. On most occasions on which I have answered the telephone, I have not been biting my nails in a passion of anxiety and impatience like Nightingale. On most such occasions, I have not been expecting the telephone to ring (not that its ringing *violates* any expectation of mine, either); with my mind still half on something else, I pick up the receiver and absently say, "Hello?" Obviously, mere habit has a lot to do with this action, but I do not propose to inquire into the nature of habit or into the extent of its involvement in such acts.

Now consider any such occasion on which I answered the telephone. I was sitting at my desk marking papers (say); the telephone rang. (I had not been expecting it to ring. I had no reason to suppose it would *not* ring.) I answered it. Without reflection or deliberation. I simply put down my pen and picked up the receiver.

Can we tell a coherent story in which (in just those circumstances) I simply ignore the telephone and go on marking papers till it stops ringing? Well, we might. Since the matter is a minor one, we need not postulate anything on the order of a religious conversion. We might simply assume that some good reason for not answering the telephone suddenly popped into my mind. (Didn't I have a letter recently from a man who claimed to be able to prove mind–body dualism from the fact that he had made several trips to Mercury by astral projection? Didn't he say that he would be calling me today to make an appointment to discuss the implications of his astral journey for the mind–body problem?) Or, again, we might imagine that I suddenly go berserk and begin to smash furniture. Or we might postulate a sudden Divine or meteorological or ballistic alteration of my circumstances. But we might also imagine that there exists no basis either in my psyche or my environment (at the moment the telephone rings) for any of these things. We may even, if you like, suppose that at the moment the telephone rings it is causally determined that no reason for not answering the phone will pop into my mind in the next few seconds, and that it is causally determined that I shall not go berserk or be struck dead.

This set of statements about me and my situation at the moment the telephone rang (and during the two or three minutes preceding its ringing) we may call the Second Telephone Story. It seems to me to be incoherent to suppose that the Second Telephone Story is true and that I, nevertheless, do not proceed to answer the telephone. And, of course, we have the following instance of Beta-prime:

N I, The Second Telephone Story is true.

N I, (The Second Telephone Story is true $\supset$ I am going to answer the telephone).

hence, N I, I am going to answer the telephone.

The conclusion may be read: 'I am going to answer the telephone and I have no choice about whether to answer the telephone'. Its connection with incompatibilism can be established by an argument not essentially different from the one already given.

It seems clear that if the premises of this third instance of Rule Beta-prime are true, then we have precious little free will – at least assuming that Beta-prime is valid. For our normal, everyday situation is represented in the Second Telephone Story. It is perhaps not clear how many of the occasions of everyday life count as "making a choice." The light turns green, and the driver, his higher faculties wholly given over to thoughts of revenge or lunch or the Chinese Remainder Theorem puts his car into gear and proceeds with his journey. Did he do something called "making a choice between proceeding and not proceeding"? Presumably not: the whole thing was too automatic. The young public official, unexpectedly and for the first time, is offered a bribe, more money than he has ever thought of having, in return for an unambiguous betrayal of the public trust. After sweating for thirty seconds, he takes the money. Did he make a choice? Of course. Between these two extremes lie all sorts of cases, and it is probably not possible to draw a sharp line between making a choice and acting automatically. But I think it is evident that, wherever we draw the line, we are rarely in a situation in which the need to make a choice confronts us and in which it isn't absolutely clear what choice to make. And this is particularly evident if we count as cases of its being "absolutely clear what choice to make" cases on which it is absolutely clear *on reflection* what choice to make. A man may be seriously consid-ering accepting a bribe until he realizes (after a moment's reflection on the purely factual aspects of his situation) that he couldn't possibly get away with it. Then his course is clear, because it has become clear to him that there is nothing whatever to be said for taking the bribe and a great deal to be said against it. He has not *decided* which of two incompatible objects of desire (riches and self-respect, say) to accept; rather he has seen that one of the two – riches – wasn't really there.

There are, therefore, few occasions in life on which – at least after a little reflection and perhaps some investigation into the facts – it isn't abso-lutely clear what to do. And if the above arguments are correct, then an incompatibilist should believe that on such occasions the agent cannot do anything other than the thing that seems to him to be clearly the only sensible thing.

Now there are *some* occasions on which an agent is confronted with alternatives and it is not clear to him what to do – not even when all the facts are in, as we might put it. What are these cases like? I think we may distinguish three cases.

First, there are what might be called "Buridan's Ass" cases. Someone wants each of two or more incompatible things and it isn't clear which one he should (try to) get, and the things are interchangeable; indeed their very interchangeability is the reason why it isn't clear to him which to try to get. (I include under this heading cases in which the alternatives are importantly different but look indistinguishable to the agent because he unavoidably lacks some relevant datum. Lady-and-tiger cases, we might call them.) Closely allied with Buridan's Ass cases, so closely that I shall not count them constituting a different kind of case, are cases in which the alternatives are not really interchangeable (as are two identical and equally accessible piles of hay) but in which the properties of the alternatives that constitute the whole of the difference between them are precisely the objects of the conflicting desires. We might call such cases "vanilla/chocolate cases." They are often signaled by the use of the rather odd phrase 'I'm trying to decide which one I want' – as opposed to '… which one to have'. I want chocolate and I want vanilla and I can't (or won't or don't want to) have both, and there is no material for deliberation, because my choice will have no consequences beyond my getting vanilla, or, as the case may be, chocolate. (Note, by the way, that someone who is trying to decide whether to have chocolate, to which he sometimes has an allergic reaction, or vanilla, which he likes rather less than chocolate, does not constitute what I am calling a "vanilla/chocolate case.") Both vanilla/chocolate cases and "Buridan's Ass proper" cases are characterized by simple vacillation. Hobbes's theory of deliberation, whether or not it is satisfactory as a general theory, is pretty uncontroversially correct in these cases. One wavers between the alternatives until one inclination somehow gets the upper hand, and one ends up with a chocolate cone or the bale of hay on the left.

The second class of cases in which it is not obvious what to do (even when all the facts are in) are cases of duty versus inclination. Or, better, cases of general policy versus momentary desire. (For what is in conflict with the agent's momentary desire in such cases need have nothing to do with the agent's perception of his moral duty; it might have no higher object than his long-term self-interest.) I have made for myself a maxim of conduct, and no sooner have I done this than, in St. Paul's words, "I see another law in my members, warring against the law of my mind." Our story of the young official and the proffered bribe is an example; further examples could be provided by any dieter. This class of cases is characterized by what is sometimes called moral struggle, although, as I have said, not all cases of it involve morality.

The third class of cases involves incommensurable values. (I owe this point to the work of Robert Kane.)[5] A life of rational self-interest (where self-interest is understood to comprise only such ends as food, health, safety, sex, power, money, military glory, and scientific knowledge, and not ends like honor, charity, and decency) versus a life of gift and sacrifice; caring for one's aged mother versus joining the Resistance; popularity with the public versus popularity with the critics. All these are cases of incommensurable values. Other cases would have to be described with more care to make sure that they fit into this class. The case of a young person wondering whether to become a lawyer or a concert pianist might belong to this class. But not if the question were, "In which profession should I make more money?" or "In which profession should I make the greater contribution to human happiness?" In those cases, values are not at issue, but only how to maximize certain "given" values; the matter is one of (at best) calculation and (at worst) guesswork. The general form of the question that confronts the agent in true cases of the third type is, What sort of human being shall I be?, or What sort of life shall I live? And, of course, this does not mean, What sort of life is dictated for me by such-and-such values (which I already accept)? *That* question is one to be decided by calculation or guesswork. In cases of the third type, the agent's *present* system of values does not have anything to tell him. His values may tell him to become a professional rather than a laborer and an honest rather than a dishonest professional, but they do not tell him whether to become a lawyer or a pianist. (It may be that the values he could expect to have as a result of the choice would confirm that choice – see Kierkegaard on the moral versus the "aesthetic" life – but that's of no help to him *now*.) The choices in the third category are those that many philosophers call "existential," but I will not use this term, which derives from a truly hopeless metaphysic. As the cases in the first category are characterized by vacillation, and the cases in the second by "moral" struggle, so the cases in the third are characterized by *indecision* – often agonized indecision. The period of indecision, moreover, may be a long one: weeks, months, or even a really significant part of the agent's life.

I believe that these three cases exhaust the types of case in which it is not obvious to the agent, even on reflection, and when all the facts are in, how he ought to choose. Therefore, if our previous arguments are correct,

⁵ R. Kane, *Free Will and Values* (Albany, NY: SUNY Press, 1985). See particularly Part II.

the incompatibilist should believe that we are faced with a genuinely free choice only in such cases. (That is: in these cases, if in any. The incompatibilist may well believe that in some of *these* cases we have no choice about how to act, or, like Holbach and C. D. Broad, that even in these cases we have no choice about how to act.) It is not clear to me that in cases of the first type – "Buridan's Ass" cases – there is any conceivable basis for saying that we have a choice about what to do. Doubtless when we choose between identical objects symmetrically related to us, or when we choose between objects that differ only in those properties that are the objects of our competing desires, there occurs something like an internal coin-toss. (My guess, for what it's worth, is that we contain a "default" decision-maker, a mechanism that is always "trying" to make decisions – they would be wholly arbitrary decisions if it were allowed to make them – but which is normally overridden by the person; I speculate that when "vacillation" occurs, the person's control over the "default" decision-maker is eventually suspended and it is allowed to have its arbitrary way.) I think that it's pretty clear that in such cases one has no choice about how one acts. If one tosses a coin, then one has no choice about whether it will land heads or tails. And, indeed, why should one want such a power – if the alternatives really are indifferent?

If this is correct, then there are at most two sorts of occasion on which the incompatibilist can admit that we exercise free will: cases of an actual struggle between perceived moral duty or long-term self- interest, on the one hand, and immediate desire, on the other; and cases of a conflict of incommensurable values.

Both these sorts of occasion together must account for a fairly small percentage of the things we do. And, I must repeat, my conclusion is that this is the *largest* class of actions with respect to which the incompatibilist can say we are free. The argument I have given shows that the incompatibilist ought to deny that we have free will on any occasions other than these. It has no tendency to show that the incompatibilist should say that we do act freely on these occasions. The argument purports to show that, given the principles from which the incompatibilist derives his position, it is impossible for us to act freely on occasions other than these. It has no tendency to show that – given the incompatibilist's principles – it is possible for us to act freely on any occasion whatever. It's like this: A biologist, using as premises certain essential features of mammals and some facts about Mars, proves that there could not be mammalian life on Mars; such a proof, even if it is beyond criticism, has no tendency to show that there *could* be any sort of life on Mars. That's as may be. His proof just tells us nothing about non-mammalian life.

I will not discuss (further) the question of how much free will we might have *within* these two categories. In the sequel, I wish to discuss the implications of what I have argued for so far for questions of moral blame.

I have argued that, if incompatibilism is true, free action is a less common phenomenon than one might have thought. It does not, however, follow that moral accountability is a less common phenomenon than one might have thought. And this is the case even on the traditional or "classical" understanding of the relationship between free will – that is, the power or ability to do otherwise than one in fact does – and accountability. Nothing that has been said so far need force the incompatibilist (the incompatibilist whose view of the relation between free will and blame is that of the classical tradition) to think that moral accountability is uncommon.

Let us see why. Would anyone want to say that the classical tradition is committed to the following thesis?: "An agent can be held accountable for a certain state of affairs only if either (a) that agent intentionally brought that state of affairs about and could have refrained from bringing it about, or (b) that agent foresaw that that state of affairs would obtain unless he prevented it, and he was able to prevent it." I don't know whether anyone would want to say this. My uncertainty is due mainly to the fact that philosophers discussing problems in this general area usually talk not about accountability for states of affairs – the *results* of our action and inaction – but accountability (or "responsibility") for *acts*. This way of talking about these matters is confusing and tends to obscure what I regard as crucial points. However this may be, the classical tradition is not committed to this thesis, though it may be that some representatives of the tradition have endorsed it. This is fortunate for the tradition, because the thesis is obviously false. This is illustrated by "drunk driver" cases: I could not have swerved fast enough to avoid hitting the taxi, and yet no one doubts that I am to blame for the collision. How can that be? Simple: I was drunk and my reflexes were impaired. Although I was unable to swerve to avoid hitting the taxi, that inability (unlike, say, my inability to read minds) was one I could have avoided having. Or again: Suppose that when I am drunk it is not within my power to refrain from violently assaulting those who disagree with me about politics. I get drunk and overhear a remark about Cuban troops in Angola and, soon thereafter, Fred's nose is broken. I was, under the circumstances, unable to refrain from breaking Fred's nose. And yet no one doubts that I am to blame for his broken nose. How can that be? Simple: Although I was unable to avoid breaking his nose, that inability is one I could have avoided having. What these examples show is that the inability to prevent or to refrain from causing a state of affairs does not logically preclude being to blame for that state of affairs. Even the most orthodox partisan of a close connection between free will and blame will want to express this connection in a principle that is qualified in something like the following way:

An agent cannot be blamed for a state of affairs unless there was a time at which he could so have arranged matters that that state of affairs not obtain.

And this principle is at least consistent with its being the case that, while we are hardly ever able to act otherwise than we do, we are nevertheless accountable for (some of) the consequences of *all* of our acts. (No one, I suppose, would seriously maintain that we can be blamed for *all* of the consequences of *any* of our acts. If I am dilatory about returning a book to the library and this has the consequence – apparent, I suppose, only to God – that a certain important medical discovery is never made, the thousands of deaths that would not have occurred if I had been a bit more conscientious are not my fault. And who can say what the unknown consequences of our most casual acts may be? Obviously, I can be blamed only for those consequences of my acts that are in some sense "foreseeable.") Consider this case. A Mafia hitman is dispatched to kill a peculating minor functionary of that organization. The victim pleads for his life in a most pathetic way, which so amuses the hitman (who would no more think of failing to fulfill the terms of a contract than you or I would think of extorting money from our students by threats of failing them) that he shoots the victim in the stomach rather than through the heart, in order to prolong the entertainment. Could he have refrained from killing the victim? Was it, just before he shot the victim, within his power to pocket his gun unfired and leave? If what has been said so far is true, probably not. Would it follow that he was not morally responsible for the victim's death? By no means. Given the kind of man he was, he was unable, in that situation, to have acted otherwise. But perhaps he could have avoided having that inability by avoiding being the kind of man he was. It is an old, and very plausible, philosophical idea that, by our acts, we make ourselves into the sorts of people we eventually become. Or, at least, it is plausible to suppose that our acts are *among* the factors that determine what we eventually become. If one is now unable to behave in certain ways – I am not talking about gross physical inabilities, like a double amputee's inability to play the piano – this may be because of a long history of choices one has made. Take the case of cold-blooded murder. The folk wisdom has it (I don't know if there is empirical evidence for this) that most of us have been born with a rather deep reluctance to kill helpless and submissive fellow human beings. But, if there is such a reluctance, it can obviously be overcome. And (so the folk wisdom has it) each time this reluctance is overcome it grows weaker, until it finally disappears. Suppose our Mafia hitman *did* have a free choice the first time he killed a defenseless victim. He might have experienced on that occasion – though doubtless these terms were not in his vocabulary – something like a conflict between momentary inclination and long-term self-interest. Suppose he did kill his man, however, and that he continued to do this when it was required of him until he had finally completely extirpated his reluctance to kill the helpless and submissive. If he is now unable to pocket his gun unfired and walk away, this is, surely, partly because he has extirpated this reluctance. The absence of this normal reluctance to kill is an essential component of his present inability not to kill. If the folk wisdom is right, and let us suppose for the sake of the example that it is, then it is conceivable he could have avoided having his present inability. And, therefore, it may be, for all we have said, that he can properly be held to account for the victim's death. Given the causal and psychological theses contained in the folk wisdom, he may be accountable for the victim's death for the same reason that a drunk driver is accountable for an accident traceable to his impaired reflexes. (But, of course, I don't mean to suggest that the case of a man who has turned himself into a sociopath by a long series of free choices over many years is morally *very* much like the case of a man who has turned himself into a temporarily dangerous driver by one or two acts of free choice in the course of an evening.)

I have nothing more to say on the subject of moral blame. This is a difficult topic, and one that involves many other factors than the ability to act otherwise. (Coercion and ignorance, for example, are deeply involved in questions of accountability. And there is the dismally difficult question of what it is for a consequence of an act to be "foreseeable" in the relevant sense.) My only purpose in these last few paragraphs has been to give some support to the idea that the radically limited domain of the freedom of the will that the incompatibilist must accept does not obviously commit him to a similarly radically limited domain for moral blame. It may be that we are usually right when we judge that a given state of affairs is a given person's fault, even if people are almost never able to refrain from bringing about the states of affairs they intentionally bring about, and even if people are almost never able to act to prevent the states of affairs that they know perfectly well will obtain if they do not act to prevent them. For it may be that they could have avoided having these inabilities.

CHAPTER 6

Moral Responsibility, Determinism, and the Ability to Do Otherwise

Once upon a time (or so we may suppose: historical accuracy is not my principal object in this introductory paragraph) every philosopher writing about "liberty and necessity" argued either that, because all that happened was necessary, there was no liberty of action or that, because there was liberty of action, not all that happened was necessary. In the course of time, however, there arose a sophisticated school of philosophers (Hobbes, Hume, and Mill, for example) who pointed out that the two sides in the debate about liberty and necessity shared a premise: that liberty and necessity (or, as we should say today, free will and determinism) were incompatible. And these sophisticated philosophers rejected this premise. Since free will and determinism[1] were compatible, they argued, a determined action could be free; and in fact a determined action *would* be free if it were determined in the right sort of way. (Some members of this school went so far as to contend that an action could be free *only if* it was determined in the right sort of way – and hence only if it was determined.) Subsequently to the rise of the sophisticated school, debates about the problem of free will became almost exclusively debates about whether it was the new, sophisticated philosophers or the old, naive philosophers who were right. (After all, the naive have certain advantages over the sophisticated: the Emperor may be wearing no clothes. As Orwell is supposed to have said, "There are some ideas that are so wrong that only a very intelligent person could believe them.") A wealth of bad philosophical terminology was coined in the course of these debates: 'hard determinism', 'soft determinism', 'libertarianism', 'contra-causal freedom', 'freedom in the libertarian sense'. It was not until the 1960s that the terminology of the free-will problem was

---

[1] Among the philosophers I have mentioned, only Mill would have known the word 'determinism', which was coined by Sir William Hamilton.

rationalized. Since that decade, most philosophers discussing the free-will problem have taken something like the following three terms to constitute the "basic" or "primitive" vocabulary of the problem:

> *The Free-will Thesis*   Some human beings have free will; that is, at least some human beings at least sometimes have it within their power to (are able to) act otherwise than they do
>
> *Determinism*   The past determines a unique future (given the past and the laws of nature, the future is determined in every detail)
>
> *Compatibilism*   The free-will thesis and determinism are compatible (their joint truth is possible).

(*Indeterminism* and *incompatibilism* are, respectively, the denial of determinism and the denial of compatibilism.) Compatibilism, is, of course, what the debates between the *naïfs* and the sophisticates had been about.[2] (If there is any need for the older terms, they may be defined as follows: hard determinism is the conjunction of determinism and incompatibilism – which, of course, jointly entail the denial of the free-will thesis; soft determinism is the conjunction of determinism and the free-will thesis – which, of course, jointly entail compatibilism; libertarianism is the conjunction of the free-will thesis and incompatibilism – which, of course, jointly entail the denial of determinism.)[3] The adoption of the newer, more rational terminology was no doubt progress of a sort, but, at a deeper level than terminology, the character of the free-will debate had not changed for many decades. Books and essays on free will were mainly the work of compatibilists, who had for a long time constituted the orthodox, majority party. Why these books and essays continued to be written was not clear, since they were all more or less the same; each explained wearily – more in sadness than in anger, really – that there never

---

[2]   I believe it was Keith Lehrer who coined the term 'compatibilism'.

[3]   But the need for them is very small, and they are almost always better avoided. As for 'contra-causal freedom' and 'freedom in the libertarian sense', they must be consigned to the dustbin of philosophical history. Unfortunately, the latter turns up with some frequency in current writings on free will. To my mind, seeing that the phrase 'freedom in the libertarian sense' has no possible use is the *pons asinorum* of the problem of free will, for compatibilists and incompatibilists use 'is able to do otherwise' in exactly the same sense. The reader who doubts this should consult my essay "When Is the Will Free?" (Chapter 5 of the present volume). This reader should consult particularly the long paragraph starting on p. 63 that begins "Before going further … " I regard this paragraph as the single most important paragraph I have ever written about the free-will problem. I wish people would pay more attention to it.

had been a problem of free will and determinism because free will and determinism were compatible – for exactly the reasons that had been given by Hobbes, Hume, and Mill. (That is to say, for exactly the reasons that had been given by Hobbes.) There were, however, a few able and respected philosophers who continued to defend incompatibilism. (C. D. Broad in his Cambridge inaugural lecture; R. M. Chisholm; Carl Ginet. The arguments of these incompatibilists were, of course, technically far superior to arguments of Bishop Bramhall, who had debated what was essentially the compatibilism–incompatibilism issue with Hobbes, but they were not fundamentally different. As one who has made some contribution to getting the argument for the incompatibility of free will and determinism clearly stated, I don't mind admitting that none of us incompatibilists has ever contributed much but increased clarity to the debate: there is essentially *one* argument – a very powerful one – for the incompatibility of free will and determinism, and the major contribution of us incompatibilists to the ongoing discussion of the problem of free will has been to make sure that the force of this argument is appreciated.)

In 1969, however, something new happened. Harry Frankfurt published a remarkable (and now classic) essay in which he denied that the debate between the compatibilists and the incompatibilists had the significance that most members of both parties had attributed to it.[4] The main interest of the free-will problem, for most philosophers, derived from their belief that moral responsibility was impossible without free will – without the ability to do otherwise. This belief was the main reason most philosophers had for *caring* about free will enough to invest time and ink in a debate about whether anyone had it or what it was compatible with. Frankfurt argued that this belief was false. More exactly, he argued that "The Principle of Alternate Possibilities,"[5] or PAP as its friends call it, was false:

PAP A person is morally responsible for what he has done only if he could have done otherwise.[6]

---

[4] "The Principle of Alternate Possibilities," *Journal of Philosophy* 66 (1969): 829–839. Reprinted in John Martin Fischer (ed.), *Moral Responsibility* (Ithaca, NY: Cornell University Press, 1986), pp. 143–152.
[5] More properly, the Principle of Alternative Possibilities.
[6] "Principle of Alternate Possibilities," p. 829. In this principle, 'could have' must not be taken to mean 'might have'; it means 'was able to'. The ambiguity of 'could have' – the 'might have'/'was able to' ambiguity' – has caused an immense amount of confusion in discussions of PAP and in discussions of the free-will problem in general. (See Chapter 4 of the present volume for an example.) Here is a pair of examples (adapted from Austin) that illustrates this ambiguity. "You could have exposed me this morning. For God's sake, watch what you're saying when you talk to the press." "You could have exposed me this morning. I want you to know that I'm grateful you didn't."

This principle is extremely plausible, but counterexamples to it are as many and various (and almost as well known) as Gettier counterexamples in epistemology. Here is one that will do as well as any:

Suppose that Gunnar has shot Ridley and is morally responsible for having done so. (Build into the example whatever you think is needed to make this supposition true.) Now add to the case an offstage "counterfactual manipulator," Cosser, who *would have* caused Gunnar to shoot Ridley (perhaps by direct manipulation of Gunnar's brain) if Gunnar *had* shown any hesitation about carrying out his long-standing plan to shoot Ridley. (In saying that Cosser is an "offstage" manipulator, we mean that his existence, powers, and intentions are unknown to Gunnar, and that, unless Cosser were forced to carry out his "contingency plan," nothing he did would have any effect on Gunnar). But, in the event, Gunnar showed no such hesitancy and, as we have said, went ahead and shot Ridley. Obviously we do not, by adding Cosser's offstage presence and his unacted-on contingency plan to the example, make our story inconsistent: we do not contradict the supposition with which we began, that Gunnar is morally responsible for having shot Ridley. But just as obviously we *do* change the story in another way: the story now entails that Gunnar was unable *not* to shoot Ridley. Look at the matter this way. Pick some moment *t* before Gunnar shot Ridley, a moment at which Gunnar still had plenty of time to change his mind about shooting Ridley, but after Cosser had formed his contingency plan and set up his monitoring devices and instruments of neural manipulation. Various "possible futures" lead away from "the world as it was at *t*." (Only one if the world is deterministic; it may be, of course, that in accepting the above invitation to "build into the example whatever you think is needed to make this supposition true," you have built indeterminism into the example.) In *all* these possible futures, Gunnar shot Ridley. In some of them – if determinism is false and there *were* such futures – this was because Cosser caused Gunnar to shoot Ridley. In the others, Gunnar shot Ridley without being caused to do so by Cosser. Nevertheless – in *all* these possible futures, Gunnar shot Ridley. And it is not *only* true that Gunnar shot Ridley in all these possible futures. If determinism is true, in none of them did Gunnar change his mind and decide not to shoot Ridley. Even if the world is deterministic, however, it was still true that (owing to Cosser and his plans and powers) in all the closest futures in which Gunnar changed his mind and decided not to shoot Ridley, he shot Ridley. In other words, the addition of Cosser to the example has the following consequence: the story now entails that Gunnar would have shot Ridley *no matter what choices or decisions he had made*. From this it obviously follows that, at *t* and later,[7] Gunnar was unable not to shoot Ridley. But then Gunnar is morally responsible for having shot Ridley even though he was unable not to shoot Ridley.

Almost a decade after Frankfurt's essay was published, I wrote an essay[8] (the body of which is contained in my book *An Essay on Free Will*)[9] in which I argued that, although PAP might be false – for just the reasons that Frankfurt had given – there were other principles that, in conjunction with incompatibilism, entailed that moral responsibility could not exist in a deterministic world. And I argued that these principles could not be refuted by "Frankfurt-style" counterexamples. (These arguments were in aid of the following conclusion: If Frankfurt is right and PAP is false, it is nevertheless true that the compatibilism–incompatibilism debate has just the significance that philosophers who care about moral responsibility have always supposed it to have.) A few years after that essay was published, Frankfurt published a reply to my arguments for these conclusions.[10] It is that reply that I wish to consider in the present essay. I will examine just one of these "other principles" and what Frankfurt says about it. This is the principle that in earlier writings I have called PPP$_2$ – but, in the present essay, I will call it simply PPP, since I shall not discuss any principle from which it needs to be distinguished by a subscript. (The three Ps stand for 'principle of possible prevention'.) Here it is:

PPP   A person is morally responsible for a state of affairs only if (that state of affairs obtains and) he could have prevented it from obtaining.

Here is the germ of what Frankfurt has to say that is relevant to my contention that PPP is true, that it cannot be refuted by Frankfurt-style counterexamples, and that, in conjunction with incompatibilism, it entails that

---

[7] It is consistent with the way we have told the story that there was a time earlier than *t* at which Gunnar was able not to shoot Ridley. It should be obvious that a more elaborate example could have been constructed according to which there was no point in Gunnar's life at which he was able not to shoot Ridley.

[8] "Ability and Responsibility" (Chapter 1 of the present volume).

[9] Oxford: Clarendon Press, 1983. See pp. 161–182.

[10] "What We Are Morally Responsible For," in Leigh S. Cauman, Isaac Levi, Charles Parsons, and Robert Schwartz (eds.), *How Many Questions? Essays in Honor of Sydney Morgenbesser* (Indianapolis, IN: Hackett, 1982). Reprinted in John Martin Fischer and Mark Ravizza (eds.), *Perspectives on Moral Responsibility* (Ithaca, NY: Cornell University Press, 1993), pp. 286–295.

moral responsibility cannot exist in a deterministic world. He contends that PPP has 'nothing at all to do with free will'. Why not? I am not sure. It seems that Frankfurt intends the following paragraph to supply the answer to this question.

> The fact that there are ... states of affairs that a person cannot bring about plainly does not in itself mean that the person lacks free will. Given that the freedom of a person's will is essentially a matter of whether it is up to him what he does, it is more a matter of whether it is up to him what bodily movements he makes than of what consequences he can bring about by his movements. Imagine [that an equipment malfunction makes it impossible for a certain man to call the police, despite his freedom to move his body in any way he likes, and imagine that this malfunction] is due to negligence on the part of the telephone company; and imagine that because of this negligence, large numbers of people are unable to do various things. These people may quite properly be resentful. But they will be carrying their resentment too far, and attributing too portentous a role in their lives to the telephone company if they complain that the company has through its negligence diminished the freedom of their wills.[11]

I am far from sure that I see what the point of this paragraph is supposed to be. For one thing, if its point is to show that PPP has nothing to do with free will, its opening words are puzzling; one would expect it to begin

> The fact that there are states of affairs that a person was unable to prevent plainly does not in itself mean that the person lacks free will.

But this is a minor point of exposition. The important point is this: the relevance of PPP to free will could hardly be plainer. More exactly, its relevance to the proposition

> In a world without free will (i.e., in a world in which no one is ever able to act otherwise), there is no moral responsibility

could hardly be plainer. Its relevance to this proposition is shown by the fact that this proposition follows from PPP and the two premises

> In a world without free will, no one is able to prevent any state of affairs (that does obtain) from obtaining

> If there is moral responsibility, someone is morally responsible for some state of affairs.

---

[11] Fischer and Ravizza, *Perspectives on Moral Responsibility*, p. 294.

(And, of course, if there is no moral responsibility in a world without free will, and if free will implies indeterminism, then there is no moral responsibility in a deterministic world.) Both these premises seem to me to be obvious truths. But perhaps Frankfurt will deny the first of them. He seems to have very particular ideas about how the phrase 'free will' should be used: he wants to connect this phrase very closely with the idea of one's control over the movements of one's body. Perhaps his particular ideas about the proper sense of the phrase 'free will' will lead him to say that even if one has no control over the movements of one's body, one may nevertheless be able to prevent certain states of affairs from obtaining. I must say that I don't see how this could be (unless perhaps the states of affairs one is able to prevent pertain to what would normally be the causal antecedents of the movements of one's body; but I doubt whether that's his point). However this may be, let us simply avoid all issues related to the proper use of 'free will'. Let us drop the phrase from our discussion. I will now present an argument (in which the words 'free will' do not occur) for the conclusion that moral responsibility cannot exist in a deterministic world. In this argument, the variable 'p' ranges over states of affairs, and the operator 'N' is to be understood in the following sense:

$Np =$ $_{df}$ p obtains and no one is able or ever was able to prevent p (from obtaining)

(1) If determinism is true and p obtains, then Np

(2) A person is morally responsible for p only if (p obtains and) he is or was able to prevent p (from obtaining)

(3) If (2) is true and if Np, then no one is morally responsible for p

hence,

(4) If determinism is true and p obtains, no one is morally responsible for p.

Premise (1) is a fairly standard statement of incompatibilism. Now it may be that if "incompatibilism" is by definition the proposition that determinism and the free-will thesis are incompatible, and if we incompatibilists have somehow been misusing the words 'free will', the thesis expressed by premise (1) shouldn't be called 'incompatibilism'. Still, this thesis is (more or less) what we who call ourselves incompatibilists have been arguing for under the name 'incompatibilism'. It's the thesis, not the name, that is important to us. If necessary, we'll find another name for our thesis and ourselves.

Premise (2) is PPP.

Premise (3) is undeniable, for its denial is

> p obtains and someone is morally responsible for p; if p obtains and someone is morally responsible for p, he is able or once was able to prevent p; no one is able or ever was able to prevent p.

The conclusion of the argument is equivalent to, 'If determinism is true, no one is morally responsible for any state of affairs that obtains'. And this, I think suffices to show that PPP is "relevant" to the question whether moral responsibility can exist in a deterministic world.

Or so it would seem. One could, however, raise the question whether moral responsibility might exist even if no one was morally responsible for any state of affairs that obtained. (Recall that the second premise of our first argument was 'If there is moral responsibility, someone is morally responsible for some state of affairs'.) Let us examine this question that someone might raise. A good way to begin a discussion of this question is to reflect on Frankfurt's title: "What We Are Morally Responsible For." What *are* we morally responsible for? If some of the things we are morally responsible for (given that we are morally responsible for anything) are not states of affairs, then moral responsibility might, for all we have said so far, exist in a world in which no one was morally responsible for any state of affairs that obtained in that world. I myself believe that we are responsible for things in other ontological categories than states of affairs that obtain – concrete events, if nothing else.[12] Nevertheless, in my view, we *are* sometimes morally responsible for states of affairs that obtain – but let us abandon this clumsy phrase and say instead that we are sometimes morally responsible for *facts*. (A possible state of affairs that does *not* obtain – there having been a woman president of the United States before the twenty-first century, say – is simply a failed candidate for factuality; it is a thing that would have been a fact if things had gone differently, but happens not to be one.) Here is an indisputable (although, unfortunately, disputed) fact:

> Millions of Jews were horribly murdered in the Nazi death camps.

Is someone morally responsible for this fact? Well, of course – but what does it mean to say that someone is morally responsible for this fact? Just this:

> That millions of Jews were horribly murdered in the Nazi death camps *is someone's fault*.

---

[12] See "Ability and Responsibility," or chapter 5 of *An Essay on Free Will*.

Or, alternatively,

> That millions of Jews were horribly murdered in the Nazi death camps *is something for which someone can be held morally accountable.*

And who is the "someone" – or, rather, who are the "someones," for morally responsibility for a fact can be shared, and this is one of those cases. That is to say, who is morally responsible (shares in the moral responsibility) for this fact? Opinions differ. Hitler and Himmler and the inner circle of the Nazi Party, certainly. But certainly others as well, although there is legitimate dispute about where the "list" should be cut off: German industrialists, collaborators in France and Poland and other conquered territories, every citizen of the Third Reich who did not actively resist the Nazis, the Allied High Command … the members of all these groups have been said by someone to share in the moral responsibility for the fact that millions of Jews were horribly murdered in the Nazi death camps. But no one says that *no one* is morally responsible for this fact. (Not even "Holocaust deniers": they deny the *fact*; they don't say that the fact exists and no one is responsible for it.) We all agree, therefore, that some people are morally responsible for some facts. (Even those who, like Clarence Darrow, verbally deny the existence of moral responsibility demonstrate in their behavior that they hold some people morally responsible for some facts.)

But suppose we're all wrong. Suppose that *every* time someone says something like "It's your fault your mother had a miserable old age" or "Alice is to blame for the fact that the Women's Shelter had to close for lack of funds" the speaker is somehow just wrong, mistaken, saying something false. Suppose there *are* no truths of that kind. What would follow? It would follow, I think, that no one was morally responsible for anything – whether it was a fact, a concrete event, or a representative of any other ontological category. Consider, for example, concrete events. It seems evident that if a person is morally responsible for, say, Tom's death, then that person must *also* be morally responsible for some fact or facts: for the fact that a bullet entered Tom's brain, for the fact that no one called 911, for the fact that Tom was left alone with his heart medicine out of reach … for *some* fact or facts. And this, I think, is true even if (as I believe) no reductive analysis of moral responsibility for concrete events in terms of moral responsibility for facts is possible.

If, therefore, (1) [incompatibilism, or whatever the thesis should be called], and (2) [PPP] are both true, determinism is incompatible with the existence of moral responsibility.

CHAPTER 7

Free Will Remains a Mystery

This paper has two parts. In the first part, I concede an error in an argument I have given for the incompatibility of free will and determinism. I go on to show how to modify my argument so as to avoid this error, and conclude that the thesis that free will and determinism are compatible continues to be – to say the least – implausible. But if free will is incompatible with determinism, we are faced with a mystery, for free will undeniably exists, and it also seems to be incompatible with *in*determinism. That is to say: we are faced with a mystery if free will *is* incompatible with indeterminism. Perhaps it is not. The arguments for the incompatibility of free will and indeterminism are plausible and suggestive, but not watertight. And many philosophers are convinced that the theory of "agent causation" (or some specific development of it) shows that acts that are undetermined by past states of affairs can be free acts. But the philosophical enemies of the idea of agent causation are numerous and articulate. Opposition to the idea of agent causation has been based on one or the other of two convictions: that the concept of agent causation is incoherent, or that the reality of agent causation would be inconsistent with "naturalism" or "a scientific worldview." In the second part of this paper, I will defend the conclusion that the concept of agent causation is of no use to the philosopher who wants to maintain that free will and indeterminism are compatible. But I will not try to show that the concept of agent causation is incoherent or that the real existence of agent causation should be rejected for scientific reasons. I will assume – for the sake of argument – that agent causation is possible, and that it in fact exists. I will, however, present an argument for the conclusion that free will and indeterminism are incompatible even if our acts or their causal antecedents are products of agent causation. I see no way to respond to this argument. I conclude that free will remains a

I am grateful to Ted A. Warfield (*il miglior fabbro*) for reading Part I of this paper and for offering valuable criticisms. I hope I have made good use of them.

mystery – that is, that free will undeniably exists and that there is a strong and unanswered *prima facie* case for its impossibility.

I

I have offered the following argument for the incompatibility of free will and determinism.[1] Let us read 'Np' as 'p and no one has or ever had any choice about whether p'. We employ the following two inference rules

α $\Box p\,|-Np$

β $Np, N(p \supset q)\,|-Nq$.

(The box, of course, represents necessity or truth in all possible worlds.) Let 'L' represent the conjunction of the laws of nature into a single proposition. Let 'P_0' represent the proposition that describes the state of the world at some time in the remote past. Let 'P' represent any true proposition. The following statement, proposition (1), is a consequence of determinism:

(1) $\Box((P_0 \,\&\, L) \supset P)$.

We now argue,

(2)	$\Box\,((P_0 \supset (L \supset P))$	1, standard logic
(3)	$N((P_0 \supset (L \supset P))$	2, α
(4)	NP_0	Premise
(5)	$N(L \supset P)$	3, 4, β
(6)	NL	Premise
(7)	NP	5, 6, β.

Since the two premises are obviously true – no one has any choice about the past; no one has any choice about the laws of nature – (7) follows from (1) if the two rules of inference are valid.[2] And from this it follows that if determinism is true, no one has any choice about anything.

---

[1] See Peter van Inwagen, *An Essay on Free Will* (Oxford: Clarendon Press, 1983), pp. 93–104.

[2] Or this will do as a first approximation to the truth. But the statement in the text is not literally true, since at least one of the two premises is a contingent truth. ('Po' is a contingent truth, and 'NPo', which has 'Po' as a conjunct, is therefore a contingent truth. 'L' is *probably* a contingent truth, and 'NL' is therefore probably a contingent truth.) Here is a more careful statement. If the two rules of inference are valid, then an argument identical in appearance with the argument in the text can be constructed in any possible world and premises (4) and (6) of any of these arguments will be true in the possible world in which it is constructed if 'Po' expresses a proposition that describes the state of the world (= 'universe') in that possible world before there were any human beings, and 'L' expresses the proposition that is the conjunction of all propositions that are laws of nature in that possible world. Thus it can be shown (if the two rules of inference are valid) with respect to each possible world that if determinism is true in that world, then none of its inhabitants has any choice about anything. And if this can be shown with respect to each possible world, then free will is incompatible with determinism.

Are the two rules of inference valid? Rule α obviously is, whatever Descartes would have us believe about God. The question of the soundness of the argument comes down to the question whether β is valid. And, although β does not, perhaps, share the "luminous evidence" of α, it nevertheless seems pretty plausible. One way to appreciate its plausibility is to think in terms of regions of logical space. By logical space, I mean a space whose points are possible worlds. (Distances between points correspond to the "distances" that figure in a Lewis–Stalnaker semantics for counterfactual conditionals; areas or volumes represent probabilities.)[3] Consider Figure 1.

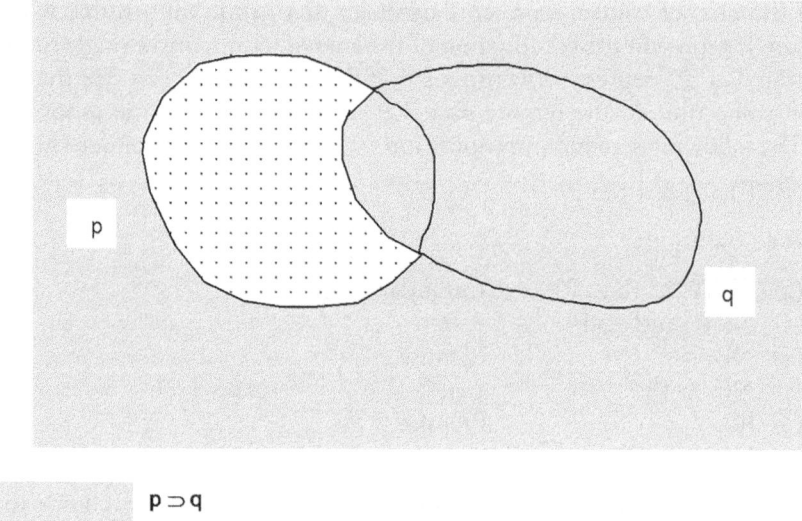

p ⊃ q

Figure 1

Suppose Alice is inside *p* and has no choice about that; suppose she is also inside the region that corresponds to the material conditional whose antecedent is *p* and whose consequent is *q* (the heavily shaded region) – and has no choice about *that*. Alice will, of course, be inside the intersection of *p* and *q*, and hence inside *q*.[4] Has she any choice about that? It

---

[3] That is, if a region of logical space occupies 23.37 percent of the whole of logical space, the probability of its being actual (containing the actual world) is 0.2337: the "intrinsic probability" of a proposition that is true in just that region of logical space is 0.2337. See my "Probability and Evil," in *The Possibility of Resurrection and Other Essays in Christian Apologetics* (Boulder, CO: Westview Press, 1997), pp. 69–87.

[4] In this paper, the symbols '*p*' and '*q*' and so on will sometimes be schematic letters representing sentences and sometimes variables ranging over propositions or regions of logical space. Although I

would seem not. As an aid to our intuitions, let us think of the regions displayed in the diagram as physical regions. Examination of the diagram shows that any way out of q – any escape route from q, so to speak – will either take Alice out of p or out of the shaded region. Therefore, *because* Alice has no way out of p and no way out of the shaded region ($p \supset q$), she has no way out of q. To be inside a region and to have no way out of it is to be inside that region and to have no choice about whether one is inside it. Rule β, therefore, would seem to be valid. This intuitive, diagrammatic argument is very plausible, and at one time I found it, or something very like it, cogent. Unfortunately, as any student of geometry knows, figures can be misleading, since a figure may have unintended special features that correspond to unwarranted assumptions. And this must be so in the present case, owing to the fact that McKay and Johnson have discovered what is undeniably a counterexample to β.[5]

McKay and Johnson begin by noting that α and β together imply the rule of inference that Michael Slote has called Agglomeration:

$Np, Nq \mid - N(p \ \& \ q)$.

(To show this, assume Np and Nq. The next line of the proof is '$(p \supset (q \supset (p \ \& \ q)))$'. The proof proceeds by obvious applications of α and β.) Rule α is obviously correct. To show β is invalid, therefore, it suffices to produce a counterexample to Agglomeration. McKay and Johnson's counterexample to Agglomeration is as follows.

Suppose I have a coin that was not tossed yesterday. Suppose, however, that I was able to toss it yesterday and that no one else was. Suppose that if I had tossed it, it might have landed "heads" and it might have landed "tails" and it would have landed in one way or the other (it's false that it might have landed on edge, it's false that a bird might have plucked it out of the air …), but I should have had no choice about which face it would have displayed. It seems that

N The coin did not land "heads" yesterday

N The coin did not land "tails" yesterday

are both true – for if I had tossed the coin, I should have had no choice about whether the tossed coin satisfied the description 'did not land

normally deprecate this sort of logical sloppiness, it does have its stylistic advantages, and it is easily eliminable at the cost of a little verbal clutter. Similar remarks apply to '&' and '⊃' and '□'.

[5] Thomas McKay and David Johnson, "A Reconsideration of an Argument against Compatibilism," *Philosophical Topics* 24 (1996): 113–122.

"heads"', and I should have had no choice about whether the tossed coin satisfied the description 'did not land "tails"'. But

> N (The coin did not land "heads" yesterday & the coin did not land "tails" yesterday)

is false – for I did have a choice about the truth-value of the (in fact true) conjunctive proposition *The coin did not land "heads" yesterday and the coin did not land "tails" yesterday*, since I was able to toss the coin and, if I had exercised this ability, this conjunctive proposition would have been false.

The case imagined is, as I said, undeniably a counterexample to Agglomeration. Agglomeration is therefore invalid, and the invalidity of β follows from the invalidity of Agglomeration. Our diagrammatic argument for the validity of β therefore misled us. But what is wrong with it?

We may note that a similar intuitive, diagrammatic argument could have been adduced in support of Agglomeration. Imagine two intersecting regions, p and q. Their region of overlap is, of course, their conjunction. Suppose one is inside p and has no way out of p; and imagine that one is inside q and has no way out of q. One will then be inside p & q; but does it follow that one has no way out of p & q? Inspection of the simple diagram that represents this situation shows that any way out of p & q must either be a way out of p or a way out of q. What is wrong with *this* argument?

To answer this question, we must examine the concept of "having a way out of a region of logical space." Suppose we know what is meant by "having access to" a region of logical space. (A region of logical space corresponds to a proposition, or to a set containing a proposition and all and only those propositions necessarily equivalent to it. To have access to a region of logical space is to be able to ensure the truth of the proposition that corresponds to that region, or to be able to ensure that that region contains the actual world. If one is inside a region one *ipso facto* has access to that region. If one has access to p, one *ipso facto* has access to the regions of which p is a subset – to the "superregions" of p.) To have a way out of a region p of logical space that one is inside is then defined as follows: to have access to some region that does not overlap p – or to have the ability to ensure that the proposition that corresponds to p is false. Now consider Figure 2.

Suppose I am "inside" the region p & q. Suppose I have access to and only to the following regions: (a) p & q and the other regions I am inside, and (b) r and the superregions of r. ("But what about the subregions of r?" From the fact that one has access to a certain region of logical space, it does

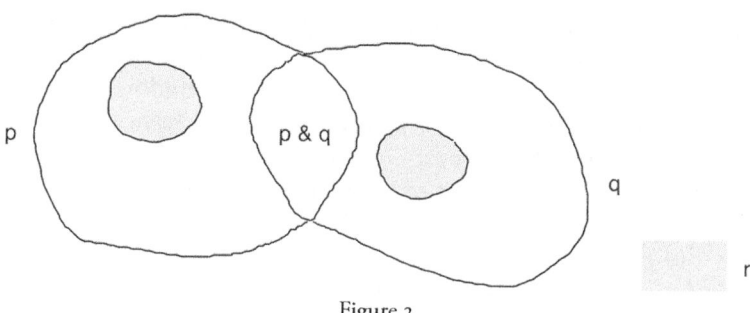

Figure 2

not follow that one has access to any of its proper subregions. I may, for example, be able to ensure that the dart hit the board, but unable to ensure with respect to any proper part of the board that it hit that proper part.) It follows from these suppositions that I am inside *p* and have no way out of *p* – for every region to which I have access overlaps *p*. (And, of course, the same holds for *q*: every region to which I have access overlaps *q*.) But I do have a way out of *p* & *q*, for I have access to a region – *r* – that does not overlap *p* & *q*. (It is not essential to the example that *r* be a non-connected region. It might have been "horseshoe-shaped" or a "ring." What is essential is that *r* overlap *p* and overlap *q* and not overlap *p* & *q*.)

If one thinks about the issues raised by McKay and Johnson's counterexample in terms of diagrams of logical space, it is easy enough to construct a counterexample to β itself (at least in the sense in which Figure 2 represents a counterexample to Agglomeration).[6] Here is a simple counterexample to β. Consider three regions of logical space, related to one another as in Figure 3.

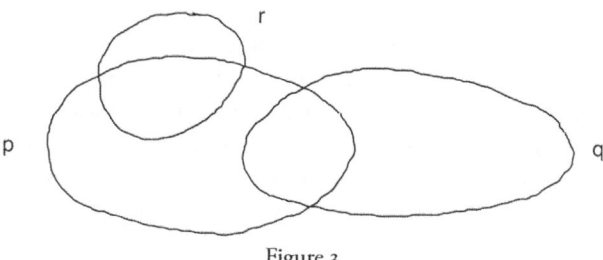

Figure 3

---

[6] The McKay–Johnson counterexample to Agglomeration is not a counterexample to β – although, since the validity of β entails the validity of Agglomeration, the existence of a counterexample to Agglomeration entails the existence of counterexamples to β.

Suppose I am inside p and inside $p \supset q$. (Or, what is the same thing, suppose I am inside p & q.) Suppose I have access to and only to the following regions: (a) the regions I am inside, and (b) r and its superregions. Then I have no way out of p (every region to which I have access overlaps p) and no way out of $p \supset q$ (every region to which I have access overlaps $p \supset q$), but I have a way out of q, for I have access to a region – r – that does not overlap q.

How did Figure 1 and the intuitive argument based on it mislead us? The answer is simple. The informal argument invited us to think of "having a way out of a region" as something like having available a path or line leading from a particular point inside that region *to a particular point* outside that region. (Recall our use of the term "escape route.") That, after all, is what it is normally like to have a way out of a region of physical space, and our intuitive grasp of any sort of space is mainly by way of analogy with physical space. But if we exercise our imaginations, we can think of ways in which one might have an ability to change one's position in physical space that is entirely different from the ability to follow a path that leads to a given point. We might for example suppose that one can bring it about that one changes one's position in space without moving – by magic, perhaps – and that when one changes one's position by this means, one might arrive at *any* of the points that make up some extended region.

Now consider once more Alice and Figure 1 (but add to Figure 1 a region r that is related to p and q just as r is related to p and q in Figure 3). Our intuitive argument for the conclusion that a way out of q must either be a way out of p or a way out of $p \supset q$ (the shaded region) was this:

As an aid to our intuitions, let us think of the regions displayed in the diagram as physical regions. Any way out of q – any escape route from q, so to speak – will either take Alice out of p or out of the shaded region.

As long as Alice moves by following a continuous path through space (an "escape route"), this is correct: any continuous path that leaves both p and the shaded region must leave q. But suppose that although Alice has no way of crossing any of the boundaries shown in the diagram by following a continuous path through space, she has a single magical resource: a magical lamp such that if she rubs it, the Slave of the Lamp will instantaneously translate her to a randomly chosen point inside the region r. Has Alice a way out of p? Has she a way out of $p \supset q$? The answers to these questions, perhaps, depend on how one defines 'a way out'. But if we define 'a way out' in a way parallel to our definition of 'a way out of a region of logical space', i.e.,

If one is inside a region of space *r*, one has a way out of *r* just in the case that one is able to ensure that one is inside a region that does not overlap *r*,

the answer to both questions is No: she has no "way out" of either of these regions. But Alice *does* have a way out of *q*: rubbing the lamp constitutes a way out of *q*, for rubbing the lamp will ensure that she is not in *q*. Our intuitions about physical space therefore misled us. As the world is, the only way to leave a region of physical space is to follow a continuous path out of that region, and our intuitions reflect this fact. Our diagrams of logical space are, of course, drawn in physical space and the diagrams therefore invite us to think of one's having access to a region *r* of logical space (a false proposition, a region not containing the actual world) in terms of one's ability to move along a line drawn from the point in the diagram that represents the actual world to some point inside the section of the diagram that represents *r*. Our "diagrammatic" argument misled us into thinking that there could be no counterexample to β (or to Agglomeration) because nothing in the concept of "access to a region of logical space" corresponds to the "continuous path" requirement that the real world imposes on our intuitions about "access to a region of physical space." A continuous path through physical space terminates in a single point, not in an extended region. To "have access" to an extended region of physical space is therefore (normally) to have access to one or more of the points that make up that region. To have access to a region of logical space, however, is in no possible case to have access to a point in logical space (a single possible world): Since one's power to direct the course of events is limited, from the fact that one is able to ensure that *some* possible world in which, say, the coin is tossed is actual it does not follow that one is able to ensure with respect to any given world in which the coin is tossed that one will be able to ensure that *that* world is actual. And of course, one never is able to ensure this; if one were one would not only be able to ensure that a tossed coin land on one particular face, but one would be able to determine the truth-value of every contingent proposition.

Our definition of 'N*p*' was '*p* and no one has or ever had any choice about whether *p*'. The *definiens* is equivalent to

> *p* and every region of logical space to which anyone has, or ever had, access overlaps *p*.

Why? Well, suppose that *p*, and that I did not do but was able to do X (and was able to do nothing else that was relevant to the truth-value of

p), and that if I had done X, p might have been true and might have been false. It seems wrong in that case to say that I had a choice about the truth-value of p. If, for example, the coin was untossed and I was able to toss it, and if I had tossed it, it might have fallen "heads" and might not have fallen "heads," it is wrong to say that I had a choice about the truth-value of the (true) proposition that the coin did not land "heads." (This point is the essence of the McKay–Johnson counterexample to Agglom-eration.) Now if it were important that the coin have landed "heads" (if someone's life depended on its landing "heads," say), there would be something wrong with my defending my failure to toss the coin by saying, "Look, the coin *didn't* land heads, and I didn't have any choice about that." And it is perhaps intuitively plausible to suppose that if p and if I had no choice about whether p, then I cannot properly be held morally responsible for p. But I don't think that this consideration has any tendency to show that I had a choice about how the coin fell. If I did offer the imagined lame excuse, the proper response would not be, "You did too have a choice about whether the coin landed 'heads'"; it would rather be, "You had a choice about whether the coin was tossed, and if you had tossed it, it might have landed 'heads.' What you are to blame for is not doing your best to bring it about that the coin landed 'heads.'" In sum, if p is a true proposition, having a choice about the truth-value of p implies being able to *ensure* that p is false.[7] And, as we have seen, the following is possible: p is true and no one is able to ensure that p is false; the conditional whose antecedent is p and whose consequent is q is true, and no one is able to ensure that that conditional is false; someone is able to ensure that q is false.

McKay and Johnson are therefore right. Rule β is invalid, and my argu-ment for the incompatibility of free will and determinism is invalid.

This, of course, does not imply that free will and determinism are com-patible, or that there is no plausible argument for the incompatibility of free will and determinism. I think, in fact, that the above argument for the incompatibility of free will and determinism can be turned into a valid argument by a minor modification of Rule β.[8] Suppose that, instead of defining 'Np' as 'p and no one has, or ever had, any choice about p' – that

---

[7] It implies more than this. It implies something about knowledge, generally knowledge of cause and effect. If p is true, and if p would be false if I did X (which I was able to do), for me to have a choice about the truth-value of p, I must have known (or at least be such that I *should* have known) that doing X would result in the falsity of p.

[8] Other ways to repair the argument have been suggested. One of these ways – it is similar to my own proposal – has been suggested by McKay and Johnson themselves; see their "Reconsideration of an

is, as '*p* and every region to which anyone has, or ever had, access overlaps *p*' – we were to define 'N*p*' as follows:

> *p* and every region to which anyone has, or ever had, *exact* access *is a sub-region of p*.

One has *exact* access to a region if one has access to it *and to none of its proper subregions*. Intuitively, one has exact access to *p* if one can ensure the truth of *p* but of nothing "more definite." The properties of the "exact access" relation differ from those of the "access" relation in several important ways. If I am inside a region, I do not in general have exact access to that region. (This is an understatement: the only region I am inside and have exact access to is the actual world.)[9] If I have exact access to a region, then, by definition, I have exact access to none of its (proper) superregions.[10] If I have exact access to the region of logical space in which Hillary Clinton proves Goldbach's Conjecture, it follows that I do *not* have exact access to the region in which *someone* proves Goldbach's Conjecture – although it follows that I *do* have *access* to that region. It is, unfortunately, impossible to give a plausible example of a non-actual region to which I have exact access. Suppose that, although I do not throw the dart, it is within my power to ensure that it hit the board – *and* that, for no proper part of the board is it within my power to ensure that the dart hit that part. Do I have exact access to a region in which the dart hits the board? Presumably not, for presumably I have access to a region in which the dart hits the board *and* I exclaim, "Ah!" For one to have exact access to the non-actual region *p* it must be the case that one can ensure the actuality of *p* but not the joint actuality of *p* and any logically independent region. If one could ensure the actuality of some non-actual *world*, one would have exact access to that world, of course, but obviously no one can do that – or no one but God. Still, it seems evident that there must be regions of logical space to which any given human being has exact access, simply because a human being's ability to ensure the truth of things, to "fine tune" his actions and their consequences, must come to an end somewhere.

Argument against Compatibilism," pp. 118–121. For a different suggestion, see Alicia Finch and Ted A. Warfield, "The *Mind* Argument and Libertarianism," *Mind* 107 (1998): 515–528.

[9] This statement assumes that no non-actual world is as close to the actual world as the actual world is to itself. Without this assumption, we should have to say: the only region I am inside and have exact access to is the set of worlds that are as close to the actual world as it is to itself.

[10] Suppose I have exact access to *r*. Then I have access to *r*. Let R be any (proper) superregion of *r*. If I have exact access to R, I have exact access to a region and to one of its proper subregions (*r*) – which is contrary to the definition of exact access.

Consider now our operator 'N', redefined as I have suggested. I think that this is what I was trying to capture when I defined 'Np' as 'p and no one has, or ever had, any choice about p'. What McKay and Johnson's counterexample shows is that the concept 'not having a choice about' has the wrong logical properties to capture the idea I wanted to capture – the idea of the *sheer inescapability* of a state of affairs. But if 'N' is redefined in the way I have proposed, the redefined 'N' does capture this idea. If every region to which I have access overlaps p, it may nevertheless be true that there is some action I can perform such that, if I did, then p *might* be false. But if every region to which I have *exact* access *is a subregion of* p, every action I can perform is such that, if I did perform it, p would be true: it is not the case that p might be false.

Now if 'N' is redefined as I have suggested, Rule β is valid – for the simple reason that every set that is a subset of both p and $p \supset q$ (that is, of p & q) is a subset of q. Thus, if every region of logical space to which anyone has exact access is within both p and $p \supset q$, every region of logical space to which anyone has exact access is within q. (And, of course, Rule α is valid: every region of logical space to which anyone has exact access is a region of logical space.)

What about the two premises of the argument for the incompatibility of free will and determinism? These both seem true – or at least the reasons for thinking them true are no worse than they were on the "no choice" understanding of 'N'. Every region of logical space to which anyone has exact access will be a subregion of P_0; every region of logical space to which anyone has exact access will be a subregion of L. (The compatibilist will disagree. The compatibilist will define 'is able' in some way – will no doubt employ some version of the "conditional analysis of ability" – that will have the consequence that each of us is *able* to perform various acts, such that, if he or she did perform them, then the conjunction of P_0 and L would be false. Thus, the compatibilist will argue, we do have exact access to regions that are not subregions of both P_0 and L. But this is an old dispute, and I have nothing new to say about it. I will say only this – and this is nothing new. The compatibilist's "move" is contrived and *ad hoc*; it is "engineered" to achieve the compatibility of free will and determinism; it *seems* that our freedom can only be the freedom to add to the actual past;[11] it *seems* that our freedom can only be the freedom to act in accordance with the laws of nature.)

---

[11] Cf. Carl Ginet, *On Action* (Cambridge University Press, 1990), pp. 102–103.

It seems, therefore, that I now have what I thought I had when I thought Rule β was valid on the "no choice" understanding of 'N': a valid argument for the incompatibility of free will and determinism whose premises seem to be true. And this, *mutatis mutandis*, is all that can be asked of any philosophical argument. At any rate, no more can be said for any known philosophical argument than this: it is valid and its premises seem to be true.

II

Free will, then, seems to be incompatible with determinism. But, as many philosophers have noted, it also seems to be incompatible with *in*determinism. The standard argument for this conclusion (which I have called the *Mind* Argument because it has appeared so frequently in the pages of *Mind*) goes something like this:

If indeterminism is to be relevant to the question whether a given agent has free will, it must be because the acts of that agent cannot be free unless they (or perhaps their immediate causal antecedents) are undetermined. But if an agent's acts are undetermined, then *how* the agent acts on a given occasion is a matter of chance. And if how an agent acts is a matter of chance, the agent can hardly be said to have free will. If, on some occasion, I had to decide whether to lie or to tell the truth, and if, after much painful deliberation, I lied, my lie could hardly have been an act of free will if whether I lied or told the truth was a matter of chance. To choose to lie rather than tell the truth is a *free* choice only if, immediately before the choice was made, it was up to the agent whether he lied or told the truth. That is to say, before the choice was made, the agent must have been able to lie and able to tell the truth. And if an agent is faced with a choice between lying and telling the truth, and if it is a *mere matter of chance* which of these things the agent does, then it cannot be up to the agent which of them he does.

(At any rate, this is one way to formulate the *Mind* Argument. Other statements of the argument are available, including some that do not appeal to the concept of chance. I will presently return to this point.) In *An Essay on Free Will*, I tried to show that the *Mind* Argument depended on the "unrevised" version of Rule β. If this is correct, then, since "unrevised β" is invalid, the *Mind* Argument is invalid. But perhaps I was wrong to think that the *Mind* Argument depended on "unrevised β," at least in any essential way. Perhaps the *Mind* Argument depends only on the employment of some rule of inference *of the same general sort* as "unrevised β." Perhaps, indeed, the Mind Argument could be rewritten so as to depend only on "revised β." I will not consider these possibilities. I will not try to answer the question whether the *Mind* Argument is in fact valid. I have a different project. I wish to consider the *Mind* Argument in a very informal, intuitive form, to contend that in this intuitive form the argument has a great deal of plausibility, and to use this contention as the basis of an argument for the conclusion that the concept of *agent causation* is entirely irrelevant to the problem of free will. This is no trivial conclusion. Most philosophers who have thought carefully about the problem of free will maintain that the concept of agent causation is incoherent – and perhaps also maintain that if, *per impossibile*, this concept were coherent, it would be contrary to naturalism or to some other important philosophical commitment to suppose that it applied to anything in the real world. A sizable and respectable minority of the philosophers who have thought carefully about the problem of free will maintain that the concept of agent causation is coherent and, moreover, that agent causation is real and figures in an essential way in the acts of free agents. But almost everyone seems to think that if there really *were* such a thing as agent causation, its reality would constitute a solution to the problem of free will. I am going to try to show that even if agent causation exists, even if it is an element in the acts of free agents, the problem of free will is just as puzzling as it would have been if no one had ever thought of the idea of agent causation. I am going to try to show that even if agent causation is a coherent concept and a real phenomenon, and we know this, this piece of knowledge will be of no help to the philosopher who is trying to decide what to say about free will.

I begin my argument by characterizing the problem of free will and the concept of agent causation.

The problem of free will in its broadest outlines is this. Free will seems to be incompatible both with determinism and indeterminism. Free will seems, therefore, to be impossible. But free will also seems to exist. The impossible therefore seems to exist. A solution to the problem of free will would be a way to resolve this apparent contradiction. There would seem to be three forms a solution could take, three ways in which one might try to resolve the apparent contradiction. One might try to show, as the compatibilists do, that – despite appearances – free will is compatible with determinism. Or one might try to show, as many incompatibilists do, that – despite appearances – free will is compatible with indeterminism. Or one might try to show, as many "hard determinists" do, that the apparent reality of free will is mere appearance. (To be reasonably plausible, a solution of the third type would probably have to incorporate some sort of argument for the conclusion that moral responsibility does not, as it appears to, require free will – or else an argument for the conclusion that a belief in the reality of moral responsibility is not, as it appears to be, an indispensable component of our moral and legal and political thought.) This is the problem to which, in my view, agent causation is irrelevant. (Perhaps there is some *other* problem that could reasonably be called 'the problem of free will' and to which agent causation *is* relevant. I can only say that if there is such a problem, I don't know what it is.)

Agent causation is, or is supposed to be, a relation that agents – thinking or rational *substances* – bear to events. Agent causation is opposed to *event* causation, a relation that events bear to events. The friends of agent causation hold that the causes of some events are not (or are only partially) earlier events. They are rather substances – not *changes* in substances, which are of course events, but "the substances themselves." Thus, they say, Thomas Reid caused the movements of his fingers when he wrote the sentence, "There is no greater impediment to the advancement of knowledge than the ambiguity of words." These movements, they insist, were caused simply by *Reid*, and not by any change in Reid. Or, speaking more carefully, since they are aware on empirical grounds that these movements were in fact caused by changes in Reid's hand and arm and spinal cord and brain, they will say that there were *some* events, events that occurred no more than a few seconds before these movements and were among their causal antecedents, events that presumably occurred within the motor centers of Reid's brain, that were caused by Reid and not by any prior events. Speaking even more carefully, they may say that at any rate there were causal antecedents of the movements of Reid's fingers to whose occurrence Reid, Reid himself, the thinking substance, *contributed causally* – thus allowing the possibility that earlier events in Reid's brain *also* contributed causally to the occurrence of these events.

Let this suffice for a characterization of the problem of free will and the concept of agent causation. Now how is the concept supposed to figure in a solution of the problem? In this wise, I believe: the reality of agent causation is supposed to entail that free will and indeterminism are compatible. The idea is something like this. A certain event happens in Reid's brain, an event that, through various intermediate causes, eventually produces a bodily movement that constitutes some voluntary action of Reid's – say, his writing the sentence, "There is no greater impediment to the advancement of knowledge than the ambiguity of words." (Perhaps we need not attempt to explain the notion of a bodily movement's "constituting" a voluntary action. The idea is illustrated by this example: certain movements of Reid's arm and hand and fingers constitute his writing the sentence, "There is no greater impediment, *etc.*") And Reid is, let us suppose, the agent-cause of the aforementioned brain-event that was a causal antecedent of his writing this sentence – or at any rate he contributes agent-causally to its occurrence. (From this point on, I will neglect the distinction between agent-causing an event and contributing agent-causally to its occurrence.) The action, or the event that is Reid's performing it, is not determined by the state of the universe at any time before the antecedent brain-event occurred. (And why not? Well, because the event that was his agent-causing the antecedent brain-event was not determined to occur by any prior state of the universe. And if that event – his agent-causing the antecedent brain-event – had not occurred, his hand and fingers would not have moved and he would not have written the sentence.) And yet it is as obviously true as anything could be that he is responsible for this event, for he was its cause: it occurred because *he* caused it to occur. It was therefore an act of free will, and free will is therefore consistent with indeterminism.

In the sequel, I will take it for granted that the relevance of the concept of agent causation to the problem of free will is supposed to be found in the supposed fact that the reality of agent causation entails that free will is compatible with indeterminism. And I will take it for granted that the argument of the preceding paragraph is a fair representation of the argument that is supposed to establish this compatibility. If there is some other reason agent causation is supposed to be relevant to the problem of free will, or if the argument of the preceding paragraph is a poor or incomplete representation of the reasons for supposing that the concept of agent causation can be used to establish the compatibility of free will and indeterminism, then the argument of the remainder of this essay will be at best incomplete and at worst entirely beside the point.

In my view, this argument does not succeed in showing that the reality of agent causation entails the compatibility of free will and indeterminism. Its weak point, I believe, is the reasoning contained in its last two sentences: "And yet it is as obviously true as anything could be that [Reid] is responsible for [the antecedent brain-event], for he was its cause: it occurred because *he* caused it to occur. It was therefore an act of free will, and free will is therefore consistent with indeterminism." It is not my plan to make anything of the fact that Reid knew even less than I about what goes on in the motor centers of human brains – or of the fact that other agents, agents who act freely if anyone does, do not even know that they *have* brains. Any doubts about the argument that might be based on these facts have to my mind been adequately answered by Chisholm, and I shall not bother about them.[12] Nor shall I raise questions about the cause of the event "its coming to pass that Reid is the agent-cause of the antecedent brain-event."[13] Again, I think Chisholm has seen what the friends of agent causation should say about the cause of this event, to wit, that Reid was its agent-cause – and was, moreover, the agent-cause of the event "its coming to pass that Reid is the agent-cause of the event 'its coming to pass that Reid is the agent-cause of the antecedent brain-event'," and so *ad infinitum*.[14] Some may object to the thesis that, as an indispensable component of his writing a certain sentence, Reid, without being aware of it, became the agent-cause of an infinite number of events; I don't.

In order to see what I *do* object to in the argument, let us return to the question why some have thought that free will was incompatible with indeterminism. Let us, that is, return to the "mere matter of chance" argument. Let us try to state this argument more carefully. (In *An Essay on Free Will*, I had a very short way with any attempt to state the *Mind* argument in terms of an undetermined act's being a random or chance occurrence.[15] I argued there that the words 'random' and 'chance' most naturally applied to *patterns* or *sequences* of events, and that it was therefore not clear what these words could mean if they were applied to single events. It will be evident from what follows that I no longer regard this argument as having any merit.) Let us suppose undetermined free acts occur. Suppose, for example, that in some difficult situation Alice was faced with a choice between lying and telling the truth and that she freely chose to tell the truth – or, what is the same thing, she seriously considered telling the truth, seriously considered lying, told the truth, and was able to tell the lie she had been contemplating. And let us assume that free will is incompatible with determinism, and that Alice's telling the truth, being a free act, was therefore undetermined. Now suppose that immediately after Alice told the truth, God caused the universe to revert to precisely its state one minute before Alice told the truth (let us call the first moment the universe was in this state 't_1' and the second moment the universe was in this state 't_2'), and

---

[12] "Freedom and Action," in Keith Lehrer (ed.), *Freedom and Determinism* (New York: Random House, 1966), pp. 11–44; see pp. 20–21.

[13] The event "its coming to pass that Reid is the agent-cause of the antecedent brain-event" is the same event as "Reid's acquiring the property *being the agent-cause of the antecedent brain event*." Presumably, there is a moment of time before which Reid has not agent-caused the antecedent brain-event and after which he has, and that is the moment at which this event occurs.

[14] At any rate, I *believe* that Chisholm has considered this problem and has defended the "and so *ad infinitum*" solution. But I have been unable to find this solution in his writings.

[15] Pp. 128–129.

then let things "go forward again." What would have happened the second time? What would have happened after t_2? Would she have lied or would she have told the truth? Since Alice's "original" decision, her decision to tell the truth, was undetermined – since it was undetermined whether she would lie or tell the truth – her "second" decision would also be undetermined, and this question can therefore have no answer; or it can have no answer but, "Well, although she would either have told the truth or lied, it's not the case that she would have told the truth and it's not the case that she would have lied; lying is not what she would have done, and telling the truth is not what she would have done. One can say only that she *might* have lied and she *might* have told the truth."

Now let us suppose that God *a thousand times* caused the universe to revert to exactly the state it was in at t_1 (and let us suppose that we are somehow suitably placed, metaphysically speaking, to observe the whole sequence of "replays"). What would have happened? What should we expect to observe? Well, again, we can't say what would have happened, but we can say what would *probably* have happened: sometimes Alice would have lied and sometimes she would have told the truth. As the number of "replays" increases, we observers shall – almost certainly – observe the ratio of the outcome "truth" to the outcome "lie" settling down to, converging on, some value.[16] We may, for example, observe that, after a fairly large number of replays, Alice lies in thirty percent of the replays and tells the truth in seventy percent of them – and that the figures 'thirty percent' and 'seventy percent' become more and more accurate as the number of replays increases. But let us imagine the simplest case: we observe that Alice tells the truth in about half the replays and lies in about half the replays. If, after one hundred replays, Alice has told the truth fifty-three times and has lied forty-eight times,[17] we'd begin strongly to suspect that the figures after a thousand replays would look something like this: Alice has told the truth four hundred and ninety-three times and has lied five hundred and eight times. Let us suppose that these are indeed the figures after a thousand replays. Is it not true that as we watch the number of replays increase, we shall become convinced that what will happen on the *next* replay is a matter of chance? (The compulsive gamblers among us might find themselves offering bets about what Alice would do on the next replay.) If we have watched seven hundred and

---

[16] "Almost certainly" because it is *possible* that the ratio does not converge. Possible but most unlikely: as the number of replays increases, the probability of "no convergence" tends to 0.

[17] After 100 replays, Alice has told the truth or lied 101 times.

twenty-six replays, we shall be faced with the inescapable impression that what happens on the seven-hundred-and-twenty-seventh replay will be due simply to chance. Is there any reason we should resist this impression? Well, we certainly know that there is nothing we could learn about the situation that could undermine the impression, for we already know everything that is relevant to evaluating it: we know that the outcome of the seven-hundred-and-twenty-seventh replay will not be determined by its initial state (the common initial state of all the replays) and the laws of nature. Each time God places the universe in this state, both "truth" and "lie" are consistent with the universe's being in this state and the laws of nature. A sheaf of possible futures (possible in the sense of being consistent with the laws) leads "away" from this state, and, if the sheaf is assigned a measure of 1, surely, we must assign a measure of 0.5 to the largest subsheaf in all of whose members Alice tells the truth and the same measure to the largest subsheaf in all of whose members she lies. We must make this assignment because it is the only reasonable explanation of the observed approximate equality of the "truth" and "lie" outcomes in the series of replays. And if we accept this general conclusion, what other conclusion can we accept about the seven-hundred-and-twenty-seventh replay (which is about to commence) than this: each of the two possible outcomes of this replay has an objective, "ground-floor" probability of 0.5 – and there's nothing more to be said. And this, surely, means that, in the strictest sense imaginable, the outcome of the replay will be a matter of chance.

Now, obviously, what holds for the seven-hundred-and-twenty-seventh replay holds for all of them, including the one that wasn't strictly a *re*play, the initial sequence of events. But this result concerning the "initial replay", the "play," so to speak, should hold whether or not God bothers to produce any replays. And if He does not – well, that's just the actual situation. Therefore, an undetermined action is simply a matter of chance: if it was undetermined in the one, actual case whether Alice lied or told the truth, it was a mere matter of chance whether she lied or told the truth. If we knew beforehand that the objective, "ground-floor" probabilities of Alice's telling the truth and Alice's lying were both 0.5, then (supposing our welfare depended on her telling the truth) we could only regard ourselves as *fortunate* when, in the event, she told the truth. But then how can we say that Alice's telling the truth was a free act? If she was faced with telling the truth and lying, and it was a mere matter of chance which of these things she did, how can we say that – and this is essential to the act's being free – she was *able* to tell the truth and *able* to lie? How could anyone be able to determine the outcome of a process whose outcome is a matter of objective, ground-floor chance?

This is the plausible, intuitive version of the *Mind* Argument that I have promised to discuss. What I must do now is show that the concept of agent causation cannot be used to undermine the intuitive plausibility of this argument.

Let us suppose that when Alice told the truth, she agent-caused certain brain-events that, in due course, resulted in those movements of her lips and tongue that constituted her telling the truth. And let us again suppose that God has caused the universe to revert to precisely its state at t_1, and that this time Alice has lied. I do not see how to avoid supposing that in this "first replay," Alice *freely* lied – for if one has to choose between telling the truth and lying, and if one freely chooses to tell the truth, then it must be the case that if one had chosen instead to lie, the choice to lie would have been a free act. (One cannot say that an agent faces exactly two continuations of the present, in one of which he tells the truth but was able to lie and in the other of which he lies and was *un*able to tell the truth.) Now if Alice's lie in the first replay was a free act, she must – according to the friends of agent causation – have been the agent-cause of some among the causal antecedents of the bodily movements that constituted her lying. And so, of course, it will be, *mutatis mutandis*, in each successive replay. If God produces one thousand replays, and if (as I have tacitly been assuming) the state of the universe at t_1 – the common initial state of all the replays – determines that Alice will *either* tell the truth or lie, then, in each replay, Alice will *either* agent-cause cerebral events that, a second or so later, will result in bodily movements that constitute her telling the truth or agent-cause cerebral events that, a second or so later, will result in bodily movements that constitute her lying. She will, perhaps, agent-cause events of the "truth antecedent" sort five hundred and eight times and events of the "lie antecedent" sort four hundred and ninety-three times. Let us suppose once more that we are somehow in a position to observe the sequence of replays. We may again ask the question, "Is it not true that as we watch the number of replays increase, we shall become convinced that what will happen in the *next* replay is a matter of chance?" I do not see why we should not become convinced of this. And what might we learn, what is *there* for us to learn, that should undermine this conviction? What should lead us to say that the outcome of the next replay, the seven hundred and twenty-seventh, will not be a matter of chance? What should lead us to say that it is anything other than a matter of chance whether Alice will agent-cause truth-antecedent cerebral events or lie-antecedent cerebral events in the about-to-occur seven-hundred-and-twenty-seventh replay? Well, one might say this: If it turns out that Alice agent-causes truth-antecedent cerebral events, this will not be a matter of chance because it will be she, *Alice*, who is the cause of the event "its coming to pass that Alice agent-causes truth-antecedent cerebral events." But have we not got every reason to regard the occurrence of *this* event – that is, the occurrence of "its coming to pass that Alice agent-causes the event 'its coming to pass that Alice agent-causes truth-antecedent cerebral events'" – as a matter of chance? If the three events "the truth-antecedent cerebral events"/ "its coming to pass that Alice agent-causes the truth-antecedent cerebral events"/ "its coming to pass that Alice agent-causes the event 'its coming to pass that Alice agent-causes truth-antecedent cerebral events'" are the first three terms of an infinite series of agent-caused events, is not the simultaneous occurrence of all the events in this sequence (as opposed to the simultaneous occurrence of all the events in an infinite sequence of agent-caused events whose first member is "lie-antecedent cerebral events") a mere matter of chance?

Nothing we could possibly learn, nothing God knows, it would seem, should lead us to distrust our initial inclination to say that the outcome of the next replay will be a matter of chance. If this much is granted, the argument proceeds as before, in serene indifference to the fact that we are now supposing Alice to be the agent-cause of various sets of cerebral events that are antecedents of the bodily movements that constitute her acts. And the argument proceeds to this conclusion: If it is undetermined whether Alice will tell the truth or lie, then – *whether or not* Alice's acts are the results of agent causation – it is a mere matter of chance whether she will tell the truth or lie. And if it is a mere matter of chance whether she will tell the truth or lie, where is Alice's free will with respect to telling the truth and lying? If one confronts a choice between A and B and it is a matter of chance whether one will choose A or B, how can it be that one is *able* to choose A?

I close with an example designed to convince you of this.[18]

You are a candidate for public office, and I, your best friend, know some discreditable fact about your past that, if made public, would – and should – cost you the election. I am pulled two ways, one way by the claims of

---

[18] The example that follows in the text rests on a mistake. (I am grateful to Michael Bratman for opening my eyes to this mistake.) See Chapter 11 of the present volume. In that chapter, I present an argument for the incompatibility of free will and indeterminism that appeals to a revised version of the example.

citizenship and the other by the claims of friendship. You know about my situation and beg me not to "tell." I know (perhaps God has told me this) that there exist exactly two possible continuations of the present – the actual present, which includes your begging me not to tell and the emotional effect your appeal has had on me – in one of which I tell all to the press and in the other of which I keep silent; and I know that the objective, "ground-floor" probability of my "telling" is 0.43 and that the objective, "ground-floor" probability of my keeping silent is 0.57. Am I in a position to promise you that I will keep silent? – knowing, as I do, that if there were a million perfect duplicates of me, each placed in a perfect duplicate of my present situation, forty-three percent of them would tell all and fifty-seven percent of them would hold their tongues? I do not see how, in good conscience, I could make this promise. I do not see how I could be in a position to make it. But if I believe that I am able to keep silent, I should, it would seem, regard myself as being in a position to make this promise. What more do I need to regard myself as being in a position to promise to do X than a belief that I am *able* to do X? Therefore, in this situation, I should not regard myself as being able to keep silent. (And I cannot see on what grounds third-person observers of my situation could dispute this first-person judgment.) Now suppose God vouchsafes me a further revelation: "Whichever thing you do, whether you go to the press or keep silent, you will be the agent-cause of events in your brain that will result in the bodily movements that constitute your act." Why should this revelation lead me to conclude that I am in a position to promise to keep silent – and therefore that I am able to keep silent? Its content simply doesn't seem to be relevant to the above argument for the conclusion that it is false that I am able to keep silent. I confess I believe there *is* something wrong with this argument. (I expect I believe this because I fervently *hope* that there is something wrong with it.) But it seems clear to me that if there is, as I hope and believe, something wrong with the argument, its flaw is not that it overlooks the possibility that my actions have their root in agent causation.

CHAPTER 8

Genes, Statistics, and Desert

Suppose there is a population in which a certain type of criminal behavior is much more common than it is in most other populations that have been studied. To what extent can the relatively high frequency of that type of behavior in that population be ascribed to genetic, as opposed to environmental, factors? In the real world, this is always a very difficult question.

Let us suppose that – in some case, in respect of some type of behavior – this difficult question has been answered. Let us suppose that the high frequency of a certain type of criminal behavior in "population A" has been shown (to the satisfaction of all of the statisticians, criminologists, sociologists, and so on – of all political persuasions and ideologies – who have studied the matter) to be, to a significant degree, a product of genetic factors. I want to investigate the consequences of this supposition for certain questions about punishment and desert. Before I turn to these questions, however, I will say something about how such a conclusion could be established.

Suppose it has been established that if, starting at a certain date, the babies born to parents belonging to population A and the babies born to parents belonging to a second population, population B – in which the incidence of the type of criminal behavior under investigation is significantly lower than it is in A – were exchanged in their cradles (the exchange being stealthy enough that the parents do not notice), the statistical profile of population A would – assuming no very important changes in the environmental conditions under which its members live – after an appropriate amount of time had passed, become significantly more like the present profile of population B. (And, of course, *vice versa*: the statistical profile of population B would become significantly more like the present profile of population A.) And let us suppose that a

I wish to thank the following people for valuable comments and criticism: Marcia Baron, Jorge Garcia, Patricia Greenspan, Michael Slote, Alan Strudler, Laurence Thomas, and David Wasserman.

similar result has been obtained with respect to A and "population C," with respect to A and "population D" – and so on, for a large and varied family of populations, populations in which the environments in which children are raised vary widely in respect of all of the environmental factors that it is reasonable to suppose have consequences for the incidence of criminal behavior in a population. (And we suppose that we have found no population in respect of which this result has not been obtained.) It must be conceded that even if there were investigators who had established the results I have imagined, they would have found no absolute proof that if they had gone on to examine one more population, they would have obtained a similar result. For all they could show without collecting further data, if they had gone on to compare population A with "population Q" (another population in which the type of criminal behavior we are interested in is low), they would have discovered that exchanging babies from A with babies from Q would leave A with the same high incidence of this behavior and Q with the same low incidence of it. Thus, even our fantastic imaginary evidence would not rule out the following possibility: the high incidence in A of the criminal behavior under investigation is due, to a very significant extent, to environmental factors that are present in A but absent from all the populations with which A has so far been compared, and might well be present in some other, unexamined populations. It does seem, however, that as the number and variety of the populations with which A has been compared in the way imagined and with the result imagined increases, the probability increases that a population with the genetic makeup of A would, in any possible human environment, exhibit a relatively high incidence of the criminal behavior being studied. And this, I suppose, is what it would mean for the relatively high incidence of some sort of criminal behavior in Population A to have a genetic cause.

To suppose that we have collected evidence of the kind I have imagined is to make an extravagant supposition, but not an impossible one. It would be possible, in principle, to collect such evidence, and therefore, possible in principle to demonstrate that it is highly probable that the high incidence of a certain sort of criminal behavior in a population is due to genetic features of that population. And it would not be necessary to exchange babies in their cradles to carry out the demonstration. When I say that it is in principle possible to collect such evidence, I am putting forward a more interesting thesis than that it is "in principle possible" actually to exchange the babies belonging to two whole populations. I am saying that it is in principle possible to determine what the results of such an exchange would be without making it. Justifying conclusions of that sort is just what statistical inference is for.

I must emphasize that I am saying only that it is *in principle* possible to determine whether, for two populations that exhibit significantly different statistical profiles as regards criminal behavior, the result of a "baby exchange" would be eventually to "reverse" (to some degree) those profiles. What is possible in principle might be forever impossible in practice. It might be that, although it is possible to say *a priori* what sort of evidence would establish or refute "reversal hypotheses" – and the even more ambitious hypotheses that ascribe the incidence of types of behavior in a population to the genetic peculiarities of that population – it is in practice impossible to collect evidence that satisfies these *a priori* requirements. However this may be, what is only in principle possible is often of considerable philosophical interest. I want to imagine a population in which a certain type of objectionable behavior is significantly more frequent than it is in most populations, and to imagine that it has been uncontroversially established that the high frequency of this behavior in this population is due to genetic features of the population. I want to imagine this because it constitutes a kind of "worst-case scenario" for those who worry about the relations between the genetic makeup of human beings and questions of punishment and desert. I want to investigate the consequences of the worst-case scenario. It might, after all, turn out that some version of the worst-case scenario is true, and there seems to be no reason to wait till some possibility materializes to start worrying about what to do about it. And even worst-case scenarios that, so to speak, never make it to the screen can be useful to theorize about, since they provide material for *a fortiori* arguments. ("If we shouldn't use nuclear weapons even if the other side attacked us with them without warning, we certainly shouldn't use them in any other case.")

Let us fill out our worst-case scenario a bit – at least to the extent of supplying a crime and a few figures. Let us say that within population A, rape is very common. One man in twenty, let us say, has at least attempted to rape someone. In population B, however, only one man in a thousand has attempted rape. We are, of course, supposing that the two populations are ones that people belong to from birth – or, better, from conception – or not at all. Population A, for example, is not supposed to be something like "inmates of federal penitentiaries." We are supposing, moreover, that if the male babies born to the parents of the two populations were (covertly) exchanged, then, after a suitable interval, the proportion of population A that were rapists would begin to decline and would eventually level out at a figure substantially lower than one in twenty; and, of course, we are supposing that the proportion of population B that were rapists would begin to rise and would eventually level out at a figure substantially higher than one in a thousand. And let us suppose that we have established similar results for A and C, A and D, and A and a great many other populations in which rape is significantly less common than it is in A – all we have been able to compare A with. If we had such evidence, we should have very good reason to believe that there was a genetic explanation for the abnormally high proportion of rapists in population A. We should not, of course, know *what* the genetic explanation was; that would be a matter for further investigation, investigation that would probably have to be carried out partly by examining human genetic material and not simply statistics about human behavior.

So much for the question how one might establish the conclusion that the high frequency of a certain type of criminal behavior in a certain population might have a genetic basis. I will now, as I have promised, turn to "certain questions about punishment and desert."

The questions that interest me are these. To what extent would the facts I have imagined, if they were real facts, provide the rapists who belong to population A with an excuse for their crimes? Should we (in that case), in writing our criminal code, be "population-blind"? Would it be *fair* to write laws that prescribed the same criminal penalties for anyone convicted of (a certain type of) rape, when we know that the proportion of the members of population A who commit rape is, because of the genetic makeup of that population, significantly higher than the proportion of the members of most other populations who commit rape? Do the members of A *deserve* to be treated the same way under the law as the members of (for example) B?

There seems to me to be one possible circumstance in which it would be absolutely clear that our laws regarding rape should in no way take into account the genetic peculiarities of A. Suppose we did indeed identify the specific genetic factor that was responsible for the relatively high proportion of rapists in A. Suppose it was discovered that the possession of "Gene Combination Alpha" was much more strongly correlated with rape than was membership in population A, and that it had been proved that almost all of the "A" rapists possessed this gene combination. And suppose it had been proved that this combination of genes was so rare in population B and most other populations as to be almost non-existent. Suppose it was shown that the distribution of this genetic factor in the various populations studied (together with the very strong correlation of this factor with rape) accounted very well for the differing proportions of rapists in those populations. Suppose that there was an easy-to-perform and reliable test that could be used to determine whether a given man possessed Gene Combination Alpha. Then it would seem to be undeniable that our laws should not take either the high proportion of rapists in A or the fact that this proportion is known to have a genetic basis into account. It is individuals and not populations that are brought to trial, at least under civilized legal systems, and any given rapist either possesses Gene Combination Alpha or he doesn't. Whether he does or does not might be a relevant matter to bring up at his trial. Whether he belongs to a population in which that combination is frequent or infrequent is certainly irrelevant.[1]

If, however, we added this kind of knowledge to our imaginary case, this would in a sense change nothing about it that was of philosophical interest. What the addition of such knowledge would change would be only the question that was the focus of philosophical interest. It would be the question 'To what extent would having Gene Combination Alpha provide an excuse for rape?' rather than the question 'To what extent would belonging to population A provide an excuse for rape?' that was the focus of philosophical interest. Let us therefore simply assume that we do not know what the genetic factors are that explain the high proportion of rapists in population A.

The interest of the question 'To what extent does belonging to population A provide an excuse for rape?' lies in the fact that members of population A do not invariably commit rape. In fact, most men who are members of A get through their lives without trying to rape anyone, even when – let us suppose – they are in circumstances in which it would be reasonable for them to believe they could get away with it. Consider, by way of contrast, "population X," in which *all* men attempt rape whenever they think they have a reasonable chance of doing so with impunity. (We suppose, again, that there is good evidence that these men would behave that way no matter what environment they were raised in.) The question 'To what extent does belonging to population X provide an excuse for rape?' is much less interesting than the question I have raised. It seems fairly clear that belonging to population X provides the rapist with a really excellent excuse, for it seems fairly clear

---

[1] This point applies not only to gene combinations, but to any factor that might be a cause or partial cause of bad behavior in an individual. We shall later apply it to desires and other psychological factors.

that in that case the rapist's behavior is genetically determined.[2] And it seems fairly clear that we do not want to blame people for engaging in behavior that is genetically *determined* (as opposed to genetically influenced). The men of population X will, it is true, have to be regarded as dangerous, but the proper attitude toward them, it would seem, ought to be like our attitude toward a typhoid carrier. We should restrict their freedom of movement, as we do with typhoid carriers, but we should feel sorry for them; we should feel sorry for them because we should feel that, however necessary it might be for us to restrict their freedom of movement, they do not *deserve* it. Just as being a typhoid carrier is a misfortune, so – I believe this would be our reaction – being genetically determined to commit rape would be a misfortune. (Of course we might blame some member of population X for being indifferent to the consequences for others of his condition – just as we blame Typhoid Mary for being indifferent to the consequences for others of *her* condition; but, presumably, we should do this only if we did not regard indifference to the consequences of one's genetically determined condition as being itself genetically determined.)

What can be said in defense of the thesis that membership in a population like population A – a population in which, for genetic reasons, the proportion of rapists is high, but in which, at least as far as anyone knows, no one is genetically determined to commit rape[3] – is at least some sort of excuse for rape? How might a convicted rapist belonging to such a population try to use this fact in court to his advantage?

Well, suppose that a man who belongs to population A has been convicted of rape, and I, who belong to population B, am presiding at his trial. The jury has just delivered its verdict, and I am about to pass sentence on him. I give him the most severe sentence the law allows, and accompany the sentencing with some remarks about the horror of rape and how mercy is entirely out of place when one is dealing with rapists. Suppose he replies,

---

[2] Marcia Baron has asked me how it can be that the behavior of the members of X is genetically determined if they are able to take into account the possibility of being punished, and (by implication) sometimes refrain from an act of rape they would otherwise have committed if they believe the risk of punishment is too high. I think we must distinguish between being determined and being irrational (that is, not being rational in the "value-free" or "Humean" sense). The men who belong to X, as I am describing them, have the following dispositional property: whenever they see an opportunity to commit rape and believe that they could get away with acting on it, they do act on it. I am supposing, moreover, that there is good evidence that it is genetically determined that they have this dispositional property.

[3] It is consistent with the evidence we have imagined that each rapist in population A was genetically determined to commit rape on the particular occasions on which he did. But the evidence would provide no reason to suppose that this was in fact the case.

"It's not your place to judge me. I am a member of population A, and you are not. I am thus laboring under a genetic burden that fortune has placed on my back and not on yours. Since you don't share my genetic burden, you are not in a position to pass moral judgment on me. What is more, it's not at all fair that I should be given the most severe sentence the law allows. If you give me that sentence, what sentence will you reserve for a member of *your* fortunate population – there are a few – who commits the same crime?" Note that in this speech the rapist presents two arguments for two different conclusions. One argument is *ad hominem*, and its conclusion is that my moral condemnation is out of place. The conclusion of his second argument – which could be addressed to any judge – is that he should not receive the most severe sentence possible.

I want to approach these two arguments by looking at some analogies. Let us look at some quite different cases of statistical correlation between criminal behavior and various genetic and environmental factors. (But *can* environmental factors provide a suitable analogy? I don't see why not. If we are interested in matters of excuse and desert, the only relevant questions to ask about a factor that has somehow influenced an agent's behavior are, Had the agent a choice about whether that factor was present? and, Had the agent a choice about whether that factor, if present, influenced his behavior? That someone who did something objectionable was drunk at the time is not much of an excuse if the agent had a choice about whether to be drunk, or if it was within his power to place himself in circumstances in which his being drunk would not have led to that sort of behavior. And features of one's environment can as easily be things that one has no choice about as the sequence of base pairs in one's DNA. No one has any choice about whether he was sexually abused at age four or was raised in grinding poverty or was born a member of a despised and visible minority.) In devising examples turning on environmental factors, I shall not, of course, assume that the populations that figure in the examples are ones a person has to be born into to belong to. In presenting the analogical cases, I shall assume that we know what explains the statistical differences between the populations that are contrasted. I shall feel free to do this because I am interested in the question, What *follows* about the responsibility of individual members of various populations between which there are statistical differences that are due to factors outside the control of their members?

Now the analogies.

There are two islands. Bank robbery is much more common on one of the islands than it is on the other: an inhabitant of Island A is in fact about twenty times more likely to rob a bank than is an inhabitant of Island B. It turns out that the explanation is not far to seek. On Island A, there are hundreds of small banks that are (as banks go) pretty easy to rob. On Island B, there are only a few large banks, and they are equipped with all sorts of state-of-the-art anti-robbery devices.

Suppose that someone who lives on Island A has been convicted of bank robbery, and I, who live on Island B, am the judge at his trail and I am passing sentence on him. I give him the strictest sentence the law allows, and accompany the sentencing with some remarks on the horror of bank robbery (I was educated in Switzerland) and how mercy is entirely out of place when one is dealing with bank robbers. Suppose the convicted bank robber replies, "It's not your place to judge me. I am a native of Island A, and you are not. I am thus laboring under an environmental burden that fortune has placed on my back and not on yours. Since you don't share my environmental burden, you are not in a position to pass moral judgment on me. What is more, it's not at all fair that I should be given the strictest sentence the law allows. If you give me that sentence, what sentence will you reserve for a member of your fortunate population – there are a few – who commits the same crime?"

I do not think that most of us would regard these arguments as very convincing. It is interesting to ask why we don't, however.

Let us look at a second case. There are two islands. Bank robbery is much more common on one of the islands than the other: an inhabitant of Island A is in fact about twenty times more likely to rob a bank than is an inhabitant of Island B. It turns out that the explanation is not far to seek. There are genetic differences between the inhabitants of the two islands, differences that have the consequence that people with the mental and physical capacities that make skilled bank robbers are much more common on Island A than on Island B. These are, let us say, manual dexterity, nerves of steel, mechanical ability, a good memory for detail, excellent spatial intuition, exceptional athletic ability ... whatever. For genetic reasons, the inhabitants of Island B tend to be nervous, clumsy, scatterbrained couch potatoes.

If we imagine a convicted bank robber from Island A arguing that he ought to receive some sort of special consideration from the court because he was born into a population that is deficient in nervous, clumsy, scatterbrained couch potatoes (or even because he himself demonstrably lacks these genetic advantages for growing up to be a non-bank robber), we shall find it difficult to imagine anyone's being convinced by his argument.

Now a third example, again turning on environmental factors. On Island A, there are secret criminal societies (like that presided over by Fagin, but with loftier criminal ambitions) that kidnap children and raise them to be bank robbers. On Island B, there are no such societies; as a consequence, bank robbery is much more common on A than on B.

A fourth example, this time involving a genetic factor. The inhabitants of A are, for genetic reasons, much harder to "socialize" than is the human norm. As children they, or at least a significant proportion of them, have a much greater tendency toward bullying, petty theft, and vandalism than the children of most populations. (The inhabitants of the island are aware of this unfortunate feature of the island's gene pool and, if possible, adopt children from off-island rather than conceive their own; well-conducted empirical studies of the careers of these adopted children confirm the intuitions of their foster-parents.) The inhabitants of A who exhibit these tendencies as children tend to rob banks when they grow up, for the simple reason that, as Willie Sutton put it, "That's where the money is." As a consequence, bank robbery is much more common on A than on B.

In these two cases, we should probably find a convicted bank robber's plea for some sort of special leniency to have some plausibility, whether or not we in the end allowed it to influence our decisions about how he or she ought to be treated by the court.

What is the lesson of these cases? It seems to me to be something like this. A factor, whether genetic or environmental, that explains why it is that a certain type of criminal behavior is more common in a certain population is not perceived as providing any sort of excuse for those who engage in that type of behavior if its effect is due to its increasing the prevalence of the skills required for that kind of behavior or the opportunities available to members of that population to engage in that sort of behavior with impunity. (The same point would apply to the easy availability of means. A convicted bomber could not plausibly ask for mercy on the ground that high explosives were easily available in his society, although he might, with some plausibility if it were true, plead that he was raised in a society in which bombers were lionized by the news media. Nor could he offer as an excuse the fact that he had inherited the – rare, let us suppose – mechanical skills necessary for constructing bombs, though he might plead that he had inherited a disposition to violence or a sociopathic disregard for human life.) But if a factor works by creating or strengthening a desire such that to act on that desire would be to engage in a certain sort of criminal behavior, we tend to regard the plea that that factor is prevalent in some population to which one belongs to be at least some sort of excuse for having engaged in that behavior. If, for example, there were a genetic factor that could be shown to produce in males an inordinately strong desire for immediate sexual release, or a desire to degrade women, the fact that this genetic factor was present in a given man who had been convicted of rape would probably be regarded as at least relevant to the question what sort of moral attitude we should take toward him and what sort of action a court should take in passing sentence. If, moreover, a factor tends to have adverse effects (adverse in our judgment) on an individual's abstract or second-order desires – the desire not to cause pain, say, or the desire not to desire to degrade women – we should probably regard the presence of that factor as relevant to questions of excuse and desert. If, for example, it could be shown that a convicted rapist had been raised by parents who taught him always to seek immediate gratification of the desires of the moment and never to consider the consequences for himself or others of his actions, we might well regard this fact about his nurture as a mitigating circumstance. If, finally, a factor tends to interfere with an individual's ability to implement his or her abstract or second-order desires – if it produces a lack of self-control, low intelligence, ignorance of generally available ways of dealing with situations in which one's momentary desires are in conflict with one's abstract or second-order desires – we should probably regard the presence of this factor as relevant to questions of excuse and desert.

Perhaps we could sum up these tendencies in the following formula. Suppose a certain kind of criminal act is significantly more prevalent in a certain population than in most other populations. If whatever factor produces this effect is "external," if it produces its statistical effect *only* by placing some of the members of that population in certain *circumstances*, if it leads them into temptation, we do not regard it as providing any sort of excuse for those members of the population that engage in that behavior – and this despite the fact that the members of the population have no choice about whether they are members of a population in which that effect is present. But if the factor is "internal," if it produces its statistical effect wholly or partly by acting on the desires and values of the members of the population (or on their ability to alter, or to act or refrain from acting in accordance with, certain desires and values), then we tend to regard this factor as something that should at least be considered when we are judging the members of the population that engage in that sort of behavior. It should be remarked that this "formula" is only a formula – an easy-to-remember device for summing up certain tendencies we have. I do not want to place too much weight on the particular terms of this formula. I particularly warn against placing too much weight on the words 'external' and 'circumstance': in the sense I am giving to these words, an agent's size and bodily strength or his possession of certain items of purely factual knowledge could count as external factors, as a component of the circumstances in which fortune has placed him.

Let us look at the case of rape. Does this tendency that I have alleged to exist manifest itself in the case of that crime? I think so. Imagine a society in which – owing to some economic necessity – women are more frequently alone and far from help than is common in most societies. For good measure, imagine that in this society, it is customary for men to cover their faces when they go out in public, like women in traditional Islamic societies. It would not be surprising if rape were markedly more common in that society than in most. But we should hardly regard the plea "I live in a society in which it's relatively easy to find opportunities for rape, and in which it's hard for the victim of rape to note any features of her assailant that might later serve to identify him – and I have no choice about whether I live in such a society" as a very effective one. Or imagine a society in which men were much larger and stronger than women – significantly more so than is in fact the norm in human populations. In this society, too, it would not be surprising if rape were more frequent than is the norm. But "I have to live in a society in which I am surrounded by women that it is physically easy for me to force myself on" is not an excuse that we should be likely to find convincing.

It might be argued that the tendency that I have alleged is less clear than I have made it out to be. One could think of cases that might tell against it. Drug addiction is more common among doctors and nurses than it is among the members of other high-stress professions (such as airline traffic controllers). The usual explanation is simply that it is much easier for doctors and nurses to get drugs than it is for most people. Assuming this to be the case, cannot doctors and nurses who are drug addicts offer the general easy availability of drugs in the medical professions as an excuse for their addiction? What about bank clerks who have embezzled money? Can't a reformed alcoholic who has relapsed plead (supposing this to be true) that people were always offering him a drink? I am inclined to account for our sympathetic reaction to these proposed excuses by pointing out that widespread opportunity can mean frequent temptation, which can, in time, increase the strength of one's desires, or weaken one's will in respect of resisting them. The most convincing of the three cases is that of the reformed alcoholic who relapses; we should note that in this case an "internal" debility was present from the start and that the frequent episodes of temptation could plausibly be supposed to have been gradually strengthening it. In short, these are not cases in which the greater-than-normal frequency of objectionable behavior in a population is due *only* to "external" factors.[4]

I continue to believe, therefore, that we do have this tendency. Is it justified? I will argue that it is not. I will begin by presenting two pairs of cases (one "environmental" pair and one "genetic" pair). Each pair will be constructed to bring out pretty strongly our tendency to regard "external" and "internal" factors as being importantly different. I will argue that there is nothing about internal and external factors that justifies us in treating them differently.

Here is the "environmental" pair. We have two societies in which rape is significantly more common than in most societies. This can be explained (we have somehow shown) entirely by features of the environments in which the members of the two societies live. The two operative environmental factors are these:

— In Society One, there is, and has been for more than a generation, legal, ubiquitous, and very well produced pornography that is essentially a glorification of rape. Even parents with the best wills in the world find it extremely difficult to prevent adolescent boys from being continually exposed to this pornography.
— In Society Two, there is an illegal but cheap and easily available drug that facilitates rape: it is tasteless, odorless, fast-acting, and easy to administer surreptitiously. It renders the victim semi-conscious and pliable. The human metabolism breaks it down into untraceable residues very fast: a few hours after it has been administered, it is undetectable by any medical test. Those who have been given this drug have afterwards only the vaguest and most confused memories of what happened while they were under its influence.

---

[4] The fact that "external" factors (like temptation) can reinforce or otherwise affect "internal" factors (like desire) suggests that the distinction between the prevalence of a kind of behavior in a population being due to external factors and its being due to internal factors is considerably more complicated than what I have said in the text allows – perhaps even that it is a dubious distinction. But if this is so, it can only strengthen the case for the conclusion that we ought to resist our tendency to regard this distinction as morally significant.

Here is the "genetic" pair. We have two societies in which rape is significantly more common than in most societies. This can be explained (we
have somehow shown) entirely by differences in the genetic makeups of
the members of the two societies. The two operative genetic factors (they
have figured in cases we have already considered) are these:

— Among the male members of Society Three, a certain gene sequence
  is very common; it has the following phenotypic effect on those men
  whose genotype contains it: they experience an inordinately strong urge
  for immediate sexual release.[5]
— In Society Four, the men are (for genetic, and not dietary or other environmental reasons) much larger and stronger than the women, significantly *more* so than is the human norm.

I take it that most of us would regard being a member of societies Two or
Four (the two "external factor" societies) as providing no sort of excuse
for rape, and that we should experience at least some tendency to regard
membership in societies One or Three (the two "internal factor" societies)
as providing at least some sort of excuse; membership in either of the latter
two societies, we are inclined to think, is a mitigating circumstance that
should be taken into account when we determine the rapist's penalty or
pass moral judgment on him. But what justification could be given for this
difference in attitude?

In each of the four societies, the rapist has certain desires, and –
whether or not he struggles against them – he acts on them and commits rape. In most cases, the more typical cases, the rapist will also
have had certain desires and tendencies that pulled him in the opposite
direction. If he is a hardened, habitual rapist, he may not have had
any opposing desires, for repeatedly acting on certain desires tends to
extinguish any desires or tendencies that oppose the desires that are
repeatedly acted on. If the hardened, habitual rapist's desire to force

[5] I am not supposing that "an inordinately strong desire for immediate sexual release" is normally
or ever the "cause" of rape. I am supposing that if an inordinately strong desire for immediate
sexual release was much more common in some population than in most, this could explain why a
higher-than-normal proportion of the men in that population were rapists. This is like supposing
that the fact that the summer of 1982 was very dry could explain why there was a higher-than-normal
number of forest fires that summer. It certainly does seem plausible to suppose that if terrorists were
to add to the New York City water supply a drug that causes men to experience an inordinately
strong desire for immediate sexual release, the number of rapes committed in New York could be
expected to increase: no doubt many men whom various factors predisposed to rape, but who would,
nevertheless, not have committed rape in the normal course of events, would be "pushed over the
edge" by ingesting the chemical.

himself on a particular woman on a particular occasion is really *unopposed* – by any values or feelings of human sympathy or preference for a sexual partner who is actually sexually aroused or even by fear of punishment – then perhaps he can't do otherwise than act on that desire. (This would be a consequence of the conclusions of my paper, "When Is the Will Free?")[6] But let us consider those much more common and typical cases in which something – human sympathy, childhood moral training, fear of punishment – opposes the rapist's momentary desire to commit the rape he is contemplating, and let us suppose that in these cases he is *able* not to act on his desire to commit the rape he is contemplating.[7]

If a man contemplating rape is indeed able to refrain from acting on his present desire, if he is indeed able to refrain from committing the rape he is considering, then I do not see why the fact that he had had that desire should, afterwards, provide him with any sort of excuse for what he has done. (And this even if his having that desire is not something he has any choice about.) The presence of this desire in his psychological economy is not a mitigating circumstance. If, moreover, the man contemplating rape is able to refrain from acting on his present desire, then I do not see how any facts about the *source* of that desire can provide him with any excuse if he decides to act on it. In Society One, the desires on which many rapists act are due to their repeated exposure during their formative years to a certain kind of particularly vicious pornography. In Society Two, the society in which the drug that facilitates rape is easily available, it is *opportunities* to commit rape, rather than momentary desires to commit rape, that are due to a corrupt environment. In Society Two there may be no one cause that produces all or most of the momentary desires to commit rape that are experienced by the men of that society; still, each particular momentary desire will have *some* cause – one that will quite possibly be outside the individual's control. In Society One, a large number of the momentary desires that issue in rape have a common cause; but why should that fact be relevant to the question how we should judge the men who act on them? The following speech, surely, is not an excuse a rapist could plausibly offer, even if everyone were wholly convinced of its truth: "I admit that I raped

---

[6] Chapter 5 of the present volume.

[7] Even the man who is now a hardened, habitual rapist will almost certainly not have been in this state "at first" – when he committed his first rape or his first few rapes. We may therefore hold him responsible for the rapes he commits in his present state, for we may hold him responsible for the fact that he now lacks the ability to resist those desires. Or at least this seems reasonable to me. I have defended a position of which this thesis is a special case in "When Is the Will Free?"

the woman who has accused me. But before I attacked her, I experienced a strong desire to rape her. And I was born a member of the Ruritanian lower-middle class, in which a higher-than-normal proportion of men experience such desires, and it has been proved that there is a common cause – some factor widespread in the Ruritanian lower-middle class – for many of these episodes of desire." If the momentary desire itself does not provide the rapist with an excuse, why should he be provided with any excuse by the existence of a factor that caused the desire, is widespread in a population to which he belongs, and produces similar desires in other members of that population?

It seems to me that internal factors like desire do not have importantly different implications for questions of excuse and desert from external factors like opportunity. Every rapist has of course had opportunities to commit rape, and an opportunity, we all agree, is no sort of excuse. If many of the opportunities to commit rape that are available to the rapists in some population have a common source (a common environmental source, as in Society Two, or a common genetic source, as in Society Four), we do not regard the existence of this common source as relevant to questions of excuse or desert. And desire would seem to be no different from opportunity in this respect: the existence of neither a (resistible) desire to commit rape nor of an opportunity to commit rape is any sort of excuse for the act; the discovery of a source of desires or a source of opportunities (whether a genetic or an environmental source) that operates across a population to which a rapist belongs would add nothing of relevance to the deliberations of those deciding how to punish or judge him. Just as a rapist cannot put forward a common, population-wide source of particular opportunities to commit rape as a mitigating circumstance, so a rapist cannot put forward a common, population-wide source of momentary desires to commit rape as a mitigating circumstance. There are, of course, other internal factors than desire that are relevant to questions of excuse and desert. There are, for example, the agent's internal resources for dealing with desires that are in conflict with his or her values or higher-order desires. But the point I am making is quite general: If the presence of some particular factor in an agent's internal economy is not an excuse for some act of the agent's, why should the fact that the agent belongs to a population in which that factor is more common than in most other populations be an excuse for that act?

Perhaps there are some who will not find this argument convincing. We might try to articulate their reservations by imagining someone who, because of his or her special relationship to a convicted rapist, is inclined to regard any circumstance that could conceivably be regarded as mitigating as really being so. We might imagine a mother who appeals on behalf of her son to the court (either a court of law or the court of public opinion) along the following lines. "You should regard my son's having grown up in a society that permits vicious pro-rape pornography as a mitigating circumstance. You should be merciful in passing sentence on him [in making moral judgments about what he did]." The plea is – to my ears, anyway – a poignant one, but I don't think we should allow it. (Unless, of course, the effect on the young man of his having grown up in an environment in which such pornography was prevalent was to render him literally *unable* to refrain from acting on the desires the pornography generated. But if that were the case – and we are supposing that it isn't – we should not have an example of a mere mitigating circumstance: we should have a case in which the rapist should be absolved of all blame, a case in which he should simply be regarded as a "rape carrier.") As long as we are convinced that the rapist had a choice about what he did, we should not reduce his sentence or soften the moral judgments we make about his act. What we can do, and what I believe we *should* do, is feel sorry for him.[8] And it would certainly do us no harm – the men among us, that is – to reflect that we might well ourselves have done what he did if we had been raised in the same corrupt environment. (Come to that, it would probably do us men no harm to ask ourselves seriously how we should have behaved if we had been raised in a society like Two or Four in which it was absurdly easy to commit rape with impunity.)

To have to deal with a recurrent desire (or, for that matter, with recurrent opportunities)[9] to commit some wrong act is a misfortune, a burden. We can, and should, feel sorry for those who have to bear burdens that we don't, and we may profit from asking ourselves how we should have borne up under them. We should not, however, regard them as mitigating circumstances. If a mother steals because she and her children are starving, that is a mitigating circumstance. If I betray my country or the

---

[8] I am here discussing only questions concerning the sorts of judgments we should make about, and the attitudes we should take toward, a particular individual and a particular act he has performed. I do not mean to imply that we have no obligation to try to find a way to lighten or remove the psychological burden that individual bears. And I certainly do not mean to imply that we have no obligation to try to find a way to reform the corrupt environment that has placed that burden on him.

[9] Recurrent opportunities to commit some wrong act will be a misfortune only for those who have some "standing" desire to commit that act. But then being subject to recurrent desires to commit some wrong act will not be much of a misfortune for those who have no opportunity to act on them.

Revolution (or whatever) under torture or because my family is being held hostage, that is a mitigating circumstance. If someone commits rape as the alternative to the murder of his family (one can easily imagine this alternative being forced on someone in one of the nasty little ethnic wars of the present decade), the fact that he faced this alternative is a mitigating circumstance.[10] Having a (resistible) desire to do ill that most other people do not have is, however, no more a mitigating circumstance than is having an opportunity to do ill that most other people do not have.

This general judgment applies if the (resistible) desire to do ill has a genetic cause; the source of a desire is irrelevant to the question whether its presence in an individual should be regarded as a mitigating circumstance. And it applies if the desire is significantly more common in some population to which the agent belongs than it is in most other populations; the presence of a desire in other individuals is irrelevant to the question whether its presence in a given individual should be regarded as a mitigating circumstance. It therefore applies if the desire is significantly more common in some population to which the agent belongs than it is in most other populations owing to genetic differences between that population and the populations in which it is less common. I conclude that even if it could be proved beyond the shadow of a doubt that the high incidence of some type of criminal behavior in a certain population was due to genetic causes, causes that operated by affecting "internal" factors – by producing resistible desires; by warping values that the agent could see to be warped by reflecting on other values that he or she has; by diminishing (but not eliminating) the agent's capacity to deal with desires he or she wishes not to act on – this discovery would be morally and legally irrelevant. The laws governing that sort of criminal behavior ought to be the same for, and applied with the same degree of rigor to, the members of that population

---

[10] These examples are cases in which circumstances mitigate the wrongness of an act because they are cases in which circumstances dictate that the alternative to performing the wrong act is to cause or allow something very bad to happen. (Indeed, if the alternative is bad enough, most of us will want to say that the act was not, in the circumstances, wrong; most of us would probably judge that it is not wrong to steal food if one's children are starving. But the examples can easily be modified so that they are clear cases of wrong acts whose wrongness is mitigated by the circumstances under which they are performed. Suppose, for example, that the children in the "starving children" case are in fact not starving but are nevertheless painfully thin and ill-nourished, and that the mother steals food from a family even more needy than hers.) But there is no "bad alternative" to rape – except in extremely rare cases like the one imagined in the text. It may be that the rapist would regard the existence of an unfulfilled desire to commit rape as a "bad alternative," but most of us will not, and we shall therefore say that the presence in him of a desire to commit rape was not a mitigating circumstance.

as everyone else.[11] And we should make the same moral judgments about those who are members of that population and engage in that behavior that we make about those who are not members of that population and engage in that behavior.

---

[11] At least if the only thing the legislatures and the courts are considering is the *fairness* of the laws and the sentences. If deterrence is a factor in their considerations, it might be advisable for them to adopt a different legal strategy with respect to members of that population.

CHAPTER 9

Freedom to Break the Laws

Philosophers are unable to agree about free will. Some are determinists[1] who deny free will, some determinists who affirm free will. Some philosophers think that free will is incompatible with determinism *and* with indeterminism – and hence that free will is impossible – while others say that we are free and that our free actions are and must be undetermined; yet others say that we are free and that our free actions are and must be determined. Some philosophers believe that acts of free will involve a special kind of causation, agent causation (whereby a substance causes alterations in the world without itself undergoing any alteration), and others respond to appeals to agent causation with incredulous stares. Some say that free will is an unintelligible notion, and others say that, whether the *thing* free will exists or not, the *concept* "free will" is a paradigm of intelligibility. Some say that although free will is incompatible with determinism, this fact is of little consequence because moral responsibility (which is what is really at issue in debates about free will) *is* compatible with determinism; their opponents reply that it is *evident* that moral responsibility cannot exist without free will. I could go on, but I trust I have made my point: the problem of free will is a typical philosophical problem.

I

Disagreement in philosophy is pervasive and irresoluble. There is almost no thesis in philosophy about which philosophers agree. If there is any philosophical thesis that all or most philosophers affirm, it is a negative thesis: that formalism is not the right philosophy of mathematics, for

---

[1] Or "near determinists": with a polite bow in the direction of quantum mechanics, these philosophers insist that there is no more indeterminism in the workings of a human being than there is in the workings of a digital computer.

example, or that knowledge is not (simply) justified, true belief.[2] (See the long quotation from David Lewis a few paragraphs on: "Gödel and Gettier may have done it.")

That is not how things are in the physical sciences. I concede that the "cutting edge" of elementary-particle physics looks at lot like philosophy in point of pervasive and fundamental disagreement among its respected practitioners. But there is in physics a large body of settled, usable, uncontroversial theory and of measurements known to be accurate within limits that have been specified. The cutting edge of philosophy, however, is pretty much the whole of it.[3]

That is not how things are in history. I concede that the historian Peter Geyl was making a true and important point when he said that history was argument without end. Nevertheless, there is no controversy whatever about whether Queen Anne is dead. Unlike the physical sciences, history does not have "a large body of settled, usable, uncontroversial theory" at its disposal but, like the physical sciences, it does have a large body of established and incontrovertible fact to work with. In philosophy, however, there is neither settled theory nor incontrovertible fact.[4]

And that is not how things are in mathematics, the biological sciences, economics, linguistics, archaeology ... The fundamental, pervasive, and irresoluble disagreement that afflicts philosophy is certainly uncommon. It is a defensible position that it is unique.

How do philosophers react when this state of affairs comes to their attention? In the seventeenth and eighteenth centuries, generally by proclaiming some new philosophical method that would finally put the feet of philosophy on the sure path of science. Such proclamations have been rare or non-existent for quite a long time now, and understandably so.

---

[2] I used to think that all philosophers, or at least all philosophers of mathematics and all philosophically minded logicians, accepted Church's Thesis (which is a philosophical thesis). I was wrong. See László Kalmár, "An Argument against the Plausibility of Church's Thesis," in A. Heyting (ed.), *Constructivity in Mathematics* (North Holland: Amsterdam, 1959), pp. 72–80.

[3] It is uncontroversial that the general theory of relativity may be used to calculate the loss of energy due to gravitational radiation in a pair of rotating neutron stars: that that theory, properly applied, will yield accurate results in the "regime" to which such a system belongs. It is uncontroversial that the statement 'The rest-mass of the electron is 9.11×10^{-31} kg' is accurate to within the displayed number of decimal places.

[4] For a remark on one attempt of philosophers to find themselves a body of uncontroversial data, see the quotation from Lewis that we are moving toward in the text (the remark on "linguistic intuition"). Another such attempt is represented by Husserl's slogan, "back to the phenomena." *Every* such attempt has generated the following reaction: some philosophers deny that the supposed foundational data are data; others deny that they are foundational; still others say that even if they are data and are foundational (in the sense that they are self-evident and require no justification beyond themselves), not much philosophy can be based on them.

Present-day analytical philosophers tend simply not to permit the fact that philosophical disagreement is irresoluble to come to their attention. One analytical philosopher who did not ignore this fact was David Lewis.[5] Here is the long quotation I have been promising. It is from the introduction to the first volume of his collected *Philosophical Papers*.[6]

> The reader in search of knock-down arguments in favor of my theories will go away disappointed. Whether of not it would be nice to knock disagreeing philosophers down by sheer force of argument, it cannot be done. Philosophical theories are never refuted conclusively. (Or hardly ever. Gödel and Gettier may have done it.) The theory survives its refutation – at a price. Argle has said what we accomplish in philosophical argument: we measure the price. Perhaps that is something we can settle more or less conclusively. But when all is said and done, and all the tricky arguments and distinctions and counterexamples have been discovered, presumably we will still face the question which prices are worth paying, which theories are on balance credible, which are the unacceptably counterintuitive consequences and which are the acceptably counterintuitive ones. On this question we may still differ. And if all is indeed said and done, there will be no hope of discovering still further arguments to settle our differences.
>
> It might be otherwise if, as some philosophers seem to think, we had a sharp line between "linguistic intuition," which must be taken as unchallengeable evidence, and philosophical theory, which must at all costs fit this evidence. If that were so, conclusive refutations would be dismayingly abundant. But, whatever may be said for foundationalism in other subjects, this foundationalist theory of philosophical knowledge seems ill-founded in the extreme. Our "intuitions" are simply opinions; our philosophical theories are the same. Some are commonsensical, some are sophisticated; some are particular, some general; some are more firmly held, some less, But they are all opinions, and a reasonable goal for a philosopher is to bring them into equilibrium. Our common task is to find out what equilibria there are that can withstand examination, but it remains for each of us to come to rest at one or another of them. If we lose our moorings in everyday common sense, our fault is not that we ignore part of our evidence. Rather, the trouble is that we settle for a very inadequate equilibrium. If our official theories disagree with what we cannot help thinking outside the philosophy room, then no real equilibrium has been reached. Unless we are doubleplusgood doublethinkers, it will not last. And it should not last, for it is safe to say that in such a case we will believe a great deal that is false.

---

[5] Another is Colin McGinn. See his *Problems in Philosophy: The Limits of Inquiry* (Oxford: Blackwell, 1993).

[6] David Lewis, *Philosophical Papers, Volume I* (Oxford University Press, 1983), pp. x–xi. There are several footnotes to this text. The reader may wish to consult the original.

Once the menu of well-worked-out theories is before us, philosophy is a matter of opinion. Is that to say that there is no truth to be had? Or that the truth is of our own making, and different ones of us can make it differently? Not at all! If you say flatly that there is no god, and I say that there are countless gods but none of them are our worldmates, then it may be that neither of us is making any mistake of method. We may each be bringing our opinions to equilibrium in the most careful possible way, taking account of all the arguments, distinctions, and counterexamples. But one of us, at least, is making a mistake of fact. Which one is wrong depends on what there is.

Let me say something to tie what I have been talking about (pervasive and irresoluble philosophical disagreement) to what Lewis was talking about (the absence of knock-down arguments from philosophy).[7]

What could put an end to disagreement in philosophy if not knock-down arguments? Philosophical agreement will come to pass when, and only when, for each important philosophical thesis, there is a knock-down argument either for that thesis or for its denial.[8] In saying this, I suppose that philosophical theses are, at least for the most part, genuine propositions (proper objects of affirmation or denial; possessed of truth-values).[9] (I suppose this, as does Lewis: "mistake of fact"; "depends on what there is.") If they are pseudo-propositions of some sort, then the resolution of philosophical disagreement (or pseudo-disagreement) will require not argument but therapy.[10]

The question whether philosophical theses are genuine propositions is important enough in relation to the topic of philosophical disagreement to be worth a brief digression.

What can be said in support of the philosophical thesis that philosophical theses are genuine propositions? I offer the following argument. At least *some* philosophical theses must be genuine propositions. For consider

---

[7] In the opening sentences of the quoted passage, Lewis speaks only of the (near) absence of knock-down *refutations* from philosophy. But, as the passage continues, it becomes clear that he means to assert the absence from philosophy of knock-down *arguments* – whether proofs or refutations.

[8] The disjunction is exclusive. There cannot be a knock-down argument both for a thesis and for its denial. If, *per impossibile*, this situation did obtain, there would be, in Hume's phrase, "a mutual destruction of arguments," and neither argument would be knock-down after all.

[9] I use the terms 'proposition' and 'thesis' as stylistic variants.

[10] I use the term 'pseudo-proposition' because of its important role in twentieth-century thinking about the nature of philosophy. But my use of the term should not be taken to imply that I suppose that there are things that appear to be propositions but aren't. I suppose, rather, that there are sentences that appear to express propositions but don't. The writers who first used the term 'pseudo-proposition' used it to designate what *I* should call 'sentences that appear to express propositions but don't' – and used the word 'proposition' to designate what I should call 'sentences that express propositions'.

the proposition that all philosophical theses are pseudo-propositions. This proposition is itself a philosophical thesis, for philosophy is a part of its own subject matter: "What is a philosophical thesis?" is a philosophical question. This proposition is therefore a pseudo-proposition if it is true. The best course for those who *want* to say that all philosophical theses are pseudo-propositions (and who have seen that if they do say what they want to say, they will be either affirming a falsehood or attempting to affirm a pseudo-proposition) is to affirm some instance of the following schema: The members of a certain proper subset φ of the set of philosophical theses are pseudo-propositions; those philosophical theses that are *not* pseudo-propositions are theses *about* the members of φ, theses that ascribe certain intrinsic or relational properties to the members of φ ("Every member of φ is a pseudo-proposition" being of course one of them). Those who have reluctantly abandoned the thesis that all philosophical propositions are pseudo-propositions could, of course, try to find a revised version of this thesis that sounds more like the original than the revision *I* have suggested. They could insist upon applying the term 'philosophy' only to the members of φ (whatever φ may be), and they could invent a new name for what otherwise would have been called 'philosophical theses about the members of φ' (no doubt the name would be 'metaphilosophical theses'). But this would be a merely verbal maneuver and would accomplish no more than any other merely verbal maneuver. Giving a new name to a certain class of philosophical theses (and denying them the old name 'philosophical thesis') is not going to change the fact that, whatever they are called, all "metaphilosophical" theses are the objects of irresoluble disagreement. Philosophers exhibit no more tendency to agree about theses like "The sentence 'Human beings have free will' expresses no proposition" than they do about theses like "The sentence 'Human beings have free will' expresses a false proposition."[11]

---

[11] Do I not by offering this argument contradict myself, at least pragmatically? Do I not represent the argument in the text (the argument whose conclusion is 'At least some philosophical theses are genuine propositions') as a knock-down argument? No, I offer it only as an argument. I could write a "Wittgensteinian" reply, or, better, response, to it, the core of which would be something like this: "The philosopher who follows the proper method never asserts anything – not even the proposition that the philosopher who follows the proper method never asserts anything. All my assertions, even this one, are parlor tricks played with linguistic props, directed illusions, conceptual sleight-of-hand, whose purpose is to get my audience to see the supposed problems of philosophy in a new way. And this seeing-in-a-new-way is not a matter of belief. When someone sees things as I want him to see them, he will have gained no new beliefs and will have lost no old ones, just as the person who now sees a duck where a moment ago he saw a rabbit has gained no new beliefs and has lost no old ones. I expect my audience, at the outset, to treat texts like the one you are now reading as comprising assertions; in the end, however, if I am successful and my audience does see things the way I want

Some philosophers have thought that they or their teachers had invented a new philosophical method, the application of which would (finally!) yield knock-down philosophical arguments. Others, most present-day analytical philosophers among them, eschew methodological questions and simply soldier on, applying the traditional methods of philosophy to "first-order" philosophical problems (that is, problems about things like the mind or morality or being and non-being, as opposed to problems concerning the nature of the philosophical enterprise). (They carefully define terms of art. They propose analyses of concepts. They advance counterexamples to analyses. They construct theories. They search out possible ambiguities in philosophically important words and phrases. They point out that this or that argument is not formally valid unless this or that proposition is added to its premises. They insist that one of the premises of an argument assumes the very point at issue. They contend that the philosophers who have favored a certain thesis would look much less favorably on one of its hitherto unnoticed consequences. They assign the burden of proof to one of the sides in a philosophical debate. They introduce into discussions of traditional philosophical questions considerations gleaned from the physical and biological sciences.)

And what *about* these present-day analytical philosophers, these philosophers who do not claim to present knock-down arguments as the result of having discovered some new philosophical method? Do they claim to present knock-down arguments as the result of having used traditional philosophical methods? Well, they rarely if ever make this claim in so many words. But I would point out that when they present the fruits of their researches in print, they employ in almost every paragraph of their books and essays phrases whose use suggests, and more than suggests, that their own philosophical work (they could hardly believe this about the central arguments of their opponents in philosophical debate) contains knock-down arguments. ('I shall now show'; 'This proof'; 'The demonstration in the previous section'; 'We see therefore'.) It would seem that, like Kant and the logical positivists and all the other philosophers who have claimed to have discovered a new philosophical method, they do believe that there are knock-down arguments in philosophy. (And it is certainly true that they

them to see them, they will no longer see anything I have said in the course of the cognitive therapy I have led them through as an assertion. Not that they will *have the belief* that the things I said were not assertions ..." (And so on. And so on.) And I do not claim that the argument presented in the text calls into question the validity (or whatever it should be called) the line of thought (or whatever it should be called) represented by this response.

believe that there *could* be.) But whether one supposes that knock-down arguments in philosophy are the fruit of a new philosophical method or the fruit of some recent application of the perennial methods of philosophy (an application of these methods that one presumably supposes to be more painstaking and insightful than almost all the applications of these methods that are to be found in the history of philosophy), one must suppose that philosophical agreement will come to be only in the wake of the discovery of some knock-down philosophical arguments. One must, in fact, suppose this even if one believes that there can be no knock-down arguments in philosophy.

Lewis (in the quotation) and I (in the opening paragraphs of the present essay) are therefore talking about the same topic: the possibility of knock-down philosophical arguments and the possibility of agreement in philosophy are the same topic.[12]

As the quotation shows, Lewis is not a typical present-day analytical philosopher: he does not believe that knock-down philosophical arguments are possible, and he does not believe that it will ever happen that most philosophers agree that some given important and positive philosophical thesis is true. (It will "hardly ever" happen that most philosophers come to agree that a certain analysis or theory is wrong; it will never happen that most philosophers come to agree that a certain analysis or theory is right.)

What the philosopher can hope for, Lewis says, is to reach what Rawls has called "reflective equilibrium" in philosophical matters – philosophical equilibrium for short. When one is in a state of philosophical equilibrium, one accepts certain answers to certain philosophical questions. One is, of course, aware of many philosophical "considerations" – arguments, definitions, principles, distinctions, and so on – that are (widely believed to be) relevant to the project of finding the correct answers to those philosophical questions to which one has accepted answers, and one believes that one has made a really serious attempt to survey all known philosophical

---

[12] My thesis about the relation between the possibility of knock-down philosophical arguments and the possibility of philosophical agreement is not based on any consideration peculiar to philosophy. I claim for it no plausibility beyond such plausibility as can be supplied by general reflection on the basis of agreement in any theoretical discipline. Consider those enviable theoretical disciplines in which "pervasive agreement" is the order of the day. Consider any proposition that, as the result of the researches of the experts in these disciplines, is generally agreed to be true ('The continents are in motion'; 'The strands of the double helix are held together by hydrogen bonding'; ...). Will there not in every case be at least one knock-down argument for the truth of this proposition (or at least an argument that the experts *regard* as a knock-down argument)?

considerations that are relevant to answering those questions. (One may or may not oneself have invented or discovered some of these considerations; one need not be an *original* philosopher to reach philosophical equilibrium.) And, finally, one is satisfied that one "knows what to say" about each of the considerations one is aware of that tells against or seems to tell against the answers one accepts. In particular, if the "consideration" is a valid argument for the denial of one of one's philosophical beliefs, one is prepared to say which of its premises one believes to be false and to explain why one believes them to be false. (An extreme case: "which of its premises" might be nothing more than the disjunction of its premises; but one would hope to do better than that.)

2

I see certain difficulties with Lewis's notion that a state of philosophical equilibrium is the best that one can hope for in philosophy. (The best one can hope for in respect of what? I mean something like this: the best that one can hope for in respect of warrant or justification or "positive epistemic status.") I will try to give a statement of the difficulties I think I see.

Let us call the set of philosophical propositions one accepts (at a given moment at which one is in a state of philosophical equilibrium) one's point of philosophical equilibrium (at that moment). Let us call two philosophers "co-workers" if their work is mutually relevant. (Whether two philosophers are co-workers will be a matter of degree, of course, and perhaps the degree to which two philosophers are co-workers will sometimes be a matter of opinion. But the notion of the degree to which two philosophers are co-workers is not an entirely subjective one. I would judge it to be uncontroversial that the degree to which Hartry Field and Martha Nussbaum are co-workers is negligible. Each is an excellent philosopher, but one would not expect the work of either to contain many citations of the work of the other.)

The following five theses seem to be true. (1) It is rare for two co-workers to reach the same point of equilibrium. (2) Pick some pair of co-workers at random (and to make our case as strong as possible, let's suppose that the two are anglophone analytical philosophers born in the same decade). Their points of philosophical equilibrium will probably be very different. (3) And not only very different, but inconsistent. And radically inconsistent: that is, these points of equilibrium could not be rendered consistent by "minor surgery," by making minor, superficial adjustments to either point of equilibrium or to both. (4) The intersection of all points of philosophical equilibrium will be a very small set of propositions, far too small to be itself anyone's point of philosophical equilibrium. (5) Consider, in fact, the intersection of the points of equilibrium that have been reached by ten randomly chosen anglophone analytical philosophers, born in the 1950s, who are all co-workers with one another to a fairly high degree. Even this intersection will (in all probability) be too small a set of propositions to be itself anyone's point of philosophical equilibrium.

Suppose I take a few moments to reflect seriously on the epistemological implications of these theses. Assume I have reached a certain point of philosophical equilibrium. What should occur to me in the matter of the degree of "warrant" (in the epistemological sense of the term) that this point of philosophical equilibrium enjoys (for me; in my present epistemic situation)? Let's assume that I know what this point of philosophical equilibrium I have reached is. Let's suppose, that is, that I am capable of setting out a certain list of philosophical propositions and that I am in a position to say truly: The point of philosophical equilibrium that I have reached contains the propositions in this list and all their logical consequences and no other propositions. (There may be difficulties with what I am asking you to suppose. How can I be certain that I accept all the logical consequences of some rich set of philosophical propositions? Might not this proposition about the membership of my point of philosophical equilibrium be itself a philosophical proposition, and, if so, might that fact not engender some paradox of self-reference? Let us ignore the possibility of such difficulties.) If I do know what my point of philosophical equilibrium is, then I think that it, that point of philosophical equilibrium, is *true* (that is, that all the beliefs it contains are true). This follows for the same reason as the reason for which it follows from my believing that snow is white and grass is green (and knowing that I believe these things) that I believe that the set of all the logical consequences of these two beliefs is true. (Maybe the valid deduction of this conclusion requires the additional premise that I understand the concept of the set of the logical consequences of a set of propositions. Consider it added.)

But what justifies me in accepting the proposition that my point of philosophical equilibrium is true? The totality of the arguments I endorse whose conclusions are members of my point of equilibrium? But consider: lots of other philosophers know about these arguments (they could state them as convincingly as I) and nevertheless occupy other points of philosophical equilibrium than mine. If the philosophical arguments I endorse have the power to confer warrant or justification (or whatever the most general terms of epistemic commendation are) on the proposition that

my point of philosophical equilibrium is true, why don't these other philosophers come to rest at the same point of equilibrium as I? It would
seem that no set of arguments could have the power to confer warrant on
two inconsistent points of equilibrium. The arguments I endorse therefore
confer warrant on one point of equilibrium (given that no other point
of equilibrium is consistent with mine) or none. And if it is one and not
none, I must suppose that it is mine. But why don't those of my co-workers who are familiar with and understand all the philosophical arguments
I endorse *see* this? It is not easy to answer this question.

I should know how to answer it if I thought I was a significantly better
philosopher than all those of my co-workers whose points of equilibrium
were inconsistent with mine (that is to say: if I thought I was a significantly
better philosopher than *all* my co-workers).[13] I should know how to answer
it if I thought that some fortunate combination of chance advantages had
enabled me to "see" some complex of philosophically relevant factors (one
so subtle that I have not yet succeeded in putting it into words and have
thus been unable to communicate it to my co-workers) that confers warrant on my point of equilibrium and on no other. But what would justify
me in believing either of these things?

Can I in fact even *reach* philosophical equilibrium once the above considerations have occurred to me? When they have occurred to me, should
I not then say something like this to myself: "Why, as far as the warrant
or justification that belong to my point of equilibrium are concerned, I
might as well have adopted it by opening a book that listed a thousand
mutually inconsistent points of philosophical equilibrium and choosing
one of them at random. Someone who did that would certainly not have
been justified in thinking that the point of philosophical equilibrium he
occupied was true. I say that I "might as well" have done that, but it is no
mere fanciful metaphor to say that "that" is pretty much what nature and
nurture and fortune have done *with me*. The point of philosophical equilibrium I occupy depends (perhaps) on predispositions to belief inherent
in my genes, (very likely) on what my parents taught me about morals and

---

[13] Members of the Flat Earth Society occupy points of geomorphic equilibrium (so to call them)
different from mine. They are aware of all the arguments I could give for the earth's being spherical,
and have ingenious (one has to admit) "refutations" of these arguments. I nevertheless believe that
the arguments I can give for the earth's being spherical confer warrant on my belief that the earth
is spherical. I answer the challenge to my belief (the one about warrant) that is presented by the
existence of other points of geomorphic equilibrium by saying simply that I am better at evaluating
arguments concerning the shape of the earth than are the occupants of the other points. I am not
willing to make the corresponding response to the challenge to my beliefs presented by the existence
of other points of philosophical equilibrium than mine.

politics and religion when I was a child, and (certainly) on what university I selected for graduate study in philosophy, who my departmental colleagues have been, the books and essays I have read and haven't read, the conversations I have had at APA divisional meetings as a result of turning right rather than left when I was wandering aimlessly about at a reception … Other philosophers have reached different points of philosophical equilibrium simply because these factors have operated differently in the course of the formation of their opinions. These reflections suggest – and the suggestion is very strong indeed – that I ought to withdraw from the point of philosophical equilibrium I occupy and become a skeptic about the answers to almost all or almost all philosophical questions.

Well, enough. I have raised certain difficulties for Lewis's views on philosophical method. I have nothing to say about how someone who holds these views should respond to the difficulties I have raised, and nothing to say about how Lewis might have responded to them. As I see matters, very similar difficulties face anyone who proposes *any* philosophical methodology – provided only that one feature of that methodology is that, whatever other goals philosophy may have, one of its goals is to make true philosophical statements. These difficulties are raised by the fact of pervasive and irresoluble philosophical disagreement. What I have tried to do is simply to suggest that Lewis's philosophical methodology (or his epistemology of philosophy, or whatever it should be called) seems unable to provide its adherents with any reason to suppose that it is epistemically permissible to believe that thoughts are brain processes, that causal relations supervene on the spatiotemporal distribution of local qualities, or that free will is compatible with determinism … or to accept any substantive philosophical thesis whatever. Lewis's thesis about the goals of philosophy may be superior to some other theses about the goals of philosophy. It may be superior to any thesis that entails that the primary task of philosophers is to search out knock-down arguments for and against philosophical propositions. But it is no more able than any other such thesis to explain how (in light of the fact of pervasive and irresoluble philosophical disagreement) anyone can be justified in believing anything of philosophical consequence.

3

I will set the difficulties to which Section 2 was devoted aside. I will assume Lewis is right about what philosophers should be aiming at and look at how what he says about free will looks from the point of view provided by his theory of the aims of philosophy.

Lewis believes that free will is compatible both with indeterminism (that is, he believes that a free act can be an undetermined act) and with determinism. It is with the latter belief that I shall be concerned. The most interesting and original aspect of Lewis's compatibilism – presented in his classic essay "Are We Free to Break the Laws?"[14] – is his response to the standard argument for incompatibilism. Versions of this argument (or at least vague intuitions whose articulation would issue in something like this argument) are as old as philosophical concern with free will, but it was not till the 1960s and 1970s that the argument was carefully formulated.[15] In those years, David Wiggins, Carl Ginet, Charles Lamb, and I formulated versions of what I am calling the standard argument. I will consider only my own version of the argument, since that is the one Lewis discusses.[16] The argument, in the form in which Lewis discusses it, turns on the notion of "being able to render a proposition [a proposition that is in fact true] false." The argument begins with the story of a judge (J) who did not raise his hand at a certain moment (T) when his doing so would have prevented a prisoner's being put to death. I claimed to be able to derive the following consequence from the conjunction of this story with determinism: J was not able to raise his hand at T.[17] (That is: "J lacked the ability to raise his

---

14 David Lewis, "Are We Free to Break the Laws?," *Philosophical Papers, Volume ii* (Oxford University Press, 1987), pp. 291–298. The paper first appeared in *Theoria* 47 (1981): 113–121. Citations are from *Philosophical Papers II*, which is available online at www.andrewmbailey.com/dkl/Free_to_Break_ the_Laws.pdf. For an important point about the argument of Lewis's paper that is not made in the present chapter, see Chapter 14, note 36 below.

15 There is one important exception to this generalization: C. D. Broad's Knightsbridge inaugural lecture, "Determinism, Indeterminism, and Libertarianism." This lecture (as far as I know) first appeared in print in Broad's collection *Ethics and the History of Philosophy* (London: Routledge & Kegan Paul, 1952). It must have been composed in the 1930s, however, since Broad became Knightsbridge Professor in 1933. If this lecture had received the attention it deserved, discussion of the problem of free will would have emerged from a very long period of sterile, textbook exchanges thirty years earlier than it did.

16 That is, the argument as it was presented in "The Incompatiblity of Free Will and Determinism," *Philosophical Studies* 27 (1975): 185–199. I presented a rather different version of the "standard argument" in "A Formal Approach to the Problem of Free Will and Determinism," *Theoria* 40 (1974): Part I, pp. 9–22. (Lewis cites the latter essay, but does not explicitly discuss the version of the standard argument it contains.) Both versions of the argument appeared, with minor revisions, in chapter 4 of *An Essay on Free Will* (Oxford: Clarendon Press, 1983), which also contains a third version of the argument.

17 In my statement of the argument (and in Lewis's discussion of it) the consequence is stated in these words: J could not have raised his hand at T. In both "The Incompatibility of Free Will and Determinism" and *An Essay on Free Will*, I expressed the idea of ability by using 'can' and 'could have'. I now know that the use of 'could have' in discussions of the free-will problem is liable to create confusions in the minds of some philosophers (David Lewis is not among them), owing to the fact that these words can mean both 'was able to' and 'might have'. For a discussion of these confusions, see my critical study of Daniel Dennett's *Elbow Room* (Chapter 4 of the present volume). In more recent

hand in such a way that the rising of his hand would have been *complete* at T (and at no earlier moment)"; this statement must not be confused with the following statement: "J lacked the ability to raise his hand in such a way that the rising of his hand would have *begun* at T.") Determinism, I said, implies the following thesis: If P_0 is a proposition that describes the state of the world (in every detail, however minute) at some moment in the remote past and if L is the conjunction of all laws of nature into a single proposition, then the conjunction of P_0 and L entails every truth. I then set out an argument whose conclusion was

If determinism is true, J was not able to raise his hand at T.

This conclusion follows (by sentential logic) from the six premises of the argument. Lewis's discussion of the argument is concerned entirely with two of its six premises:

(5) If J was able to render the conjunction of P_0 and L false, J was able to render L false

(6) J was not able to render L false.

Lewis contends that one or the other of these premises is false (or would be false in the circumstances imagined); *which one* is false will depend on what is meant by 'is able to render *p* false'. (Why does the argument contain this odd form of words, anyway? For the following reason. Determinism is a thesis about the logical relations that hold among certain propositions – those that are laws of nature and those that assert that, at a specified time, the world is in a certain "total state." If one is to investigate the question of the compatibility of determinism and the thesis that human beings are sometimes able to act otherwise than they do, one will need some way to describe an agent's abilities in terms of the agent's power "over" the truth-values of propositions. Infinitival constructions like 'is able to raise his hand' do not satisfy this need, nor do most other ordinary idioms. I coined the form of words 'is able to render *p* false' to satisfy it.)

We can, Lewis says, distinguish a *weak* and a *strong* sense in which one may be said to be able to render a proposition false. If 'was able to render false' (let us call this the Suspect Phrase) is understood in the weak sense, Lewis contends, the compatibilist should deny premise (6) of the

---

writings on free will, I have made it a policy always to use 'is able to' instead of 'can' in present-tense ascriptions of ability, and 'was able to' instead of 'could have' in past-tense ascriptions of ability. I have decided to adhere to this policy in the present essay, despite the fact that this decision entails changing both the wording of the argument Lewis discusses and the wording of his discussion.

argument. (That is to say, on the weak interpretation of the Suspect Phrase, a free agent in a deterministic world is able to render L false.) And if the Suspect Phrase is understood in the strong sense, the compatibilist should deny premise (5). These contentions are perfectly correct, and I will not explicitly discuss the strong and weak definitions of the Suspect Phrase or Lewis's arguments concerning the consequences of these definitions for the truth-values of premises (5) and (6). One might of course want to ask what should be made of the fact that compatibilism entails that there are possible circumstances in which an agent is able to render L false (in *any* plausible sense of 'able to render false'). I will, in fact, presently raise just this question, but in relation to my own definition of the Suspect Phrase (which is not the same as either of Lewis's definitions). It is, as Lewis notes, open to me to define the Suspect Phrase in any way I like. He says (rightly), "It does not matter what 'could have rendered false' means in ordinary language; van Inwagen introduced the phrase as a term of art. It does not even matter what meaning van Inwagen gave it. What matters is whether we can give it any meaning that would meet his needs – any meaning that would make all his premises defensible without circularity" (p. 296). (Note that the Suspect Phrase does not appear in the conclusion of the argument.)

In "The Incompatibility of Free Will and Determinism," I did not define the Suspect Phrase. Instead of providing a formal definition of 'can render false', I simply gave a few instructive examples (I hoped they were instructive) of cases in which an agent was (or was not) able to render some specified proposition false.[18] In *An Essay on Free Will*, however, I did define 'can render false'. *An Essay on Free Will* was not yet published when Lewis wrote "Are We Free to Break the Laws?" Apparently, however, I had communicated the definition that was to appear in the book to him in a letter. He discusses this definition in a footnote.[19] This is the definition (as Lewis formulates it – but I have substituted 'was able to' for Lewis's 'could have'):

> An agent was able to render a proposition false if and only if he was able to arrange things in a certain way, such that his doing so, together with the

---

[18] Lewis rightly notes the weakness of this method (p. 297, final paragraph): If one attempts to support a principle *p* by giving examples, one's examples may (at best) support only a principle of the form 'if *q* then *p*', where *q* is some contingent truth that happens to be true in all the states of affairs laid out in one's examples.

[19] This definition was not constructed to block Lewis's argument. It was the outcome of some discussions I had been having with Mark Heller (then a graduate student). Heller had convinced me of the importance of providing an explicit definition of 'is able to render *p* false'.

whole truth about the past, strictly implies the falsity of the proposition. (p. 296, n. 5)[20]

If I understand Lewis, his position is that if I use this definition, the meaning I thereby provide for 'was able to render false' is not a meaning that makes all my premises "defensible without circularity." In that case, he maintains, the problematical premise is (6). Lewis says,

> On this definition, Premise 6 simply says that I could not have arranged things in any way such that I was predetermined not to arrange things in that way. It is uninstructive to learn that the soft determinist [the determinist who believes that people are sometimes able to do otherwise] is committed to denying Premise 6 thus understood. (p. 296, n. 5)

These words are harder to understand on the third or fourth reading than they seem to be on the first. If, as I say, I understand Lewis, he is implying that if the Suspect Phrase is defined in the way I have proposed, then my argument for incompatibilism is circular or begs the question against the compatibilist or something of that sort. (I have never been able to get very clear about what a circular argument is – or begging the question, either. I am reminded of a remark that Roderick Chisholm once made in response to a charge of having committed one or the other of these offenses: "I seem to have been accused of the fallacy of affirming the antecedent.") If we are to evaluate this charge, it will be useful to have an unambiguous statement of the argument to which it applies. Let us use the name 'the Fully Explicit Argument' for the argument of "The Incompatibility of Free Will and Determinism," modified as follows: all occurrences of the Suspect Phrase are removed from the argument by replacing them with the *definiens* I have proposed. The charge Lewis has made may now be put in these words: the Fully Explicit Argument is circular (or begs the question against the compatibilist). Let us see what we can make of this charge.

In the above quotation, Lewis points out (at least this is very close to what he points out) that the following entailment holds:

> L conjoined with the whole truth about the past strictly implies every truth (that is to say: everything that is so is predetermined to be so)

and

> J did not raise his hand at T but was able to raise his hand at T

---

[20] Lewis's strict implication is my entailment. Since the quotation from Lewis has introduced the term 'strictly implies' into the discussion, and since theses about entailment are going to turn up very frequently in the sequel, I will sometimes myself use 'strictly implies', simply to avoid inelegancies like 'That this entailment holds entails …'

jointly entail

> J was able to arrange things in a way such that he was
> predetermined not to arrange things in that way.

Let us call this the Trivial Entailment (since it is "uninstructive" to be informed that it holds). Let us give the name 'the Antecedent' to the conjunction of determinism ('L conjoined with the whole truth about the past strictly implies every truth') and the thesis that J did not raise his hand at T but was able to raise his hand at T.

Now consider the following argument for incompatibilism, which takes the Trivial Entailment as its starting point:

Here is another way of stating the Trivial Entailment: the Antecedent entails

> J was able to arrange things in a way such that L conjoined with the
> whole truth about the past strictly implies that he did not arrange
> things that way.

It follows that the Antecedent entails

> J was able to arrange things in a way such that his arranging things
> in that way conjoined with the whole truth about the past strictly
> implies the falsity of L.

> And no one has this ability. No one could *possibly* have this
> ability. But the Antecedent entails that J has this ability, and the
> Antecedent is a possible state of affairs if free will and determinism
> are compatible. It follows that free will and determinism are not
> compatible.

This argument and the Fully Explicit Argument do not, I think, differ in any important way. The two arguments are simply two formulations of the standard argument for incompatibilism. In aid of our attempt to understand Lewis's charge of circularity or question-begging, let us ask what Lewis would have said about this second argument (or this second formulation of the standard argument) – for if the argument in the passage I have quoted from Lewis's footnote shows that the Fully Explicit Argument is circular, it certainly shows that this little argument (to which it is more directly applicable) is circular. Well, he would certainly have rejected one of its premises. He would certainly have rejected *this* premise: 'No one could possibly have this ability'. Well and good: if he doesn't believe it, he doesn't believe it and the obvious thing for him to do is to say so. What interests me just at present is not whether this premise is true but why I should be accused of circularity or question-begging because I have employed it. (I don't see what *other* premise of the argument such an accusation could be based on.) Is *any* argument for incompatibilism that contains this premise *ipso facto* a "circular" argument? Do I, simply in virtue of employing this premise, "beg the question" against the compatibilist? If so, what would the general lesson be: that no one, in offering a (valid) argument for not-*p* may include in that argument a premise such that *p*-ists, on examining the argument, would seize on it and say, "That's the premise that we reject"? That seems to me to be a rather extreme thesis. It seems evident to me that an acceptable philosophical argument may include such a "crucial" premise, and, I think, if there are any good philosophical arguments, most of them do. Most carefully formulated philosophical arguments contain one premise such that (when all terms of art have been unambiguously defined) *that* is the premise philosophers will want to argue about.

It should be evident both from what I said in Section 1 and what I said in the preceding paragraph that I do not regard either the Fully Explicit Argument or the little argument based on the Trivial Entailment or any other argument for incompatibilism as a knock-down argument. Lewis and I agree that the search for knock-down arguments in philosophy is an unrealistic goal. But if that is so, need Lewis pay any attention to any of these arguments? Of what interest could they be to him and to those who share his views on free will? Well, let us look at the present dialectical situation – the dialectical situation in which Lewis and I find ourselves when I have said that it is obviously impossible for one to be able so to arrange things that one's so arranging them together with the whole truth about the past strictly implies the falsity of L, and he has pointed out that compatibilism entails that this *is* possible – in the terms provided by Lewis's own theory of the goals of philosophy. What my argument enables compatibilists like Lewis to do is (in Lewis's words) to measure the price. The cost of compatibilism, or part of the cost, is this: the compatibilist, the philosopher who believes in the possibility of free agents in a deterministic world, must believe that a free agent in a deterministic world is able to arrange things in such a way that one's so arranging them, together with the whole truth about the past, strictly implies the falsity of at least one law of nature. Recall Lewis's words:

> Argle has said what we accomplish in philosophical argument: we measure the price. Perhaps that is something we can settle more or less conclusively. But when all is said and done, and all the tricky arguments and distinctions and counterexamples have been discovered, presumably we will still face the

question which prices are worth paying, which theories are on balance cred-
ible, which are the unacceptably counterintuitive consequences and which
are the acceptably counterintuitive ones. On this question we may still differ. And if all is indeed said and done, there will be no hope of discovering
still further arguments to settle our differences.

The question confronting Lewis and me is not, or *should* not be, whether,
in employing either the premise 'No one could possibly have this ability'
or Premise (6) of the Fully Explicit Argument –

> J was not able to arrange things in any way such that his doing so,
> together with the whole truth about the past, strictly implies the
> falsity of L –

I render my argument circular or beg the question. The question should
be: How plausible are these premises? Lewis thinks they are implausible.
His reason for thinking them implausible seems to be this: He finds compatibilism very plausible indeed and he sees that the compatibilist must
deny them. He finds this price, these things that the compatibilist must
deny, to be, if counterintuitive, at any rate "acceptably" counterintuitive.
I find the denials to which the compatibilist is committed implausible,
"unacceptably counterintuitive." He and I have, therefore, reached different points of philosophical equilibrium (or we have reached different
points of philosophical equilibrium as regards one philosophical question:
What should one believe about the standard argument for the incompatibility of free will and determinism?).

Is there anything more to say? Well, I could say something about why I
find 'No one could possibly have this ability' and Premise (6) of the Fully
Explicit Argument plausible. I could and I will.

Suppose that Elijah, who is currently in Jerusalem, claims that he is
able to be in Babylon ten minutes from now. Suppose further that we, his
audience, are able to convince him that the laws of nature and the whole
truth about the past together strictly imply that he will not be in Babylon
ten minutes from now. Then, surely, Elijah must either withdraw his claim
to be able to be in Babylon ten minutes from now or else claim to be able
to perform a miracle – for that is what his being in Babylon ten minutes
from now would be if the past and the laws of nature together entail that
he is not going to be in Babylon ten minutes from now: a miracle.

It is entirely plausible, it is unexceptionable, to define a miracle as an
event or state of affairs whose occurrence would be inconsistent with the
whole truth about the past and the laws of nature. It would be a mistake
to insist that a miracle should be defined as an event whose occurrence

would be inconsistent with the laws of nature *tout court*. (Imagine this exchange: "I can perform miracles. I am, for example, able to be in Babylon ten minutes from now." "Oh, that wouldn't be a miracle. A miracle is an event that contradicts the laws of nature. And your being in Babylon ten minutes from now is consistent with the laws of nature, for the laws of nature don't have anything to say about who is where when." It would be a miracle, though.) It is, therefore, entirely plausible to define the *ability* to perform a miracle as the ability to bring about an event or state of affairs whose occurrence would be inconsistent with the whole truth about the past and the laws of nature.

If I had proposed these definitions in an essay that was not about free will but about, say, the concept of the miraculous, no one would have taken exception to them. But these plausible definitions have the following consequence. The ability that premise (6) of the Fully Explicit Argument says that J does not have is the ability to perform a miracle. And since it's entirely plausible to suppose that ordinary people in ordinary circumstances are not able to perform miracles, it's entirely plausible to suppose that (6) is true.

This was my promised argument for the plausibility of (6). It is not, I concede, a knock-down argument for (6) or even for the plausibility of (6). It simply sets forth a price that the compatibilist must pay. Free will in a deterministic world – the argument demonstrates – strictly implies the ability to perform miracles. The compatibilist believes that there are deterministic worlds in which agents have free will; the compatibilist must therefore grant that in all such worlds, all free agents are able to perform miracles. The compatibilist must grant that, in a deterministic world, freedom is freedom to break the laws. (It is therefore the compatibilist and not the incompatibilist who believes in the possibility of "contra-causal freedom.") But, if my experience of compatibilists is to be trusted, the compatibilist will regard the price as worth paying. Indeed the *soft determinist* (the compatibilist who believes that the actual world is one of the worlds in which determinism and freedom coexist) will no doubt find the price worth paying. I would expect the typical soft determinist to say something along these lines: "That all free agents are able to perform miracles is perhaps a counterintuitive consequence of soft determinism, but it's an *acceptably* counterintuitive consequence. (And, anyway, it's a consequence only on your definition of 'able to perform a miracle'; no doubt other definitions are possible.) Accepting this consequence is a price worth paying. The price is worth paying because it's just evident that we *are* free and *are* determined (at least for all practical purposes; quantum indeterminacy obviously plays no part in the causal genesis of human action). Note that this acceptably counterintuitive consequence does not entail that anyone is a miracle-worker, that any agent ever does so arrange things that the whole past and the laws of nature together strictly imply that things are not arranged that way. For in every case in which an agent is able so to arrange things, it will be determined that the agent not act on that ability."

My arguments for incompatibilism are therefore like almost all other philosophical arguments: they are not knock-down arguments. They are not arguments that will force the compatibilist to become an incompatibilist on pain of irrationality or cognitive dissonance. They are not arguments that have the enviable property imagined by Robert Nozick: anyone who understands their premises and does not accept their conclusion will *die*. But they are not, on that account, arguments that have no power to affect people's opinions. They are not simply "feel good" arguments for incompatibilists, arguments that incompatibilists can call to mind when they feel their incompatibilist faith flagging. They have in fact demonstrated that they have the power to form philosophical opinion: they have convinced some philosophers who were trying to decide whether to be compatibilists or incompatibilists to become incompatibilists.[21]

---

[21] I think it is very probable that "they have convinced some philosophers" is a gross understatement. I think it is very probable that they have convinced a great many philosophers. Speaking at a conference on free will in the early nineties, I made a remark to the effect that compatibilism was the standard view among philosophers. Michael Slote, who was in the audience, said that he thought that, on the contrary, incompatibilism had become the standard view, or at least the majority view. A few years later, I asked Ted Warfield whether he thought that was right. Warfield, who comes as close as is humanly possible to knowing what every analytical philosopher thinks about anything and is very knowledgeable indeed about the ins and outs of the free-will controversy, replied that he thought that the majority of analytical philosophers who had actually worked on the free-will problem were incompatibilists, and that the majority of analytical philosophers (full stop) were compatibilists. If it is indeed true that the majority of analytical philosophers who have actually worked on the free-will problem are incompatibilists, a very large part of the explanation of this fact lies in the influence of the various versions of the "standard" argument for the incompatiblity of free will and determinism on philosophers who were graduate students in the seventies and eighties. (Cf. note 6 to the introductory essay to this volume.)

How to Think about the Problem of Free Will

Perhaps we should begin with this question: What *is* the "problem of free will"? Like those other great "problem" phrases of which philosophers are so fond – "the mind–body problem," "the problem of universals," "the problem of evil" – this phrase has no clear referent. There are obviously a lot of philosophical problems about free will, but which of them, or which combination of them, is *the* problem of free will? I will propose an answer to this question, but this proposal can be no more than that, a proposal. I propose that we understand the problem of free will to be the following problem.

There are seemingly unanswerable arguments that (if they are indeed unanswerable) demonstrate that free will is incompatible with determinism. And there are seemingly unanswerable arguments that (if indeed ...) demonstrate that free will is incompatible with indeterminism. But if free will is incompatible both with determinism and indeterminism, the *concept* "free will" is incoherent, and the *thing* free will does not exist. There are, moreover, seemingly unanswerable arguments that, if they are correct, demonstrate that the existence of moral responsibility entails the existence of free will, and, therefore, if free will does not exist, moral responsibility does not exist either. It is, however, evident that moral responsibility does exist: if there were no such thing as moral responsibility nothing would be anyone's fault, and it is evident that there are states of affairs to which one can point and say, correctly, to certain people: "That's *your* fault." It must, therefore, be that at least one of the following three things is true:

> The seemingly unanswerable arguments for the incompatibility of free will and determinism are in fact answerable; these arguments are fallacious
>
> The seemingly unanswerable arguments for the incompatibility of free will and indeterminism are in fact answerable; these arguments are fallacious

The seemingly unanswerable arguments for the conclusion that the existence of moral responsibility entails the existence of free will are in fact answerable; these arguments are fallacious.

The "problem of free will" is just this problem (this is my proposal): to find out which of these arguments is fallacious, and to enable us to identify the fallacy or fallacies on which they depend.

Having set out a philosophical problem, and having, tendentiously, identified this problem with the problem of free will, I will define the important terms that occur in the statement of the problem.

Since I'm presenting a paper that consists largely of advice, I will preface these definitions with some advice about how to frame definitions.

(1) Define every term you use that is neither a word or phrase of ordinary language nor a technical term of some discipline other than philosophy (in which discipline, one supposes, it will have been given an adequate definition). Do not waive this requirement in the case of some term simply because philosophers use that term a lot. If you think that some term you will use has been given an adequate definition in the philosophical literature, repeat that definition.

This, at any rate, is the ideal. It will often be impossible to write an essay (as opposed to a very long book) that conforms to this ideal. But, insofar as one's essay does not conform to this ideal, one has issued a promissory note: definitions of all one's technical terms should be available on request.

I have talked of defining terms, but that was loose talk. Here's a second piece of advice about framing definitions: define sentences, not terms. Do not, for example, define 'cause' or 'causation' or 'causality'; rather, define 'x is the cause of y' or 'x is a cause of y' or 'x causes y'. Do not define 'knowledge'; rather, define 'x knows that p'. And a definition of, e.g., 'x causes y' should take this form: a sentence that can replace 'x causes y' at all its occurrences, a sentence in which 'x' and 'y' and no other variables are free, together with a specification of the kinds of object over which 'x' and 'y' range. A definition of 'x knows that p' should contain the free variable 'x' and the schematic sentence-letter 'p' and no other free variables or schematic letters.

This stern requirement – the "Chisholm requirement" so to call it – can be softened in one way: it is permissible to define nouns and noun-phrases ("terms" in the strict sense of the word) if they are the names of theses or propositions. Thus, a proper definition can consist of the phrase, 'Ethical naturalism is the thesis that' followed by a declarative sentence, or a series of them, that spells out what the philosopher offering the definition takes to be the content of the thesis called 'ethical naturalism'. This is a softening of the Chisholm requirement, and not a contradiction of it, because, like the pristine Chisholm requirement, it demands a definition whose *definiens* contains a complete declarative sentence (or a series of them). Why, you may ask, do I "privilege" *declarative sentence* over the many other syntactic categories in this way? My answer is this: the declarative sentence is the natural unit of clear statement.

The following series of definitions conforms to my second requirement. Note, for example, that my first definition is a definition of 'the free-will thesis' and not of 'free will'.[1] (Unfortunately, one of the definitions does not conform to my *first* requirement: the definition of 'determinism' contains the phrases 'the laws of nature' and 'determine a unique future', neither of which is either ordinary language, a technical term of some science like physics or geology, or defined. My excuse is the one I have mentioned: this is a paper, not a book. I remind you, however, that I *have* written a book.)

These definitions serve to explain the system of concepts everyone who thinks about the free-will problem should use – or so *I* say.

The free-will thesis is the thesis that we are sometimes in the following position with respect to a contemplated future act: we simultaneously have both the following abilities: the ability to perform that act and the ability to refrain from performing that act. (This entails that we *have been* in the following position: for something we did do, we were at some point prior to our doing it able to refrain from doing it, able not to do it.)[2]

Determinism is the thesis that the past and the laws of nature together determine, at every moment, a unique future. (The denial of determinism is indeterminism.)

---

[1] The phrase 'free will' – whether it occurs by itself or within the phrase 'the free-will thesis' – hardly exists except as a philosophical term of art. Its non-philosophical uses are pretty much confined to the phrase 'of his/her own free will', which means 'uncoerced'. When, in the movie *Devil's Advocate*, Keanu Reeves says to Al Pacino, "But suppose I sell my soul to you, and then repent on my deathbed …," and Pacino, the Devil, replies, "Yeah – free will. That one's a *bitch*," the latter is using a term from philosophy: a technical term from philosophy that, by way of theology, has achieved everyday currency with little if any distortion of the meaning it has in philosophy, a very uncommon fate for a technical philosophical term. 'Free will', although a technical term, was, for centuries, bandied about without any real attempt at a definition – like 'continuous function' in pre-nineteenth-century mathematics. It is my position that the definition of 'the free-will thesis' that follows in the text provides a philosophically adequate definition of this old technical term.

[2] Whatever you do, do not define 'free will' this way: 'Free will is whatever sort of freedom is required for moral responsibility' (or 'Free will consists in having whatever sort of access to alternative possibilities is required for moral responsibility').

Compatibilism is the thesis that determinism and the free-will thesis could both be true. (And incompatibilism is the denial of compatibilism.)[3]

Libertarianism is the conjunction of the free-will thesis and incompatibilism. (Libertarianism thus entails indeterminism.)

Hard determinism is the conjunction of determinism and incompatibilism. (Hard determinism thus entails the denial of the free-will thesis.)

Soft determinism is the conjunction of determinism and the free-will thesis. (Soft determinism thus entails compatibilism.)

I must emphasize that I intend these definitions to be entirely neutral as regards competing positions about the relations between free will and determinism and entirely neutral as regards competing accounts of the nature of free will. In principle, of course, as a matter of logical *theory*, a definition cannot favor one thesis over its logical contraries. A definition is a declaration about how words are to be used, and a rose would smell as sweet even if we all agreed to use the word 'rose' to mean 'chamber pot'. Roses and their scents are elements of reality, and reality is serenely indifferent to the ways in which human beings use words. In practice, however, one has to admit that – owing to the perverse human tendency to confuse words and things – definitions can be tendentious. I contend that my definitions are not tendentious. I contend that agreement to abide by the above set of definitions will not confer any hidden advantage on any position that figures in philosophical debates about free will – including, of course, my own. In defense of this contention, I cite the fact that the finest essay that has ever been written in defense of compatibilism – possibly the finest essay that has ever been written about any aspect of the free-will problem – David Lewis's "Are We Free to Break the Laws?,"[4] opens with definitions of 'determinism', 'soft determinism', 'hard determinism', and 'compatibilism' that are equivalent to the definitions I have set out above. (Lewis gave no definition of 'libertarianism' because he had no use for the term. I have no use for it either, but, in point of fact, my series of definitions contains definitions of several terms that I have no use for. But

---

[3] Whatever you do, do not use 'compatibilism' as a name for the thesis that *moral responsibility* is compatible with determinism. This can only cause confusion. If you must have a name for this thesis, invent a new one: 'MR-compatibilism' or some such.

[4] *Theoria* 47 (1981): 113–121. Reprinted in Lewis's collected *Philosophical Papers, Volume II* (Oxford University Press, 1987), pp. 291–298. It is available on line at www.andrewmbailey.com/dkl/Free_to_Break_the_Laws.pdf

some people do use these terms, and I am laying down the law about what someone who does use them should mean by them.)

Since 'moral responsibility' figures prominently in my statement of the free-will problem, one might expect that at this point I should define this term, or at least define some sentence or sentences in which it occurs – 'x is morally responsible for y', perhaps. I won't do this. If I *did* offer a definition in this general area, it would be something like this:

x is morally responsible for the fact that $p =$ $_{df}$ It is x's fault that p.

But so much confusion attends the phrase 'moral responsibility' (the confusion is of our own making; as Berkeley said, "we have first raised a dust, and then complain we cannot see") that I despair of straightening it all out in a paper that is not devoted to that topic alone. In the sequel, instead of discussing free will and moral responsibility, I'll discuss a simpler (but obviously closely related) topic, free will and negative moral judgments. A fully adequate discussion of the problem of free will, however, would require a discussion of the relations that hold between free will and moral responsibility.

The last three "-isms" in my list, libertarianism, hard determinism, and soft determinism, are conjunctions of more fundamental theses. Although the terms 'libertarianism', 'hard determinism', and 'soft determinism' are perfectly well defined, I very strongly recommend that philosophers never use them – except, of course, when they are forced to because they are discussing the work of philosophers who have been imprudent enough to use them. (This was what I was alluding to when I said that I had no use for several of the terms for which I provided definitions.) Writers on free will who do not take my advice on this matter are continually saying things that they would be better off not saying – and they wouldn't say these unfortunate things, they would automatically avoid saying them, if they confined their list of technical terms to 'the free-will thesis', 'determinism', 'compatibilism', and 'incompatibilism'. A minor example is this: There is a tendency among writers on free will to oppose 'compatibilism' and 'libertarianism'; but the fundamental opposition is between compatibilism and incompatibilism. Here is a major example (not entirely unconnected with my minor example). Philosophers who use the term 'libertarianism' apparently face an almost irresistible temptation to speak of "libertarian free will."

What is this libertarian free will they speak of? What does the phrase 'libertarian free will' mean? Since I'm discussing the usage of others, of certain people who have perversely chosen not to follow my advice about the proper way to frame definitions, I am going to have to try to answer a question about the meaning of an abstract noun-phrase. And this faces me with some very real semantical difficulties. I generally have trouble understanding writers who do not take my advice about how to frame definitions. Noun-phrases like 'free will' and 'compatibilist free will' and 'libertarian free will' are particularly difficult for me. I find it difficult to see what sort of thing such phrases are supposed to denote. In serious philosophy, I try never to use an abstract noun or noun-phrase unless it's clear what ontological category the thing it purports to denote belongs to. For many abstract noun-phrases, it's not at all clear what sort of thing they're supposed to denote, and I therefore try to use such phrases only in introductory passages, passages in which the reader's attention is being engaged and a little mush doesn't matter. In serious philosophical argument about free will, I try to restrict my use of abstract noun-phrases to phrases that indisputably denote *propositions* (such as 'the free-will thesis' and 'determinism'). If I had to guess what sort of thing 'free will' etc. denoted, one guess I might make is that they denote a certain *properties*. On that guess, 'free will' is a name for the property *is on some occasions able to do otherwise*. But then what properties are denoted by 'compatibilist free will' and 'libertarian free will'? Well, presumably, e.g., 'libertarian free will' denotes whatever it is that 'free will' denotes when libertarians use it. And 'free will' denotes the same thing when anyone uses it. So, if 'free will' denotes the property *is on some occasions able to do otherwise*, there's really nothing for 'libertarian free will' to denote but that same property. Another guess about what 'free will' might denote is: it denotes a certain power or ability: the power or ability sometimes to do otherwise than what one in fact does. (That is, of course, *another* guess only if a power is something other than a property.) If that's what 'free will' denotes, a power, then, by an argument parallel to the above, 'libertarian free will' and 'compatibilist free will' denote that same power.

The operative word in both guesses is 'able' – as in 'Jill says she's able to do what I've asked'. Many philosophers, in attempting to spell out the concept of free will, use the phrase 'could have done otherwise'. I did so myself in *An Essay on Free Will*.[5] Nowadays, however, I very deliberately avoid this phrase. I avoid it because 'could have done otherwise' is ambiguous and (experience has shown) its ambiguity has caused much confusion in discussions of free will. My advice to all philosophers who write about free will in English is that they should avoid this phrase as well. A

---

[5] Oxford: Clarendon Press, 1983.

whole chapter of Daniel Dennett's first book on free will (*Elbow Room*)[6] was written to no purpose because he didn't realize that 'could have done' sometimes means 'might have done' [and this 'might' is itself ambiguous: it has both an ontological and an epistemic sense] and sometimes 'was able to do'. J. L. Austin was very clear about this in his classic paper "Ifs and Cans,"[7] but subsequent writers on free will have not learned what he had to teach.[8] (I can't resist the temptation to mention a passage in Austin's essay – page 163 – that delights me because it is such a perfect reflection of a vanished culture. Being a Englishman with a pre-war public school education speaking to an audience of his cultural peers, Austin found it natural to explain the two senses of 'could have' by contrasting a case in which a Latin speaker would have said '*potui*' and a case in which he would have said '*potuissem*'.) This ambiguity in the phrase 'could have done otherwise' has led a considerable body of philosophers to think that to say that someone could have done otherwise is to imply something having to do with "alternative possibilities," to imply that the person's act was undetermined. And, indeed, when it means 'might have done otherwise' (in the ontological, as opposed to the epistemic, sense of 'might have'), that is just what 'could have done otherwise' *does* imply. But those who have defined free will in terms of the phrase 'could have done otherwise' were using the phrase in its other sense: 'was able to do otherwise'. They would have done better simply to have avoided the ambiguous phrase and to have used 'was able to'.

All the phrases that have been used in definitions of 'free will' (and in statements of the free-will thesis) can be defined in terms of, or dispensed with in favor of, 'able'. For example, the much used phrase 'within one's power' can be defined like this: 'It is within x's power to' means 'x is able to'. Having said this about the word 'able' I want to make what seems to me to be an important point, a point that is, in fact, of central importance if one wishes to think clearly about the freedom of the will: compatibilists and incompatibilists mean the same thing by 'able'. And what do both

---

[6] *Elbow Room: The Varieties of Free Will Worth Wanting* (Cambridge, MA: MIT Press, 1984). See Chapter 6, "Could Have Done Otherwise."

[7] In J. L. Austin, *Philosophical Papers* (Oxford: Clarendon Press, 1961), pp. 153–180. *Philosophical Papers* was edited by J. O. Urmson and G. J. Warnock.

[8] The chapter of Dennett's *Elbow Room* cited in note 5 contains a rather lengthy discussion of "Ifs and Cans." In this discussion Dennett presents telling criticisms of some of Austin's arguments (I would call your attention to his excellent discussion of the notorious "I could have holed it" example). But Dennett does not see the point I am calling attention to – although he sometimes dances maddeningly close to it. For more on this topic, see my critical study of *Elbow Room*, Chapter 4 of this volume.

compatibilists and incompatibilists mean by 'able'? Just this: what it means in English, what the word means. And, therefore, 'free will', 'incompatibilist free will', 'compatibilist free will', and 'libertarian free will' are four names for one and the same thing. If this thing is a property, they are four names for the property *is on some occasions able to do otherwise*. If this thing is a power or ability, they are four names for the power or ability to do otherwise than one in fact does.

All the compatibilists I know of believe in free will. Many incompatibilists (just exactly the libertarians: that's how 'libertarian' is defined) believe in free will. And it's one and the same thing they believe in. Compatibilists say that the existence of this thing (whose conceptual identity is determined by the meaning of the English word 'able', or of some more or less equivalent word or phrase in some other language) is compatible with determinism; incompatibilists say that the existence of this thing is incompatible with determinism. If Alice used to be an incompatibilist and has been converted by some philosophical argument to compatibilism, she should describe her intellectual history this way: "I used to think that free will was incompatible with determinism. I was blind but now I see: Now I see that *it* is compatible with determinism." And her use of 'it' does not have to be apologized for: this very thing she used to think was incompatible with determinism, she now thinks is compatible with determinism. (Compare: I used to think that knowledge was incompatible with the logical possibility of a Universal Deceiver. Now I see that *it* is compatible with the logical possibility of such a being.) What Alice should *not* say is this:

I used to think that free will was one thing, a thing incompatible with determinism. Now I think it's another thing – I mean I think that the words 'free will' are a name for another thing – a thing compatible with determinism. The thing I used, incorrectly, to call 'free will' *is* incompatible with determinism; I was right to think it was incompatible with determinism. But it doesn't exist (I mean no agent has it), and it couldn't exist, and if it did exist, it wouldn't be right to call it 'free will'.

Talk of 'libertarian free will' is therefore at best useless. Taking this phrase seriously as a denoting phrase would be like taking 'materialist pain' (or 'pain according to the materialists') seriously as a denoting phrase. Suppose someone said that 'pain according to the materialists' purported to denote some particular sort of brain process, and that it therefore didn't exist unless materialism was the right philosophy of mind. That would be silly. Materialists and dualists and idealists all use 'pain' to refer to the same thing.

Let me break off at this point and remark that the fallacy of which I'm accusing those who speak of libertarian free will is a very general sort of fallacy whose pernicious effects extend far beyond the problem of free will. The fallacy need not involve abstract nouns like 'free will'. I have seen a very pure instance of it that involves the most concrete of all nouns, 'God'. I have seen a letter to the editors of the *Chicago Tribune* the author of which contended that it could not be that (as had been maintained by the author of an earlier letter) Christians and Muslims worshiped the same God, since the Christian God was incarnate in Jesus Christ and the Muslim God was not. But, of course, 'the Christian God' can only mean 'the God worshiped by Christians' and 'the Muslim God' can only mean 'the God worshiped by Muslims'. And the three phrases 'God' and 'the God worshiped by Christians' and 'the God worshiped by Muslims' all denote the same being. Even if there is no God, this statement is true, as it were, counterfactually: if any of the three phrases *did* denote something, the other two would also denote it. (As to the letter-writer's logic, one might as well argue that since, in the writings of Malcolm Muggeridge, Mother Theresa was a saint, and, in the writings of Christopher Hitchens, Mother Theresa was a charlatan, Muggeridge and Hitchens were therefore not writing about the same woman.)

If the materialists (to return to our primary example) are wrong about pain being a physical process, they've nevertheless been referring to it all along. On conversion to some other view, they shouldn't say, "I see now that there is no such thing as what I called 'pain'." They should say, "I see now that pain doesn't have some of the properties I thought it had; for one thing it isn't a physical process." And libertarians who become compatibilists shouldn't say, "I see now that there is no such thing as what I called 'free will'." They should say, "I see now that free will doesn't have some of the properties I thought it had; for one thing, it isn't incompatible with determinism."

Use of the phrase 'libertarian free will' can lead critics of libertarianism into confusion about what it is that libertarians believe. I can only tear my hair out when I read the following statement:[9]

> Van Inwagen has said of an argument concluding that libertarian free will is incompatible with *in*determinism, "I fervently hope that there is something wrong with it."

[9] Lynne Rudder Baker, "Why Christians Should Not Be Libertarians: An Augustinian Challenge," *Faith and Philosophy* 20 (2003): 460–478; see n. 48, p. 476.

I would never (except in discussions of the work of others) use the phrase 'libertarian free will'; and nothing I have written can be accurately paraphrased using that phrase. The conclusion of the argument to which Professor Baker refers[10] was that free will *simpliciter*, that one free will that both compatibilists and incompatibilists believe in, was incompatible with indeterminism. The argument that I said I hoped was defective was a version of the "*Mind* Argument." I will discuss the *Mind* Argument later in this essay. Here I will note only that most of the proponents of the *Mind* Argument have been *compatibilists*, who have used it to defend the conclusion that free will – not compatibilist free will, not libertarian free will, but free will full stop – is incompatible with indeterminism. (The *Mind* argument is perhaps the sharpest arrow in the compatibilist's quiver. It is a sharp arrow for two reasons: (i) it is very hard to answer, and (ii) it follows from its conclusion that if free will is possible, free will is compatible with determinism.)

The pernicious phrase 'libertarian free will' has led critics of libertarianism to misunderstand not only what libertarians believe but the motives that underlie their beliefs. Professor Baker, for example, has supposed (in the article I have cited) that libertarians "want" libertarian free will – which means, presumably, both that they want to have it (as they no doubt want to be wise and virtuous) and that, in some more purely intellectual and disinterested way, they want libertarianism to be the correct theory of free will.[11] These are, I suppose, natural things for someone to suppose if that person thinks that there is something called 'libertarian free will' and that it is a different thing from "compatibilist free will." But, as I have said, insofar as it makes sense to treat 'libertarian free will' as a

---

[10] See my essay "Free Will Remains a Mystery," Chapter 7 of the present volume. The words Baker quotes occur on p. 110.

[11] Baker's essay is primarily an argument for the conclusion that *Christian* philosophers should not be libertarians. In the matter of motives and desires, she is primarily concerned to defend the position that Christian philosophers should not want to have "libertarian free will" or want libertarianism to be true. All but one of the reasons for wanting libertarianism to be true that she canvasses and rejects in the section of the paper called "Motives for Belief in Libertarian Free Will," however, have nothing in particular to do with theism in general or Christianity in particular: libertarian free will is required for moral responsibility; without libertarian free will, we'd be puppets; libertarian free will is presupposed by the principle '"ought" implies "can"'. The single "motive for belief in libertarian free will" she considers that would be a motive only for Christians (or at any rate, only for theists) is that libertarian free will is (supposedly) essential to an effective reply to the argument from evil. In this essay, I am concerned to address only the motives of libertarians that are essentially connected with what I am calling "the problem of free will." I am not concerned to address motives that a libertarian might have that arose from beliefs he or she had that (like theism) were not consequences of the premises that generate the problem of free will.

denoting term, it has to be regarded as a name (a rather misleading name) for free will – for free will *simpliciter,* free will *tout court,* free will full stop, free will period. And this one thing, free will, is what *both* libertarians and soft determinists want to have. It's simply not true that there are two distinct things, libertarian free will and compatibilist free will, and that libertarians want the one and don't regard the other as worth having (regard what the compatibilists offer as "free will" as, in Kant's words, *ein elender Behelf* – a miserable substitute). There is, I concede, some historical justification for this. Kant, if I read him right, saw Hume as offering a substitute for free will, an *ersatz* free will that was a mere pretender to the name. But this is not the way present-day incompatibilists view what their compatibilist colleagues call free will. We present-day incompatibilists see the free will that compatibilists believe in as the genuine article; their only mistake, in our view, is to suppose that it, the genuine article, is compatible with determinism.

Let us turn from what libertarians want to have to what they want to be true. Do libertarians want libertarianism to be true? Well, libertarianism is the conjunction of the free-will thesis and incompatibilism. To want libertarianism to be true, therefore, would be to want both the free-will thesis and incompatibilism to be true. I will stipulate, as the lawyers say, that libertarians want the free-will thesis to be true. (And who wouldn't? Even hard determinists, or most of them, seem to regard the fact – they think it's a fact – that we do not have free will as a matter for regret.) But do libertarians want incompatibilism to be true? Perhaps some do. I can say only that *I* don't want incompatibilism to be true. Just as hard determinists regard the non-existence of free will as a matter for regret, I regard the fact – *I* think it's a fact – that free will is incompatible with determinism as a matter for regret. But reason has convinced me that free will is incompatible with determinism, and I have to accept the deliverances of reason, however unpalatable they may be. I should think that any philosopher in his or her right mind would *want* compatibilism to be true. It would make everything so *simple.* But we can't always have what we want and things are not always simple.

I have used Professor Baker as an example of a philosopher who has misunderstood what libertarians believe and want because she provides a recent and very clear example of such a philosopher. But heaven forbid that I should be thought to have implied that she's unique or even unusual in this respect. I could cite similar mistakes on the part of many others. Consider Daniel Dennett, a philosopher always worth considering. The same sort of mistake is on display in his title "On Giving Libertarians

What They Say They Want" (and in the essay whose title it is).[12] I repeat: What libertarians want is identical with what soft determinists want: free will, the ability to do otherwise. (There *is* something we libertarians want that soft determinists don't want. We libertarians want to know what's wrong with the well-known arguments for the incompatibility of free will and indeterminism. Soft determinists don't want this, or most of them don't, because they, or most of them, don't think that there is anything wrong with those arguments. But this is not the thing that libertarians say they want that Dennett was talking about.) We may consider also in this connection the subtitle of *Elbow Room*, "*The Varieties of Free Will Worth Wanting*." There is only one variety of free will worth wanting because there is only one variety of free will: the ability to do otherwise. And everyone wants that, both those who think human beings have it (libertarians and soft determinists and compatibilists who are not determinists) and most of those who think they don't (most hard determinists).

I should at some point, and this is as good a point as any, make a remark about the phrase 'libertarian free will' that I have found it rather hard to find a natural place for it in my discussion of the phrase. There is a way to define 'libertarian free will' that does not have the consequence that 'libertarian free will' is simply another name for free will *simpliciter*. One *might* define 'libertarian free will' like this:

x has libertarian free will = $_{df}$ *x* has free will *simpliciter* and free will *simpliciter* is incompatible with determinism.

Similarly, one might offer this definition of compatibilist free will:

x has compatibilist free will = $_{df}$ *x* has free will *simpliciter* and free will *simpliciter* is compatible with determinism.

Given these definitions, libertarian free will is not identical with compatibilist free will. Libertarian free will and compatibilist free will are logical contraries: they can't both exist.

I can only say that no libertarian has ever used 'free will' to mean 'libertarian free will' in this sense, and that no compatibilist has ever used 'free will' to mean 'compatibilist free will' in this sense. It is therefore hard to see what point these definitions might have. "Libertarian free will" in the present sense is by definition incompatible with determinism, and "compatibilist free will" is by definition compatible with determinism. If,

---

[12] In *Brainstorms: Philosophical Essays on Mind and Psychology* (Cambridge, MA: MIT Press/Bradford Books, 1978), pp. 286–299.

therefore, libertarians had used 'free will' to mean 'libertarian free will' it is hard to see why they would have bothered to offer arguments for the incompatibility of free will and determinism. And if compatibilists had used 'free will' to mean 'compatibilist free will', it is hard to see why they would have bothered to offer arguments for the compatibility of free will and determinism. (Insofar as they have. I concede that my argument on this point is somewhat weakened by the fact that it is pretty rare for a compatibilist actually to present an argument for compatibilism. The more usual procedure among compatibilists is to treat compatibilism as the "default" position concerning the relation between free will and determinism, and – if they do even this much – to try to refute the standard arguments for incompatibilism.) I would also point out that, if the words are given this sense, I do not want "libertarian free will"; I want free will *simpliciter*, of course, but I should much rather have compatibilist free will than libertarian free. It would make everything so simple. Unfortunately, as I see matters, I have free will *simpliciter* if and only if I have libertarian free will (in the present bizarre sense of 'libertarian free will'). That is to say, as I see matters, free will *simpliciter* is incompatible with determinism.

What I have presented, I contend, is the free-will problem properly thought through – or at least presented in a form in which it is possible to think about it without being constantly led astray by bad terminology and confused ideas. Let me now restate the problem of free will, this time using only "basic" terminology, the undefined terms that occur in my definitions.

The following two theses are *prima facie* incompatible:

(1) We are sometimes in the following position with respect to a contemplated future act: we simultaneously have both the following abilities: the ability to perform that act and the ability to refrain from performing that act

(2) The past and the laws of nature together determine, at every moment, a unique future.

These two theses are *prima facie* incompatible because the premises of the Consequence Argument (an argument whose logical validity no one disputes) are *prima facie* true. 'The Consequence Argument' is my name for the standard argument (various more or less equivalent versions of the argument have been formulated by C. D. Broad, R. M. Chisholm, David Wiggins, Carl Ginet, James Lamb, and myself) for the incompatibility of (1) and (2). It is beyond the scope of this paper seriously to discuss the

Consequence Argument. I will, however, make a sociological point. Before the Consequence Argument was well known (Broad had formulated an excellent version of it in the 1930s, but no one was listening),[13] almost all philosophers who had a view on the matter were compatibilists. It's probably still true that most philosophers are compatibilists. But it's also true that the majority of philosophers who have a specialist's knowledge of the ins and outs of the free-will problem are incompatibilists.[14] And this change is due entirely to the power, the power to *convince*, the power to move the intellect, of the Consequence Argument. If, therefore, the Consequence Argument is fallacious (in some loose sense; it certainly contains no *logical* fallacy), the fallacy it embodies is no trivial one. Before the Consequence Argument was well known, most philosophers thought that incompatibilists (such incompatibilists as there were) were the victims of a logical "howler" that could be exposed in a paragraph or two. No one supposes that now. (I mean this to be true in the sense in which 'No one now believes in the Divine Right of Kings' is true. *Some* people, of course, do believe in the Divine Right of Kings.) The *prima facie* incompatibility of (1) and (2) is the first of three components of the problem of free will. Now the second.

The following proposition is *prima facie* true.

(3) Necessarily: If one is contemplating some possible future act, and if the past and the laws of nature do *not* together determine that one shall perform that act, then one is unable to perform that act.

Proposition (3) is *prima facie* true because the *Mind* Argument, whose conclusion it is, is, *prima facie*, a cogent argument. 'The *Mind* Argument' is my name for an argument that may be loosely stated like this: If what one does does not follow deterministically from one's previous states, then it is the result of an indeterministic process, and (necessarily) one is unable to determine the outcome of an indeterministic process. (The name 'The *Mind* Argument' is due to the fact that between 1930 and 1960, versions of the argument appeared regularly in that august philosophical journal. One example is R. E. Hobart's classic essay, "Free-Will as Involving Determination and Inconceivable without It.")[15]

---

[13] C. D. Broad, "Determinism, Indeterminism and Libertarianism," *Ethics and the History of Philosophy* (London: Routledge & Kegan Paul, 1952). "Determinism, Indeterminism and Libertarianism" was Broad's inaugural lecture as Knightsbridge Professor, in 1933.

[14] I.e., incompatibilists in the proper sense of the term (see note 3 above). There are, of course, philosophers who believe that free will and *determinism* are incompatible and who also believe that free will and *moral responsibility* are compatible.

[15] *Mind* 43 (1934): 1–27. I have myself presented a version of the *Mind* Argument in "Free Will Remains a Mystery."

Now consider this fact. Propositions (1) and (3) jointly entail proposition (2). If, therefore, (3) is true, and if (1) entails the denial of (2), then (1) is a necessary falsehood. If (1) is incompatible with (2), therefore, and if (3) is true, it is impossible for there to be agents who are able to do anything other than what they in fact do. (Indeed – whether this is so depends on how some tricky questions are answered – (3) may imply that, if the world is indeterministic, agents are not even able to do the things that they in fact *do*.)

We have, therefore, a *prima facie* case for the impossibility, the ground-floor or metaphysical impossibility, of the following proposition: When we deliberate about which of two actions, A and B, to perform, we are sometimes able to perform A *and* able to perform B. We have, to speak loosely, a *prima facie* case for the metaphysical impossibility of free will. Broad thought that the reasoning I have set out (or something very much like it) was not only *prima facie* correct but correct *tout court*, and that this proposition is in fact impossible. Might we not simply agree with him? Might we not simply agree that free will (not "libertarian free will" but free will *simpliciter*) is metaphysically impossible?

This question brings us to the third component of the free-will problem: an argument for the conclusion that moral responsibility requires the ability to act otherwise than we do. As I have said, however, owing to widespread confusions that attend the concept of moral responsibility, confusions I cannot address within the scope of this essay, I shall not present an argument for this conclusion. I shall instead present an argument for the conclusion that the truth of negative moral judgments about a person's acts implies that that person was able to do something other than the act that is the object of the moral judgment. (If you tell me that, in your view, moral judgments do not have truth-values, I will reply that my argument does not really require the premise that moral judgments have truth-values; the argument could be reconstructed in other terms.) The strategy on display in this argument, I contend, could, with minor modifications, be used to construct an equally plausible argument for the conclusion that moral responsibility implies the ability to act otherwise.

Suppose that your friend Alice has told a lie, and that you say to her (stern moralist that you are),

(a) You ought not to have lied.

Making statement (a), it would seem, commits you to the truth of

(b) You ought either to have told the truth or to have remained silent.

And (b), in its turn, commits you to the truth of

> (c) You were able either to tell the truth or [inclusive] remain silent.

Note in connection with statement (c) that we always accept "I wasn't able to do x" as an excuse for not doing x – provided, of course, that we *believe* that statement. (So I say. Some might want to dispute this in certain cases in which the inability that the speaker claims is a consequence of the speaker's own prior acts. Suppose, for example, that our Alice had replied to statement (a) by saying, "I couldn't help lying. I'd been drinking and I always turn into a pathological liar when I've had a few. When I'm drunk, I simply loose the ability to speak truthfully." You will probably want to tell me that this fails as an excuse, and I will agree. At least I'll agree to this extent: Alice can't expect you, the stern moralist of the example, to respond by saying, "Oh, I didn't know that. That's all right, then." But I don't think that what I've conceded implies that you, the stern moralist, can properly respond by saying, "Granted, but you still ought not to have lied." What you, in your stern moralist role, should say is rather, "Well, if drinking affects you that way, you shouldn't drink. You don't claim that you weren't able to refrain from drinking, do you?" If Alice replies that she is literally unable to resist the temptation to drink, you can – if you believe this statement – tell her that in that case she ought to avoid situations in which she might be tempted to drink. If she replies that she tries, and tries very hard and very intelligently, to avoid situations in which drink might be offered her, but contends that she was exposed to temptation in present instance because of humanly unforeseeable circumstances – well, perhaps at this point, assuming that everything Alice says is to be believed, even the sternest moralist ought to leave off making moral judgments.)

Statement (c) commits you to the truth of

> (d) You were able to do something you did not do,

and (d) commits you to the truth of (1), to the free-will thesis.

Therefore, if the free-will thesis is false, negative moral judgments are always false. (Or if moral judgments lack truth-values, negative moral judgments are always in some way out of place or inappropriate. Even if moral judgments lack truth-values, there's obviously *something* wrong with telling King Canute that he ought to have succeeded in halting the advance of the tide. If agents are never able to do anything other than what they in fact do, all moral judgments share whatever defect it is that that one so prominently displays.) It is, however, undeniable that people do not always behave as they ought. (In the words of the Book of Common Prayer, "We have left undone those things which we ought to have done, and we have done those things which we ought not to have done.") Denying that agents are ever able to do otherwise is therefore simply not an option.

These are the three arguments that create the problem of free will. Each of them is *prima facie* correct, but at least one of them must contain some error. But which? And where does the error (or where do the errors) lie? That is the problem of free will. I myself think that the error must lie in the *Mind* Argument. But I haven't the faintest idea what the nature of the error is. (Most of my fellow libertarians think that the error in the *Mind* Argument – they agree with my conviction that that's where the error is to be found – can be exposed by reflection on the concept of "agent causation." I cannot agree. In my view, even if agent causation exists and underlies all our free actions, this does not point to any defect in the *Mind* Argument.[16] The advice I've offered in this paper has mostly been directed at compatibilists. Here's a piece of advice for incompatibilists: do not underestimate the power of the *Mind* Argument.)

The problem of free will, I believe, confronts us philosophers with a great mystery. Under it our genius is rebuked. But confronting a mystery is no excuse for being in a muddle. In accusing others of muddle, I do not mean to imply that they are muddled because they do not believe what I do about free will. I do not mean to imply that they are muddled because they are compatibilists. I'm an incompatibilist and David Lewis was a compatibilist. But the two of us have framed the problem of free will in the same terms. I, naturally enough, don't think I'm muddled, and I don't think Lewis was either. No indeed: he saw the problem with his usual crystalline clarity. Here's my closing piece of advice for compatibilists. Study "Are We Free to Break the Laws?" carefully. *That's* the way to be a compatibilist.

---

[16] My reasons for thinking this can be found in "Free Will Remains a Mystery," Chapter 7 in this volume.

CHAPTER II

A Promising Argument

0

Let us say that it is at a certain moment *up to* one *whether* one will do A or do B if one is then faced with a choice between doing A and doing B and one is then able to do A and is then able to do B.[1] And let us say that it is at a certain moment *undetermined whether* one will do A or do B if there is a possible world in which the laws of nature are the same as those of the actual world and whose state at that moment is identical with the state of the actual world at that moment and in which one will do A *and* a world satisfying those same two conditions in which one will do B.[2]

Libertarianism is the conjunction of the following two theses:

> *The Free-will Thesis* Various human agents at various times and on various occasions have been in the following situation: they were faced with a choice between alternative courses of action (e.g., between lying and telling the truth, between becoming a physician and becoming a concert pianist, between meeting Jill in Phoenix on Thursday and not meeting Jill in Phoenix on Thursday) and it was then up to them which of these courses of the action they would pursue.

---

[1] The dummy phrases 'do A' and 'do B', when they occur in the same sentence schema are to be replaced by "incompatible" action phrases – 'tell a lie' and 'tell the truth', for example, or 'be in Phoenix at noon tomorrow' and 'be in Chicago at noon tomorrow'.

[2] None of the three propositions

> Sally is now faced with a choice between doing A and doing B
>
> It is now up to Sally whether she will do A or do B
>
> It is now undetermined whether Sally will do A or do B

entails that Sally will either do A or do B. It might be, for example, that at a certain point in her life Sally was faced with a choice between becoming a physician and becoming a concert pianist, that it was then up to her whether she would become a physician or a pianist, that it was then undetermined whether she would become a physician or a pianist – *and* that she eventually decided to pursue neither of those vocations and became a journalist.

Incompatibilism　If one is at a certain moment faced with a choice between doing A and doing B, it is then up to one whether one will do A or do B *only if* it is then undetermined whether one will do A or do B – and *necessarily* so.

I

Many philosophers have contended that libertarianism is necessarily false – that it is a metaphysically impossible or even a logically incoherent thesis. Of the various arguments that have been given for the impossibility of libertarianism, the simplest is that the impossibility of libertarianism is an immediate consequence of the following principle, which (it is contended) is a necessary – perhaps a conceptual – truth:

> *The Indetermination-Inability Principle*　If one is at a certain moment faced with a choice between doing A and doing B, and if it is then undetermined whether one will do A or do B, it is not then up to one whether one will do A or do B; in fact, one is not then able to do A *and* not then able to do B.[3]

(The impossibility of libertarianism follows from the Indetermination-Inability Principle because that principle and incompatibilism jointly entail that human agents are never in the following situation: they are faced with a choice between alternative courses of action and it is up to them which course they will pursue; and the Free-will Thesis entails that human agents are sometimes in that situation.)

But is the Indetermination-Inability Principle true? The principle can seem very plausible if one considers only cases of this sort:

Jack is deliberating about whether to hit the right-hand or the left-hand side of the dartboard. It is now undetermined whether he will hit the

---

[3] It is tempting to suppose that if one is *not able* to perform a certain contemplated action, it follows logically that one *will not* perform that action. This tempting thesis obviously entails there could be no agent who was going to do either A or B and who was neither able to do A nor able to do B. Anyone, therefore, who endorses, e.g., the conditional, 'If it is now undetermined whether Sally (who in a moment will either lie or tell the truth) will lie or will tell the truth, then Sally is not now able to lie and is not now able to tell the truth', must purport to be using 'not able' in a sense that does not have the tempting thesis as a consequence: that person must admit that there are possible (and no doubt actual) cases in which someone does something that he or she had not been able to do. But it does not seem implausible to suppose that 'not able' has a sense that permits this. It does not seem implausible to suppose that there is a sense of 'not able' in which someone who had never before touched a dart and who casually tossed a dart at a wall was, before the dart was tossed, *not able* to hit the particular square millimeter of wall in which the dart fortuitously came to rest. And it does seem plausible to suppose that if one is not able (in this sense) to do A, and not able (in this sense) to do B, then it is not up to one whether one will do A or do B. (In fact, it seems plausible to suppose that if one is not able to do A, then it is not up to one whether one will do A or do B.)

right-hand side or the left-hand side owing to the fact that it will be unde-termined at the moment the dart leaves his hand which side of the board it will hit.

It is at least very plausible to suppose that Jack is not, during the course of his deliberations, able to hit the right-hand side and is not able to hit the left-hand side. But such cases are not decisive, since they involve the concept of *success* or at least the concept of *result*: they are cases in which an agent is now faced with a choice between doing A and doing B, and in which, if the agent should endeavor to do A or should endeavor to do B, whether the agent would succeed in either endeavor is now unde-termined. But what about cases in which an agent is now faced with a choice between doing A and doing B, and in which it is now undeter-mined whether the agent will do A or do B – but in which it is now *determined* that, once the agent has decided one way or the other, the agent will succeed in doing the thing decided on?[4] Should we say that such an agent is not now able to do A and not now able to do B? That is the real question, for the Indetermination-Inability Principle implies that if one is now faced with a choice between doing A and doing B, and if it is now undetermined whether one will do A or do B, then (no matter what *else* may be determined or undetermined) one is not now able to do A and not now able to do B.

2

In "Free Will Remains a Mystery,"[5] I presented an argument for the con-clusion that if one is now faced with a choice between speaking and keep-ing silent, and if it is now undetermined whether one will speak or keep silent, then one is now unable to keep silent. (An exactly parallel argument could be used to defend the conclusion that someone in those circum-stances is now unable to speak.) I quote the argument in full:

You are a candidate for public office, and I, your best friend, know some discreditable fact about your past that, if made public, would – and should – cost you the election. I am pulled two ways, one way by the

---

[4] That is to say, there are possible futures in which the agent decides to do A and does A and possible futures in which the agent decides to do B and does B; and there are no possible futures in which the agent decides to do A and does not do A, and no possible futures in which the agent decides to do B and does not do B. (A "possible future" is a possible world in which the past, present, and laws of nature are the same as those of the actual world.)

[5] Chapter 7 of the present volume.

claims of citizenship and the other by the claims of friendship. You know about my situation and beg me not to "tell." I know (perhaps God has told me this) that there exist exactly two possible continuations of the present – the actual present, which includes your begging me not to tell and the emotional effect your appeal has had on me – in one of which I tell all to the press and in the other of which I keep silent; and I know that the objective, "ground-floor" probability of my "telling" is 0.43 and that the objective, "ground-floor" probability of my keeping silent is 0.57. Am I in a position to promise you that I will keep silent? – knowing, as I do, that if there were a million perfect duplicates of me, each placed in a perfect duplicate of my present situation, forty-three percent of them would tell all and fifty-seven percent of them would hold their tongues? [Here I should have added the qualification 'to a very high probability'.] I do not see how, in good conscience, I could make this promise. I do not see how I could be in a position to make it. But if I believe that I am able to keep silent, I should, it would seem, regard myself as being in a position to make this promise. What more do I need to regard myself as being in a position to promise to do X than a belief that I am *able* to do X? Therefore, in this situation, I should not regard myself as being able to keep silent. (And I cannot see on what grounds third-person observers of my situation could dispute this first-person judgment.)[6]

I will call this argument the Promising Argument.

Shortly before "Free Will Remains a Mystery" appeared in print, and too late for me to do anything about it, Michael Bratman convinced me (in conversation) that the Promising Argument was invalid. Here is my own statement of his diagnosis of the flaw in the argument:

You set the case up this way. Your friend wants you to promise not to reveal his misconduct, and, while you are deliberating about whether to make such a promise, you believe that it is, at that moment, undetermined whether you will tell all or keep silent. Now you might well have that belief in those circumstances and it might even be true – but, if it is true, it doesn't follow that, if you were to make the desired promise, it would *then* be undetermined whether you would tell all or keep silent. Perhaps if you were to promise to keep silent, it *would* then be determined that you would keep silent (it may for example be psychologically impossible for you to do something that you have promised not to do). If that would be

---

[6] Pp. 109–110 in the present volume.

the result of your promising to keep silent, then you *are* in a position – you are *now* in a position – to promise your friend to keep silent. Your argument was essentially this:

> If I am able to keep silent, then I am in a position to promise to keep silent
>
> If it is undetermined whether I shall keep silent, then I am not in a position to promise to keep silent
>
> *Hence*, If it is undetermined whether I shall keep silent, I am not able to keep silent.

As I have shown, the second premise of this argument is false, or at any rate, might well be false.

The flaw is real. But can the basic idea behind the argument be saved? Can the argument be revised so as to eliminate the flaw? The following section contains my best attempt at such a revision.

3

Let us consider a more elaborate version of the Indetermination-Inability Principle (the *New Indetermination-Inability Principle*):

> Where t_2 is a future moment and t_1 is a future moment earlier than t_2:
>
> > If one is now faced with a choice between doing A at t_2 and doing B at t_2, and if, at t_1, it will be undetermined whether one will do A at t_2 or do B at t_2 (and if this *would* then be undetermined whatever one might do between now and t_1), then one is not now able to do A at t_2 and one is not now able to do B at t_2.

The New Indetermination-Inability Principle may be defended by an elaboration of the Promising Argument – the *New Promising Argument*:[7]

My good friend Jake Higgins is a candidate for re-election to the Senate. He has been having a sleazy affair with Mary O'Brien, a married member of his staff, and I know all about it. Jake has learned that at a press conference tomorrow, a reporter well known for her muckraking skills plans to ask me the following question: "Are the rumors true – is Senator Higgins

---

[7] I have taken the opportunity afforded by this revision to introduce a few "improvements" into the example on which the argument rests, improvements that are not strictly needed to meet Bratman's criticism.

intimately involved with Mrs. O'Brien?" Jake knows that there is no hope of his being re-elected if I do not explicitly say that the rumors are unfounded (an evasive response to the question will be taken as confirmation of the rumors). He begs me to promise to deny everything; that is, to promise to lie to the press. How shall I respond to this request if I have the following belief?

At the moment the question is asked, it will be undetermined whether I shall respond with a lie or with the truth (and, therefore, it is *now* undetermined which I shall do): if there were a large number of perfect duplicates of me (in identical environments) at the moment the reporter asked her question, some (to a near certainty) would lie and some would tell the truth. And, moreover, it would at the moment the question was asked be undetermined how I should respond to it even if, at some moment between the present moment and that moment, I promised to lie.

(Perhaps I believe this because I believe that whichever decision I make – to lie or to tell the truth – will be a free decision and believe on philosophical grounds that free decisions must be undetermined events.) If I have this belief, it seems, I should now regard myself as *not in a position* to promise Jake to lie to the press tomorrow. (The case is not all that different from this one: Suppose I believe that when I try to start my car, it will at that moment be undetermined whether it will start – and that this will then be undetermined no matter what I do between the present moment and the moment at which I try to start the car; then I should regard myself as not being in a position to promise someone a ride.) And that means that I believe that I am not now able to lie to the press tomorrow – for if I were now able to lie to the press tomorrow, I *should* be in a position to promise Jake to lie to the press tomorrow.[8] And the same argument (*mutatis mutandis*) will continue to apply as long as there is a future moment at which it will be undetermined whether I shall lie (in response to the reporter's

---

[8] It may sound a little odd to say, "I am not *now* able to lie *tomorrow*." For that matter, it may sound odd to say, "I *am* not able to lie *tomorrow*." The oddness of both sentences is due entirely to the fact that lying is not – at least in any normal case – an action that requires some longish sequence of pre-liminary actions. We can certainly say, "I am not able to meet you in Phoenix tomorrow" (meeting you in Phoenix tomorrow might well require a longish sequence of preliminary actions), and this is essentially the same assertion as "I am not now able to meet you in Phoenix tomorrow" (that is: it's now too late for me to do all the things needed to accomplish this end) – although in the latter case the hearer might not be sure what pragmatic function the semantically redundant adverb 'now' was supposed to be performing. In any case, there is nothing puzzling about the function of 'now' in the assertion, "Yesterday, on Monday, I was still able to meet you in Phoenix tomorrow (Wednesday), but I am not now, on Tuesday, able to do that." Or if someone said to me, "Lie for me tomorrow," the reply "If I were now to promise to lie for you tomorrow, I'd be making a promise I was not able to keep" would not sound at all odd.

question) or answer honestly.[9] If, for example, it is now 11:58, and if the reporter is going to ask her question at noon, and if it will then be undetermined whether I shall respond to her question with a lie or the truth – and if this would then be undetermined even if at some point in the next two minutes I promised to respond with a lie – then I am not now, at 11:58, able to respond with a lie.[10]

I think it's fair to say that if the New Promising Argument proves that in the case I have imagined I am not now able to lie tomorrow, then an easy generalization of the reasoning it embodies establishes the New Indetermination-Inability Principle.

Well and good. But does the New Indetermination-Inability Principle – like the (original) Indetermination-Inability Principle – imply the falsity of libertarianism?

4

One can deduce the falsity of libertarianism from the New Indetermination-Inability Principle only if one can deduce from the New Indetermination-Inability Principle that no human agent x is ever in the following situation:

> x is at some given moment faced with a choice between doing A and doing B
>
> it is at that moment up to x whether x will do A or do B
>
> it is at that moment undetermined whether x will do A or do B.

And one cannot deduce from the New Indetermination-Inability Principle that no agent is ever in that situation. There are two reasons why the New Indetermination-Inability Principle does not have that consequence. These reasons can be most easily displayed in a concrete example.

Suppose that it is now 11:58 and that I am faced with a choice between lying at noon and telling the truth at noon. Suppose it is now undetermined whether I shall lie at noon or tell the truth at noon. Can we deduce from these suppositions and the New Indetermination-Inability Principle

---

[9] More exactly: Let $t2$ be the moment at which the question will be asked, and $t1$ be an earlier future moment; a similar argument will show that I am not now able to lie at $t2$, provided that (a) at $t1$ it will be undetermined whether I shall lie at $t2$, and (b) if between the present moment and $t1$ I were to promise to lie at $t2$, it would (still) be undetermined at $t1$ whether I should lie at $t2$.

[10] I contend that the New Promising Argument can be generalized so as to apply to *all* pairs of moments that satisfy the conditions specified in the previous note. I concede that this contention faces an obvious "practical" difficulty: it takes a certain amount of time to make a promise.

that it is not now up to me whether I shall lie at noon? (That is, can we deduce that I am not both able to lie at noon and able to tell the truth at noon?) We cannot – and, as I said, for two reasons.

First, it may be that 11:58, the present moment, is the *last* moment at which it is or will be undetermined whether I shall lie at noon or tell the truth at noon; it may be that at every moment between 11:58 and noon it will either be determined that I shall lie at noon or else determined that I shall tell the truth at noon – although now, at 11:58, it is – as it was at all earlier moments – undetermined *which* of these alternatives is the one that will be determined after 11:58.[11] Note that the New Indetermination-Inability Principle does not tell us that if it is now the *last* moment at which it is undetermined whether I shall lie or tell the truth at noon, then I am now unable to lie (or unable to tell the truth) at noon; it allows us to deduce that I am unable now, at 11:58, to do something at noon only given that it will be undetermined at some *later* moment, some moment between 11:58 and noon, whether I shall do that thing at noon.

Secondly, suppose that there *is* a moment between the present moment and noon – 11:59, say – at which it will be undetermined whether I shall lie or tell the truth at noon. We cannot deduce from that supposition and the New Indetermination-Inability Principle the conclusion that I am at present unable to lie (tell the truth) at noon; to reach that conclusion, we should need a further premise: that it *would* be undetermined at 11:59 whether I should lie at noon or tell the truth at noon *no matter what I might do* between the present moment and 11:59. And why should we suppose *that*? How do we know, for example, that the following statement is false?: If I *were* to promise thirty seconds from now to lie at noon, then it *would* be determined at 11:59 that I should lie at noon. (That counterfactual is certainly consistent with the proposition that it is now – at 11:58 – undetermined whether I shall lie at noon: suppose it is now undetermined whether I shall make that promise.)

I conclude that the New Promising Argument, for all its promise, is in one important respect a failure. True, it succeeds in establishing the

---

[11] It is easy to see that such "indetermination of determination" cases are possible. Imagine a deterministic mechanism that displays a red bulb and a green bulb. Imagine that there is inserted into the works of this mechanism a smaller, indeterministic mechanism that will, in its indeterministic way, at 11:58, turn a switch in the deterministic mechanism either to the right or to the left. And imagine that if the switch is turned to the right, the red bulb must light two minutes later and that if it is turned to the left, the green bulb must light two minutes later. Then at every moment between 11:58 and noon, it will either be determined that the red bulb will light at noon or else determined that the green bulb will light at noon – although it will be at 11:58 (as at all earlier moments) undetermined *which* of these alternatives will be the one that is determined after 11:58.

New Indetermination-Inability Principle, but it fails of its larger purpose, for it does not imply the falsity of libertarianism. The revisions of the Promising Argument that were needed to evade Bratman's insightful criticism of that argument have weakened the conclusion of the revised argument to the point where its conclusion does not imply the falsity of libertarianism.

I would point out that this "failure" of the New Promising Argument by no means establishes the possibility of libertarianism. After all, an argument can be the most abject failure imaginable and nevertheless have a true conclusion. For all the failure of the New Promising Argument shows, the (original) Indetermination-Inability Principle may be true, and that principle entails the falsity of libertarianism. The burden of the present section is that reasoning that turns on the relation between one's being able to do a certain thing and one's being in a position to promise to do that thing cannot establish the Indetermination-Inability Principle; such reasoning can establish only the weaker New Indetermination-Inability Principle.

5

If the New Indetermination-Inability Principle does not imply the falsity of libertarianism, it does imply the falsity of a thesis that most libertarians would be strongly inclined to accept, even if that thesis is not a strict logical consequence of libertarianism. I will call this thesis the *Deliberation-Freedom Thesis*:[12]

> At various times and on various occasions, there has been a human agent x who was in the following situation:
>
>> x was faced with a choice between doing A and doing B
>>
>> x chose to do A after an extended period (several minutes, at least) of serious deliberation
>>
>> At every moment during that period of deliberation, it was up to x whether x would do A or do B (at every moment during that period of deliberation, x could say truly, "It is now up to me whether I shall do A or do B: I am now able to do A and I am now able to do B")[13]

[12] Strictly speaking, this "thesis" is not a thesis but a thesis schema. Instances of the schema can be obtained by replacing the dummy phrases 'do A', 'do B', 'doing A', and 'doing B' with appropriate English phrases. To say, "I accept the Deliberation-freedom Thesis" is to commit oneself to the schema's having some true instances.

[13] It is a firm conviction of mine that if one is at a certain moment deliberating about whether to do A or to do B, it *follows* that one believes at that moment that one is then able to do A *and* then able

> During that period of deliberation, x was "condemned to freedom": from the moment at which x first began to try to decide whether to do A or do B till the moment at which x's choice to do A or x's choice to do B was (irrevocably) made, there was nothing x could do to change the fact that, till the choice was made, it would be up to x whether x would do A or do B (nothing, that is, short of breaking off deliberating about whether to do A or do B).

The New Indetermination-Inability Principle and incompatibilism jointly entail the falsity of the Deliberation-Freedom Thesis.[14] Libertarianism, as I have defined libertarianism, does not entail the Deliberation-Freedom Thesis, but it does seem to me to be a thesis that most libertarians would be very strongly inclined to accept. Some libertarians (and perhaps some opponents of libertarianism) might even want to say that the definition of libertarianism in Section 0 of this paper was unsatisfactory, unsatisfactory because "real" libertarians mean something more by 'libertarianism' than the rather weak thesis I gave that name to in Section 0.

Perhaps there are philosophers who would say this and perhaps they are right. And perhaps they are right because "real" libertarians accept the Deliberation-Freedom Thesis. Let us take that possibility into account by renaming the thesis that was called 'libertarianism' in Section 0: let us now call that thesis *weak* or *minimal* libertarianism. And let us call the conjunction of incompatibilism and the Deliberation-Freedom Thesis *strong* libertarianism. (Strong libertarianism obviously entails weak or minimal libertarianism.) The New Indetermination-Inability Principle argument implies the falsity of strong libertarianism but does not imply the falsity of weak or minimal libertarianism.

The New Promising Argument refutes strong libertarianism (its conclusion implies the falsity of strong libertarianism). But how important an accomplishment that is is debatable.

The following two questions are obviously relevant to the debate: *Are there in fact any strong libertarians?*; *How committed are such strong libertarians as there may be to strong libertarianism?* I am fairly sure that there are some strong libertarians, but am not at all sure how committed to strong libertarianism they may be. For all I know, most strong libertarians

---

to do B. But, of course, if one necessarily believes that p whenever one is F, it doesn't follow that it's *true* that p whenever one is F and believes that p. It follows from my "firm conviction" that philosophers who believe that the free-will thesis is false have contradictory beliefs whenever they engage in deliberation. It does not follow that the free-will thesis is true.

[14] That is, no instance of the schema is consistent with the conjunction of the New Indetermination-Inability Principle and incompatibilism.

(always assuming that there are any) would be willing to say something along the following lines: "I *did* accept 'strong libertarianism' but the New Promising Argument has convinced me that that thesis is false. Well, no matter. Strong libertarianism is not really essential to my views on free will. I'm content to make a strategic withdrawal to weak libertarianism and defend that position." If the friends of strong libertarianism are fair-weather friends of that sort, then the New Promising Argument is not as important as it would be if strong libertarianism had committed advocates.

Another sort of consideration that is relevant to the question of the importance of the New Promising Argument has to do with the implications of the argument for the construction of libertarian models or theories of free will. By this I mean models of, or theories that attempt to provide an account of, what *goes on* within an agent when that agent performs an act of free will[15] – models or theories of free will that in some way incorporate incompatibilism. (Many libertarians – I am not one of them – have attempted to construct such models or theories.) Let us say that a theory of free will is a *strong* libertarian theory if it entails both incompatibilism and the Deliberation-Freedom Thesis. And let us say that a theory of free will is a *weak* libertarian theory if it is not a strong libertarian theory and it entails both incompatibilism and the free-will thesis. (Strong libertarianism is not strong libertarian theory because it is not a theory at all; it is only a thesis or position. By the same token, weak libertarianism is not a weak libertarian theory.) The New Promising Argument may simplify the search for a libertarian theory of free will in virtue of the fact that it implies that no strong libertarian theory can be correct.

---

[15] In the language of the present paper, an act of free will may be defined in this way: If an agent was at some point faced with a choice between doing A and doing B, and if the agent did A, and if at some moment before the agent did A, it was up to that agent whether he or she would do A or do B, then the agent's doing A was an act of free will.

CHAPTER 12

Author's Preface to the French Translation of An Essay on Free Will

It has been just over thirty years since the publication of *An Essay on Free Will*. M. Michon, the translator, has suggested that this French translation might provide an occasion for the author to reflect on the book in the light of subsequent work – his own and that of other philosophers – on the problem of free will. I am happy to do so.

I will not, in these brief remarks, summarize the book. (The first chapter of the book is a summary of its content.) I will instead present some thoughts on three topics:

– The question 'If I were to revise the book today, if I were to produce a second edition, what changes would I make?'
– Aspects of the book I should like to call to the attention of readers (aspects that, in my view, readers of *An Essay on Free Will* have been insufficiently attentive to).
– The course of the discussion of the problem of free will subsequent to the publication of the book.

These thoughts are contained in the following remarks, which should be read after the reader is familiar with the book.

If I were to Revise the Book Today, what Changes would I make?

First, I would use an entirely different vocabulary to frame the problem to which the book is addressed. In the paragraphs that follow I will describe this "different vocabulary," and I shall try to explain the reasons for my present dissatisfaction with certain of the words and phrases that figured prominently in *An Essay on Free Will*.

The most salient change I would make, although perhaps not the philosophically most important one, is that I would not now use the phrase 'free will'. In fact, I would not even use the adjective 'free' – I would not speak of free actions, free agents, or free choices. Nor would I use the adverb 'freely' and the noun 'freedom'. In my view, these words have little meaning beyond that which the philosopher who uses them explicitly gives them, and yet philosophers persist in arguing about what they do or should mean. They enter into disputes about what "free will" and "free choices" and "acting freely" and "freedom" *really are*. These philosophers have fallen prey to what I may call *verbal essentialism*. That is to say, it is essential to their discussions that they involve certain *words*: 'free', 'freely', 'freedom' … It would be impossible to translate their discussions into language that did not involve those words. The essential content of *An Essay on Free Will*, however, could have been presented without using 'free' or 'freely' or 'freedom'. (I show in detail how to do this in "The Problem of Fr** W*ll.")[1] In this Preface, however, I will use the phrase 'free will' (and 'free' and 'freely') simply because there is no readily available alternative. This phrase should be understood in the sense I gave it in *An Essay on Free Will*. (Or see the definition below on pp. 182–183.)

I would, moreover, not use the phrase 'could have' – and I would be particularly careful to avoid the phrase 'could have done otherwise'. That is because these phrases are grammatically ambiguous, and this ambiguity has caused a great deal of confusion in discussions of the free-will problem in English. I will not, however, discuss this ambiguity in this Preface, because there is no parallel ambiguity in French (or in any other language of which I am aware).[2]

In the revised book, I would not use the phrase 'moral responsibility' – for, in my view, this phrase is used in current philosophy without any clear sense. I would replace all references to "moral responsibility" with references to fault or blame. (To *moral* fault or blame.) And I would speak of fault and blame only in connection with the consequences of actions (or failures to act). Thus, I would not say anything like 'Alice is morally responsible for telling lies to Frank' – for it is not at all clear what that means. I would instead say things like, 'Frank's unhappiness is Alice's fault' or 'Alice is to blame for Frank's unhappiness'. (Alice's lies would come in

---

[1] Chapter 13 of the present volume.
[2] The ambiguity is rooted in the fact that the English modal auxiliary 'can' does not govern an infinitival clause. Thus, one way of saying 'Je peux *jouer* au tennis' in English is, 'I can *play* tennis'. By contrast, the syntax of the English verb-phrase 'to be able' corresponds exactly to that of '*pouvoir*': 'I am able *to play* tennis'. In the revised book, I would replace the syntactically ambiguous 'could have done otherwise' with the syntactically unambiguous 'was able to do otherwise'.

at a later stage in a conversation about Alice and Frank: "Why is Alice to blame for Frank's unhappiness?" "Because his unhappiness is due to the scurrilous lies she told him about his wife.")

In the revised book, I would replace "Principle β" with a different principle. Principle β was:

> *p* and no one has, or ever had, any choice about that

> If *p*, then *q*, and no one has, or ever had, any choice about that

>   *hence,*

> *q* and no one has, or ever had, any choice about that.

Or, in abbreviated form,

$$N p, \, N(p \rightarrow q) \mid -Nq.$$

And Thomas McKay and David Johnson have shown that β is invalid.[3] Consider a coin that is never tossed. Suppose that I have a choice about whether the coin is tossed, but that neither I nor anyone else has, or ever had, a choice about how the coin would fall if tossed. Let '*Notheads*' abbreviate 'The coin never falls heads' and '*Nottails*' abbreviate 'The coin never falls tails'. It is obvious that

> (1) N(*Notheads* → (*Nottails* → (*Notheads* & *Nottails*))),

since '*Notheads* → (*Nottails* → (*Notheads* & *Nottails*))' is a logical truth. The following two statements are also obvious:

> (2) N *Notheads*

> (3) N *Nottails*,

owing to the fact that *Notheads* and *Nottails* are both true and no one has a choice about how the coins would fall if tossed.

If β is valid, then (1) and (2) imply

> (4) N(*Nottails* → (*Notheads* & *Nottails*)),

and (3) and (4) imply

> (5) N(*Notheads* & *Nottails*).

And (5) is false, since I have a choice about whether the coin is tossed: if I choose not to toss the coin (my actual choice), *Notheads* & *Nottails* will be

[3] Thomas McKay and David Johnson, "A Reconsideration of an Argument against Compatibilism," *Philosophical Topics* 24 (1996): 113–122.

true. If I choose to toss the coin, *Notheads* & *Nottails* will be false, since the coin must fall either heads or tails.

The reason I mistakenly supposed that β was valid was this. I mistakenly supposed that the only way in which it could be that one had no choice about the truth-value of a proposition would be for the truth-value of that proposition to be in some way so firmly "fixed" that one was unable to change it. I did not see that that there is another way for one to have no choice about the truth-value of a proposition: for that truth-value to be a mere matter of chance.

I would now formulate β differently. Or, if you like, I would substitute another principle for β, a principle that does not contain the phrase 'has no choice about'. I propose the following. Say that it is *a humanly unalterable truth* that p just in the case that p and nothing that any human being is or ever has been able to do is such that if someone were to do it, that person's action might result (could possibly result) in its not being the case that p. "Revised β" would then be

It is a humanly unalterable truth that p

It is a humanly unalterable truth that if p, then q

hence,

It is a humanly unalterable truth that q.

I believe this principle to be valid.

I now turn to another topic, the topic of psychological laws. In *An Essay on Free Will*, I said the following (pp. 63–64 in the original):

> Suppose psychologists discover that no one who has received moral training of type A in early childhood ever spreads lying rumours about his professional colleagues. Suppose you and I in fact received such training. Does it follow that we *can't* engage in this odious activity? I don't see why it should be supposed to follow … Suppose further that that you and I are in fact *able* to spread lying rumours about our colleagues. Does it follow that a statement of the regularity we have supposed psychologists to have discovered is, though true, not a law? [I do not see why it should not be regarded as a law.] "But why," someone may ask, "does this regular pattern of behavior occur if people don't *have* to conform to it?" Note that the only people in a position to depart from it are those who have in fact had training of type A. Perhaps it is just these people who *see the point* in not spreading lying rumours. To come to see the point in not exercising an ability one has is not to *lose* that ability.

Conversations with Alexander Rosenberg, and some thoughts that I had after reading a science-fiction novel called *Protector* by Larry Niven, gradually convinced me that this passage was radically confused. (The "Protectors" of Niven's novel are beings, all of them sterile males formerly capable of reproduction, each of whom, of biological necessity, ascribes intrinsic value to only one thing: the preservation of his own bloodline. Protectors, moreover, are far more intelligent than any human being, and, in consequence, each Protector almost always sees immediately, in any situation in which he finds himself, what course of action is most likely to preserve his bloodline – "and straightaway he acts." Niven has one of his Protectors say at one point, "Protectors have precious little free will." When I first read those words, my immediate reaction was to smile and to regard them as a rather typical non-philosopher's confusion about free will. A decade or so later, I realized that it was I who had been confused.)[4] My reasons for thinking this passage confused eventually found expression in a paper called, "When Is the Will Free?"[5] In that paper, I defended the position that the principles – Principle β, for example – that I used to argue for the incompatibility of free will and determinism also support the proposition that if human beings are ever able to act otherwise than they in fact do, this can be the case only very rarely. (The distinction between "Original β" and "Revised β" is not relevant to my defense of this position.) A revised version of *An Essay on Free Will* would incorporate this position.

If I were to rewrite the book, it would contain an extensive discussion of the implications of recent developments in neuroscience for the problem of free will.[6]

Since the publication of *An Essay on Free Will*, it has become increasingly clear to me that free will is a philosophical mystery – something that philosophers do not understand at all. (It is not the only one. For example, no philosopher understands conscious experience or the apparent "passage" of time.) I do not mean to imply that free will is a mystery in the theological sense: something that is beyond all possibility of human comprehension. That may or may not be the case. I contend only that as of this date, no philosopher has achieved an understanding of free will. That may be because free will is indeed something that human beings are incapable of understanding, but it may be because we human beings have not yet discovered the right way to think about free will. I will lay out the essence of this mystery in four fairly simple statements – labeled 'first', 'secondly', 'thirdly',

---

[4] When I told this autobiographical anecdote to David Lewis, who was familiar with Niven's novel, he understood my point immediately – although he did not agree with it.

[5] Chapter 5 of the present volume.

[6] Walter Sinnot-Armstrong (ed.), *Moral Psychology*, volume IV, *Free Will and Moral Responsibility* (Cambridge, MA: MIT Press, 2014), is an excellent introduction to this topic.

and 'fourthly'. First, there are excellent arguments for each of the following three propositions:

> If antecedent conditions and the laws of nature determine the way in which a human being shall act at a certain time, then that person's act at that time is not free. (This proposition, of course, is the proposition commonly called 'incompatibilism'.)

> If antecedent conditions and the laws of nature do *not* determine the way in which a human being shall act at a certain time, then that person's act at that time is not free.

> If a human being's acts are never free, then the consequences of those acts are not the fault of that human being.

Secondly, the following fourth proposition seems to be true beyond all possibility of dispute.

> Some of the consequences of some of the acts of some human beings are their fault.

Thirdly, these four propositions form a logically inconsistent set, and, therefore, either the excellent arguments for at least one of first three propositions must contain some flaw or else it must be that (to take one example among many millions of compelling examples) the deaths of six million Jews in the extermination camps were not anyone's fault. Fourthly, no one knows of even a plausible candidate for a flaw in any of the arguments for the first three of the four propositions (not, at any rate, in the arguments *I'm* thinking of), and to deny the fourth would be simply bizarre. I doubt whether many philosophers will agree with my statement that "no one knows of even a plausible candidate for a flaw in any of the arguments for the first three of the four propositions," but it represents my considered judgment. My own view is that there is a flaw in the argument (the argument that *I* think is the best argument for this conclusion) for the proposition 'If antecedent conditions and the laws of nature do *not* determine the way in which a human being shall act at a certain time, then that person's act at that time is not free'. But I haven't any idea what this flaw might be.

I would recommend that the "problem of free will" be understood as follows: it is the problem of discovering a flaw in at least one of the arguments for the first three propositions – or else of explaining how the seemingly self-evident fourth proposition, could, despite all appearances, be false. In my judgment, no one has the least idea how to solve this problem. That is what I mean by saying that "free will is a mystery." If I were to revise *An Essay on Free Will*, I would give the thesis that free will is a mystery a very prominent place in the revised work (although, as I have said, in stating and defending this thesis I would not use the words 'free will').

In my view, few if any of my fellow "libertarians" – that is, incompatibilists who accept the reality of free will – appreciate the immense power of the *Mind* Argument (the conclusion of which is the second of the propositions above: the proposition that undetermined human actions cannot be free). One typical reaction of libertarians to that argument is to declare that the problem it poses for libertarianism can be solved by positing that some events are caused not by earlier events but by *substances*, to wit, human agents. These libertarians hold that the *agent* (as opposed to some event that occurs within the agent) is sometimes the cause of the agent's actions. I have since presented arguments for the conclusion that even if "agent causation" indeed exists, it is irrelevant to the problem that the *Mind* Argument poses for libertarianism.[7] I would include these arguments in a revised version of the book.

Much of what was said about quantum mechanics in section 6.2 of the book was out of date even when the book was written – although, of course, I did not realize that at the time; I did not realize that several of the most important of my statements about quantum mechanics were based on obsolete sources (this is particularly true of my statements about von Neumann's "proof" of the impossibility of supplementing quantum mechanics with "hidden variables"). I would completely rewrite section 6.2.

Many philosophers writing on free will suppose that "libertarian free will" and "compatibilist free will" are two different things. (This is particularly true of compatibilists.) They suppose, that is, that libertarians believe in a kind of free will that is incompatible with determinism, and that compatibilists believe in a kind of free will that is compatible with determinism. They suppose that libertarians reject compatibilism on the ground that to give the name 'free will' to what the compatibilists call by that name is to be guilty of (in Kant's words) "a wretched subterfuge," and that compatibilists reject libertarianism on the ground that what libertarians give the name 'free will' to does not exist (and is, moreover, something that no one should want to have or to believe in the existence of). In my view, this position is simply false and allegiance to it has been the occasion of an immense amount of unclarity and confusion in writing on free will. (Of course this

---

[7] "Free Will Remains a Mystery," Chapter 7 of the present volume.

confusion would simply vanish if, as I recommend, philosophers were to cease to use such phrases as 'free will' and 'free agent' and 'free act'.) If I were to revise *An Essay on Free Will*, I would include a presentation of my reasons for holding this view.[8]

Aspects of the Book that Readers have been Insufficiently Attentive to

One frequently hears variants on the following challenge to libertarianism – as frequently today as thirty years ago:

If free will were, as you libertarians contend, incompatible with determinism, one could never know whether one – whether *anyone* – had free will unless one knew whether the world was governed by a deterministic set of laws. And if ascriptions of fault or blame presuppose the existence of free will, then no one could know whether anything was anyone's fault unless one first knew that determinism was false. Libertarianism thus implies that we should all be skeptics about whether anything has ever been anyone's fault. But you libertarians seem to be perfectly confident that certain states of affairs are the fault of certain people, that certain people are to blame for certain things. This is not a consistent position.

I would call the attention of anyone who accepts any argument that is even remotely similar to this argument to section 6.3 of *An Essay on Free Will*. I do not claim to be familiar with the whole of the vast literature on free will, determinism, and moral blame, but to the best of my knowledge, the arguments of that section have not only never been adequately answered, but they have never been discussed at all. In my view, anyone who accepts anything like the above argument should address the arguments of section 6.3.

I turn now to the topic of "Frankfurt counterexamples." One of the propositions that figures in the statement of "the problem of free will" above is:

(6) If a human being's acts are never free, then the consequences of those acts are not the fault of that human being.

Many philosophers suppose that this proposition was shown to be false by Harry Frankfurt in his classic paper "The Principle of Alternate

---

[8] I would direct any philosopher who thinks that "compatibilist free will" and "libertarian free will" are two different things to David Lewis's marvelous essay "Are We Free to Break the Laws?," *Theoria* 47 (1981): 113–121. Available on line at www.andrewmbailey.com/dkl/Free_to_Break_the_Laws.pdf. Lewis, with his usual clarity of mind, realized that he, a compatibilist, and I, a libertarian, were talking about the *same thing* when we spoke of agents "acting freely," and that the issue between us was whether this one thing was compatible with determinism. A revised version of *An Essay on Free Will* would certainly include an extensive discussion of "Are We Free to Break the Laws?" (See pp. 186–187 in the text.)

Possibilities."⁹ In that paper, Frankfurt presented a counterexample to the "Principle of Alternate Possibilities":

PAP   A person is morally responsible for what he has done only if he could have done otherwise.

If one restates (6) in terms of "moral responsibility" (and 'person'), one obtains something like

> (7) If a person's acts are never free, then that person is not morally responsible for the consequences of any of those acts,

which is equivalent to

> (8) A person is morally responsible for some of the consequences of some of his acts only if that person's acts are sometimes free.

If one assumes that a person's act is free just in the case that that person "could have done otherwise" (that is, was able to do otherwise, was able to do something else or nothing at all), then (8) is, more or less, equivalent to

> (9) A person is morally responsible for some of the consequences of some of his acts only if that person is sometimes (i.e., at certain points in his life) able to do otherwise.

(The reader will see that I have been attempting to transform (6) into something as similar to PAP as possible.)

It is the burden of the long discussion of Frankfurt's arguments in *An Essay on Free Will* (sections 5.3–5.7) that, even on the assumption that Frankfurt has presented a successful counterexample to PAP, (a) this counterexample is not a counterexample to (9), and (b) it is not possible to use the "general idea" behind Frankfurt's counterexample to PAP to construct a counterexample to (9). I therefore maintain that if Frankfurt has indeed refuted PAP, this refutation is irrelevant to the problem of free will, or at least irrelevant to the problem I call 'the problem of free will'. But a significant proportion of the writers on the problem of free will continue to treat "Frankfurt counterexamples" as an important contribution to our understanding of the problem of free will. I would direct their attention to sections 5.3–5.7 of *An Essay on Free Will.*

I turn, finally, to the challenge, "But what would you say if determinism, or something that might be called 'determinism for all practical purposes', turned out to be true?" I am not infrequently asked questions whose essential point may be summarized as follows.

⁹ Harry G. Frankfurt, "The Principle of Alternate Possibilities," *Journal of Philosophy* 66 (1969): 829–839. (The correct word, by the way, would have been 'alternative', not 'alternate'.)

Whatever may be the case as regards the general metaphysical thesis of determinism, it is certainly a very real possibility that human beings are "essentially deterministic systems" – in the sense in which your computer is an essentially deterministic system. (Even if there are all sorts of undetermined events going on at the quantum level inside your computer, it is vastly unlikely that these events will have the consequence that the behavior of your computer will exhibit any indeterminacy at the level of "observables" – vastly unlikely, for example, that it is indeterminate what will appear on the monitor, given a precise description of what you have done at the keyboard.) And if determinism is incompatible with the proposition that human beings have free will, then – surely? – the thesis that human beings are essentially deterministic systems is also incompatible with that proposition. What would you say if that possibility were shown by scientific investigation to be realized? What would you say if science produced a convincing demonstration that human beings were essentially deterministic systems?

I have answered this question with some care in section 6.4 of *An Essay on Free Will*, although this answer has received little or no attention from writers on free will. My answer takes the form of an argument for the thesis that the most reasonable response for me to make to such a "convincing demonstration" would be to conclude that Principle β was invalid – or, since β is invalid in any case, that "Revised β" was invalid. "Revised β" seems to me to be an obvious truth – it seems to possess a certain "luminous evidence" (Locke) or to "force itself upon the mind as true" (Gödel). But the history of philosophy provides a fund of examples of propositions that seemed to *very* able thinkers to have those features and which eventually proved to be false. One may cite Zeno's conviction that every object is motionless at an instant (a landscape painting displays the spatial relations among certain objects at an instant; if you inspect such a painting, you will observe that everything in it is *not moving*), Galileo's conviction that there are more numbers that are either even or odd than there are numbers that are odd, Frege's appeal to what we now call "the unrestricted comprehension principle" in set theory, and the status of the Galilean law of the addition of velocities in pre-Einsteinian physics.

The Course of the Discussion of the Problem of Free Will Subsequent to the Publication of *An Essay on Free Will*

I believe that the most important contribution to the literature on free will subsequent to the publication of *An Essay on Free Will* was David Lewis's essay "Are We Free to Break the Laws?"[10] (Although this essay appeared in a number of *Theoria* dated 1981, that number of the journal may well not actually have appeared till after the publication of the book. In any case, it was written before Lewis had read the book. The essay is, however, a profound critique of the argument of my own essay "The Incompatibility of Free Will and Determinism,"[11] and therefore a profound critique of one of the three arguments for incompatibilism that are presented in chapter 3 of *An Essay on Free Will*.) In my own deeply prejudiced view, it is the only publication of real philosophical significance concerning the arguments of the book. (I have replied to it in an essay called "Freedom to Break the Laws.")[12]

In my opinion the philosophical literature on free will, subsequent to the publication of my book and Lewis's essay, has degenerated into a sterile scholasticism (in the pejorative sense of the word; I do not mean to imply that scholasticism in the pejorative sense was any more common in the medieval schools than it has been in any other philosophical community). That is, there have been no new arguments or ideas of any real consequence. The parties to the discussion of the problem of free will since 1983 know all the relevant arguments and concepts that pertain to every aspect of the problem, and dispute about those arguments and concepts without saying anything that is both new and important about them. They employ, moreover, a standard or "set" vocabulary for discussing the problem that is in many respects unsatisfactory and of which they are insufficiently critical – or, to be frank, not critical at all.

I would add two qualifications to this generalization. First, in the last decade (or a bit more) neurobiologists and other scientists have had a great deal to say about free will. Whether what any of what they said is of any great philosophical importance is a difficult question to answer. As the slang phrase has it, the jury is still out. But, philosophically important or not, it is *new*, and the charge of "sterile scholasticism" that I have brought against the work of philosophers writing on free will does not apply to it. (I do not mean to imply that philosophers have been inattentive to the implications of neurobiology for the problem of free will. There has been some very interesting work by philosophers on those implications, and that work, too, must be exempted from the charge of sterile scholasticism.)

---

[10] See n. 8.
[11] *Philosophical Studies* 27 (1975): 185–199. Available on line at www.andrewmbailey.com/pvi/
[12] Chapter 9 of the present volume.

Secondly, there have been some developments in the work of philosophers on free will in the last thirty years that I would condemn on grounds other than "sterile scholasticism." I have observed, in examining this work, a phenomenon that I can only describe as "terminological degeneration." One case of this has already been mentioned: the introduction of the phrases "compatibilist free will" and "libertarian free will" into discussions of the free-will problem. I will mention two other cases – cases not unrelated to each other.

(i) There has been a tendency to use 'free will' in a sense something like this:

> To possess free will is to have open to one alternative possibilities in whatever sense of 'alternative possibilities' it is that is relevant to ascriptions of moral responsibility.

Now I have deprecated both the phrase 'free will' and the phrase 'moral responsibility'. But my reasons for disliking these two phrases are largely irrelevant to my present point. As to 'moral responsibility', if I were to change the definition in (i) to

> To possess free will is to have open to one alternative possibilities in whatever sense of 'alternative possibilities' it is that is relevant to ascriptions of moral fault or blame,

my objections to the "new" definition of 'free will' would be essentially the same. Let us therefore turn to those objections.

In discussions of the free-will problem for at least several decades before (and for perhaps a decade after) the publication of *An Essay on Free Will*, the phrase 'free will' had an agreed-upon and reasonably precise meaning:

> An agent has free will if he or she sometimes acts freely; and an agent acted freely on a certain occasion if that agent was able to have done something other than what he or she did.

My first objection can be presented as a rhetorical question: Why change the long-agreed-upon meaning a philosophically significant term has had? – the meaning, indeed, it had throughout a significant episode in the history of the problem of free will, to wit the period (1965–85) during which incompatibilism became a respectable philosophical position? (I leave aside the question whether this was the meaning that 'free will' has *always* had in philosophy and theology.)

And here is a second rhetorical question: Surely the new definition is a lot less clear than the "classical" one? It seems to me, in fact, that the very idea of adopting a new or revised definition of 'free will' rests on a confusion

– a failure to recognize that 'free will' is a philosopher's term of art, a purely technical term that does occur in everyday discourse.[13] The attempt to provide a new definition of 'free will' is an example of the above-mentioned "verbal essentialism" that infects much of the current discussion of the relations between determinism, indeterminism, and the ascription of moral blame. It rests on the false belief that the *phrase* 'free will' and the *words* 'free' and 'freely' and 'freedom' are – owing the role that they supposedly play in our everyday discourse about fault and blame – of philosophical significance, the false belief that the use of these particular verbal items is *essential* to the posing and discussion of "the problem of free will." It is this apparently widespread false belief that has led me to the conclusion that it would be a good thing if 'free will' and 'free' and 'freely' and 'freedom' were entirely eliminated from discussions of philosophical problems concerning fault and blame and the causal antecedents of human action.

(ii) There has been a tendency to change the meaning of 'compatibilism'. The original meaning of this word (I believe that the word was coined and given this meaning by Keith Lehrer in the 1960s) and the meaning it had during the "classical" period of the discussion of free will by analytical philosophers (1965–85) was

The existence of free will (the existence of human beings who sometimes act freely in the sense given above) is compatible with determinism (the thesis that at any given moment, the laws of nature permit only one possible future)'.[14]

---

[13]   This bald statement requires two qualifications. (a) 'Free will' occurs in everyday discourse as a component of the longer phrase 'of * own free will', where the asterisk represents the position of a possessive pronoun. This phrase implies nothing but the absence of coercion. To say, for example, that Kim Philby acted as a Soviet agent "of his own free will" means nothing more than his acting as a Soviet agent was uncoerced: he did not so act because he had been threatened with unpleasant consequences if he refused to be a Soviet agent. And, of course, everyone will agree the question whether a given action was coerced or uncoerced has nothing to do with the questions like 'Is the state of the world at a given time is determined by its states at earlier times?' and 'Does God foresee everything we do?' and 'Do the Libet experiments show that our actions are the result of events prior to our conscious choice to perform them?' (b) Technical terms from various sciences and disciplines ('entropy', 'catalyst', 'evolution'...) do find their way into everyday discourse, where they are used without any real understanding of their technical senses – impressionistically, as it were. And, of course, this has happened with 'free will'. If a popular science writer tells her readers that the Libet experiments prove that our belief in "free will" is an illusion, most of her readers will think that they have understood what it was that she has said has been proved to be an illusion – despite the fact that if you asked them to say *what* our belief in free will was a belief in, they could give no answer that had any intelligible content.

[14]   Two propositions are "compatible" if it is metaphysically possible for them both to be true. Thus 'compatibilism' was originally a name for the thesis that there are possible worlds in which (a) at any given moment, the laws of nature permit only one possible future, and (b) there are agents who sometimes act freely. Of course, there would be little point in one's being in that sense a compatibilist

And this is the "new" meaning of 'compatibilism':

The existence of *moral responsibility* is compatible with determinism.[15]

(Or, as I should prefer to say, the existence of human agents who can properly be blamed for some of the consequences of their acts is compatible with determinism. But my reasons for disliking the phrase 'moral responsibility' are irrelevant to my present point.) This seems to me to be a harmful terminological innovation for two reasons. First, it has the consequence that the word 'compatibilism' will have been used in two different senses at various places in the free-will literature – and it may not always be clear which of the two senses a given author means it to have. Secondly, it leaves those who use it without a name for the thesis that the existence of free will is compatible with determinism. (Unless, of course those who insist on using 'compatibilism' in the new sense invent a new word to express the old sense. But surely it would be a better procedure to let 'compatibilism' continue to mean what it originally meant, and to coin some new term – semi-compatibilism or MR-compatiblism or some such – as a name for the thesis that moral responsibility and determinism are compatible? A nice compromise, and one I should have no objection to, would be to drop 'compatibilism' *simpliciter* and to introduce two new terms to express the two senses unequivocally – perhaps 'FW-compatibilism' and 'MR-compatibilism'.)

Now giving the word 'compatibilism' this new sense would be defensible if it were clear that the question 'Is the existence of moral responsibility compatible with determinism?' could be investigated without raising and attempting to answer the question 'Is the existence of free will compatible with determinism?' And indeed many philosophers seem to think that it is possible to discuss the former question without discussing the latter – possible, that is, if 'free will' in the latter question is understood in its "classical" sense:

> An agent has free will if he or she sometimes acts freely; and an
> agent acted freely on a certain occasion if that agent was able to
> have done something other than what he or she did.

---

if one did not accept the following conditional thesis: If the *actual* world is "deterministic," then it is one of the deterministic worlds in which there are agents who sometimes act freely; but that thesis is not strictly speaking implied by "classical compatibilism."

[15] Some philosophers currently writing on the free-will problem call this thesis 'semi-compatibilism'. (That is to say, semi-compatibilism is the thesis that, *whether or not* free will is compatible with determinism, *moral responsibility* is compatible with determinism.) I have no real objection to that term.

(Of course, if 'free will' is understood in *this* sense:

> To possess free will is to have open to one alternative possibilities in whatever sense of 'alternative possibilities' it is that is relevant to ascriptions of moral responsibility,

if the concept of "free will" is defined in terms of its relation to moral responsibility, then by definition any attempt to answer the question, 'Is the existence of moral responsibility compatible with determinism?' will involve an attempt to answer the question 'Is the existence of free will compatible with determinism?')

Many philosophers, then, seem to think that is it possible to investigate the question whether the existence of moral responsibility is compatible with determinism without raising and attempting to answer the question whether the existence of agents who, on some occasions, are able to act otherwise than they have in fact acted is compatible with determinism. That thesis may be true or it may be false – *I* certainly think it's false – but it is a *substantive* philosophical thesis. The appropriation of 'compatibilism' to mean 'the thesis that the existence of moral responsibility is compatible with determinism' seems to suggest that this substantive philosophical thesis has somehow been shown to be true – which it certainly has not been. I therefore contend that the practice of using 'compatibilism' in this new sense be strongly resisted. I insist that the "standard vocabulary" employed in discussions of the problem of free will *must* include a term for the thesis that the existence of agents who, on some occasions, are able to act otherwise than they have in fact acted is compatible with determinism. I recommend (although I do not insist) that that term be 'compatibilism'. I do, however, insist that 'compatibilism' *not* be used as a name for the thesis that moral responsibility is compatible with determinism. If 'compatibilism' is not to be used in its original sense, then it should not be used at all, and, as I have suggested, some new pair of unequivocal terms (such as 'FW-compatibilism' and 'MR-compatibilism') should be devised and adopted.

CHAPTER 13

*The Problem of Fr** W*ll*

But who sees not that all the dispute is about a word?
Berkeley

A couple of years ago, I was invited to give a talk on the topic "A Philosophical Perspective on Free Will" at a "summer school" on science and religion – an occasion at which I was the only philosopher who spoke, the other speakers being scientists and theologians. I didn't choose the title of my talk. It was, rather, proposed by the organizers of the summer school, and I reluctantly accepted it. I concede that it wasn't a bad title for practical purposes; that is, it indicated in a very loose sort of way what I intended to talk about. But I disliked it. In fact, I disliked it intensely. I disliked it because it implied something that I think is false, namely that there's some reasonably well-defined thing called 'free will' and that specialists in various studies or sciences or disciplines have, or might be expected to have, different "perspectives" on it: physicists view (or might be expected to view) this thing called 'free will' from one perspective, neurobiologists from another, philosophers from a third perspective, theologians from a fourth – and so on.

Let me consider a contrastive analogy – an imaginary interdisciplinary conference on some topic on which the representatives of different disciplines might be expected to have distinct "perspectives." Let us imagine a gathering of representatives of different fields of study – let us say, astronomy, biology, communications engineering, and theology – to discuss the topic "extraterrestrial intelligent life." The idea in the minds of the organizers of the conference is that the astronomers present will discuss extraterrestrial intelligent life from one perspective, the biologists from another, the communications engineers from a third, and the theologians from a fourth. The idea of such a gathering is not at all puzzling, for – even if there are disagreements about the precise definition of 'life' or about what, exactly, 'intelligent' means – we have at least a rough-and-ready understanding of the phrase 'intelligent life', and we know what it would be to bring the perspective provided by a particular discipline to a discussion of its existence elsewhere in the universe. (We would, for example, expect the astronomers at our imaginary gathering to talk about such matters as the proportion of stars that have planets on which life is possible and the kind of observations that might indicate that a planet was inhabited by an industrial civilization, and the communications engineers to talk about the problems of sending and receiving signals across intersidereal distances and about what features would mark a signal sent by intelligent beings.)

In my view, however, there is no analogy between this wholly unpuzzling case (*sc.* of the representatives of various disciplines coming together to discuss some thing or phenomenon from different perspectives) and the idea that representatives of various disciplines might come together to discuss "free will," each from the perspective of his or her own discipline. There is no analogy between the cases because the phrase 'free will' has no agreed-upon meaning. And I don't mean that there are rival definitions of 'free will' in the way that there are rival definitions of 'life' or 'intelligence'. The case of 'free will' is much worse than that. Everyone agrees that dogs and spiders and paramecia and algae are living things, and that rocks and steam engines and neutron stars aren't. Everyone agrees that bus drivers and mathematicians and lawyers, however stupid some among them may be, exhibit "intelligence" in the sense the word has in the phrase 'The Search for Extraterrestrial Intelligence'. And everyone agrees that mice and giraffes don't. That is to say, there are perfectly clear cases of things that are "alive" and "intelligent" and there are perfectly clear cases of things that do not enjoy these distinctions, and disputes about the exact meanings of these two words are just that: disputes about the *exact* meanings they do – or should – have. But no one has any idea, any idea at all, what 'free will' means.

We may distinguish two classes of people who have no idea what 'free will' means (I mean, two classes of people among those who talk about "free will" – in the sense of engaging in discussions in which the phrase 'free will' plays some important role). I'll call these two classes of people "the scientists" and "the philosophers." (Of course, most scientists – and, for that matter, most philosophers, at least in their published work – manage to get through their careers with out mentioning free will at all.) While neither group has any idea what 'free will' means, this is true of the two groups in different ways. Scientists who discuss "free will" use the term without any attempt at a definition – or else they provide some useless piece of verbal hand-waving that they seem to regard as a definition. (In a couple of cases, they provide definitions that are clear enough but simply *bizarre*.) And that's also true of many philosophers. The people I'm calling "the philosophers," however, do provide reasonably precise and intelligible definitions of 'free will'; the trouble is, they don't all provide the same one. In fact, they provide wildly different ones. And then, to their shame, they go on to *argue* about who has the *right* one – or, as they tend to put it (again to their shame), they argue about "what free will is." And since the words 'free will' don't mean anything in particular, a dispute about "what free will is" is simply absurd. By way of analogy – if you can abide another analogy, so close on the heels of the last – one might imagine a rancorous dispute between some physicists (on the one hand) and some diplomatic historians (on the other) about what "force" is; the historians say that force is the application by a nation of military action to resolve a conflict that cannot be resolved by diplomatic means, and the physicists say that force is a vector: the net force acting on an object at an instant is the rate at which its momentum is changing at that instant. If you can imagine such a dispute, try your imagination further: imagine someone's describing it by saying that it shows that diplomatic historians and physicists "have different concepts of force."

Now you may want to tell me that what I'm saying is obviously wrong, since we do use the words 'free will' in everyday life, and we understand them as well as we understand any words we use. I reply that there is a sense in which it is true that we use the words 'free will' in everyday life (and use them in a perfectly intelligible way), but that this fact does not contradict what I have been saying. In everyday life – in the business of getting and spending, falling in love and raising families, voting in elections, consulting doctors and lawyers, and so on – when we use the words 'free will' it is almost always inside the phrase 'of one's own free will' (where 'one's' represents the position of a possessive pronoun). And there's no real dispute about what that means: if, for example, you're asked in a court of law whether you did something or other of your own free will, you're being asked whether you acted under duress – under any sort of coercion. (Were you, for example, threatened with certain untoward consequences if you did not act that way?) And everyone knows that people sometimes do things when they believe that their not doing them would have no untoward consequences. It is obvious that none of the disputes about "free will" that are so notable a part of the intellectual landscape, past and present, are about whether people ever do things without being coerced. Suppose someone asks,

How can we possibly have free will if God foresees everything we do?

Or, again, suppose someone asks,

How can we possibly have free will if a being with infinite power of calculation and a knowledge of the laws of mechanics and of the forces that particles exert on one another and a knowledge of the position and momentum of every particle of matter at any given time could calculate the position and momentum of every particle of matter at any other time?

Or, finally, suppose someone asks,

How can we possibly have free will if the Libet experiments show that physical conditions sufficient for our so-called voluntary bodily movements exist prior to our conscious decision to make those movements?

It is obvious that none of these three speakers is asking how it could be that our acts are uncoerced in the circumstances they have specified – for those circumstances don't even *seem* to be incompatible with the absence of coercion.

The ordinary meaning of the phrase 'free will' – or '*freier Wille*' or '*libre arbitre*' or what have you – simply does not explain its use in contexts like these. (Incidentally, everything I say about 'free will' will apply to any closely related words or phrases – such as 'freedom', 'free action', 'free choice' …)

"But what about your own work, van Inwagen?" the Interlocutor asks. "After all, you've written a book called *An Essay on Free Will*, and the words 'free will' occur frequently in many of your essays." Point well taken. And here is my answer to this well-taken point. In the seventies and early eighties, when I was doing most of my work on, well, free will, I was a naive product of my philosophical education. I was working within a philosophical tradition or paradigm or whatever you want to call it that I had been initiated into by my teachers Richard Taylor and Keith Lehrer – who had been in their turn initiated into it by *their* teacher, Roderick Chisholm – in which the words 'free will' had a very specific technical meaning. I simply supposed that the meaning 'free will' had in this tradition was the meaning with which all analytical philosophers used this phrase. And, oddly enough, this was, in those days, very close to the truth. Consider, for example, David Lewis's characteristically splendid paper "Are We Free to Break the Laws?"[1] – it was published in 1981 – a profound analysis and

---

[1] David Lewis, "Are We Free to Break the Laws?," *Philosophical Papers, Volume II* (Oxford University Press, 1987), pp. 291–298. The paper first appeared in *Theoria* 47 (1981): 113–121. Citations are from *Philosophical Papers II*. It is available online at www.andrewmbailey.com/dkl/Free_to_Break_the_Laws.pdf

criticism of the argument of my paper "The Incompatibility of Free Will and Determinism."[2] In his discussion of my argument, Lewis – without question or reservation or apology – used the words 'freedom' and 'free' (said of both an act and an agent) and the phrases 'free to', 'freely does', and 'act freely' in precisely the senses in which I had used them. But if it was ever the case that all or almost all analytical philosophers used these words and phrases (and the phrase 'free will') in the senses that I had supposed were their universally accepted senses, it is no longer. And it had not always been the case. If I were writing the book now, I would not identify its subject matter by reference to "free will" or by the use of any other phrase containing 'free' or 'freely' or 'freedom'.

I now turn to a statement of what seems to me to be a philosophical problem of great significance. This problem is intimately related to what *some* writers have meant by "the problem of free will." It is, in fact, closely modeled on a problem that I myself once proposed as a referent for 'the problem of free will'.[3] You will notice, however, that the adjective 'free' does not occur in my statement of the problem – nor does the noun 'freedom' or the adverb 'freely'. My statement of the problem will be, so to speak, 'free'-free. If I sometimes *mention* the f-word, generally in the course of quoting the writings or discussing the work of others, I shall at any rate not *use* it again. (And I will not use the noun 'will' again, either.) You will also notice that there will be no mention of the moral responsibility of agents for their actions in my statement of the problem. I shall indeed speak of certain states of affairs *being the fault of* various agents, or, alternatively, of those agents *being to blame for* those states of affairs, and fault and blame certainly bear some intimate relation to moral responsibility, whatever the words 'moral responsibility' may mean. I take it that a statement like

Jerry is (morally) responsible for his wife's unhappiness

can be nothing more than a philosopher's needlessly technical way of saying 'Jerry is to blame for his wife's unhappiness' or 'It's Jerry's fault that his wife is unhappy'. (I'm not much interested in what a philosopher might mean by saying that someone – Jerry, say – was "morally responsible" for some *good* state of affairs. I suppose it would be something like "Jerry gets the credit for it.") So I propose to speak of fault and blame instead of moral responsibility. And note that if one has decided to speak of fault and blame (as opposed to moral responsibility), and if that decision leads one to reflect on how judgments of fault and blame are framed, one will

[2] *Philosophical Studies* 27 (1975): 185–199.   [3] See Chapter 10 of the present volume.

realize that the objects of those judgments are states of affairs and not actions. That is to say, the things that can be said to be someone's fault (or for which someone can be blamed) are states of affairs that are in some way or other causally related to that person's actions (or inactions), not the actions themselves. The statement "It's Fred's fault she was elected; he cast the deciding vote" makes perfect sense. But what could a statement like "It's Fred's fault that he raised his hand when the chair said, 'All in favor?'" mean? In the unlikely event that someone did say that, I'd have to cast about for an interpretation; I suppose I'd decide that the speaker must have regarded some consequence of the hand-raising as a bad thing and had chosen a rather puzzling way of saying that that bad thing was Fred's fault.

Finally, I will not use the treacherous – because radically ambiguous – phrase 'could have done otherwise'.[4] (I will, in fact, not use 'could have' at all.)

So much for the words and phrases that will not occur in my statement of the philosophical problem I have promised you. Now the problem.

Four Theses

I begin by stating four theses. I am not affirming these theses; I am rather stating them so that I can refer to them in the statement of the problem. Two of the theses have familiar names: 'determinism' and 'indeterminism'. I'll state the other two first, however. These theses have no "standard" names, so I shall have to invent my own names for them. In order to ensure that these names are not tendentious, I will call them simply 'Thesis One' and 'Thesis Two'. Here is Thesis One:

> On at least some occasions when a human agent is trying to decide between two or more incompatible courses of action, that agent is able to perform each of them.[5]

---

[4] See Chapter 4 of the present volume.

[5] Alfred R. Mele has suggested to me that I should say something about the ambiguity of 'able to'. And this was a useful suggestion, for the phrase has many senses. In the text, I alluded to the "radical ambiguity" of 'could have done otherwise', and it is my firm opinion that 'was able to ...' is less *dangerously* ambiguous – less likely to slip from one of its senses to another in the course of a philosophical argument – than 'could have ...' Nevertheless, the phrase 'is able to' (whatever its tense; whatever the infinitive it governs) *is* ambiguous. For example: Grisha Sokolov has been stranded on a desert island; is he able to play the piano? In one sense, Yes, in another, No. Or: The loan officer at the First National Bank knows that she would lose her job if she approved your application for a loan; is she able to approve it? Of course: she has only to sign this piece of paper; and yet she tells you, "I'm afraid I'm unable to approve the loan you've applied for." Is she mistaken? Lying? I have discussed ambiguities of these and various other kinds that attend the phrase 'is able to' in section 1.4 (pp. 8–13) of *An Essay on Free Will* (Oxford: Clarendon Press, 1983). But the sense

If, for example, the following story is true, there has been one such "occasion." Early last January, Sally was admitted both to Julliard to study piano and to the Harvard Law School. At that time she wanted very much to become a concert pianist (for reasons of personal fulfillment). She also wanted very much to become a lawyer (in this case, her reasons were moral and political). She spent the month of January trying to decide whether to study piano at Julliard or law at Harvard (or, more immediately, whether to accept the Julliard offer and decline the Harvard offer or to accept the Harvard offer and decline the Julliard offer). At every moment during the course of these deliberations, she was able to do this:

> accept the Julliard offer and decline the Harvard offer,

and she was able to do this:

> accept the Harvard offer and decline the Julliard offer.

That is to say, at every moment in the course of her deliberations she had *both* those abilities. (Of course, having both the ability to do A and the ability to do B is not the same thing as having the ability to do both A and B.)

And here is Thesis Two (note that Thesis Two refers to Thesis One):

> If the bad consequences of a decision are ever the fault of the person who made the decision, then Thesis One is true.

An alternative formulation of Thesis Two:

> If anyone can rightly be blamed for the bad consequences of some decision he or she has made, then Thesis One is true.

---

of 'is able to' that figures in the argument of this paper may be specified by a simple device – by considering what is involved in being in a position to make a promise. Suppose that Alice asks Tim to give her a ride to work the next day (it's a serious matter; she'll lose her job if she counts on Tim for a ride and he fails to provide it). A necessary (and I think sufficient) condition for Tim's being in a position to promise to give Alice the requested ride is that he believe that he *is able to* give her a ride. And those italicized words have, in that context, the sense I mean 'is able to' to have in the argument in the text. Suppose Winifred and Sokolov are both castaways on the same island; able though he is to play the piano (in one sense of 'able'), he is not in a position to promise Winifred that he will play the piano that evening. And the loan officer is no doubt in a position to promise you to approve the loan ("no doubt": it might be that she is unsure whether it is psychologically possible for her to sign the piece of paper in those circumstances) – although of course it would be either foolish or dishonest of her to *make* such a promise. Having said all these things in response to Professor Mele's suggestion, I must concede that he will probably not regard what I have said as satisfactory. See his closely reasoned paper "Agents' Abilities," *Noûs* 37 (2003): 447–470. There are many points in this paper in which he and I are in fundamental disagreement, and an adequate discussion of them would require a separate paper. For a more extensive discussion of these points, see Chapter 14 of the present volume.

Consider, for example, the following story of a decision that has had bad consequences. One of Frank's students offered to have sexual intercourse with him if he would give her an A in his ethics course. Frank thought it over and decided to accept her offer – a decision that led to his losing his job, his family's being in serious financial need, and his wife's being driven nearly mad with rage and jealousy.

Now most people, on hearing this story, would say that all these bad things – Frank's losing his position, his family's severe need, his wife's near madness – were *his fault*. They would say that he was to *blame* for them. Let us suppose that most people are right: these things were Frank's fault and he can rightly be blamed for them.

Thesis Two implies that it follows from these bad consequences of Frank's decision being his fault that Thesis One is true. It follows, that is, that it is false that it is *never* the case that when a human agent is trying to decide between two or more incompatible courses of action, that agent is able to perform each of them.

We next state the other two theses, determinism and indeterminism, that will figure in the statement of the problem.

> *Determinism* is the thesis that the past and the laws of nature determine a unique future.

> *Indeterminism* is the thesis that the past and the laws of nature do not determine a unique future.

We now proceed to a description of the dialectical situation that, as it were, generates the problem.

The Dialectical Situation

There are seemingly unanswerable arguments that (if they are indeed unanswerable) demonstrate that Thesis One is incompatible with determinism. I allude, of course, to the various versions of the Consequence Argument, as it is known in the trade. And there are seemingly unanswerable arguments that (if indeed ...) demonstrate that Thesis One is incompatible with indeterminism (this part needs a little work, since indeterminism does not imply that a *given person's* actions are undetermined; the work can be done). I allude, of course, to the various versions of the *Mind* argument – named in honor of the august journal in which so many variants on it have appeared. But if Thesis One is incompatible with both determinism and indeterminism, then Thesis One is false – necessarily false, in fact.

There are, moreover, seemingly unanswerable arguments that, if they are correct, demonstrate the truth of Thesis Two. (But what about Frankfurt's refutation of the Principle of Alternative Possibilities? Has Frankfurt not shown that – or at any rate, can his arguments not easily be adapted to show that – a certain state of affairs can be someone's fault even if no one trying to decide whether to do A or to do B has ever been able to do A *and* able to do B? I can only say that I explained many years ago why Frankfurt's arguments do not show any such thing, and that if people have not been listening, it's *not my fault.*[6] But this is really beside the point. I am stating a problem, not discussing possible solutions to that problem. And I am not stating this problem with an eye towards presenting a solution of my own to it. Frankfurt's arguments are best looked at as a proposed solution to the problem I am in the process of stating. Similar remarks apply to supposed refutations of the Consequence Argument and the *Mind* Argument.)[7]

But if Thesis One is false and Thesis Two is true, then nothing is ever anyone's fault. And it is evident that it is simply *false* that nothing is ever anyone's fault. It must, therefore, be that at least one of the following four propositions is true:

> The seemingly unanswerable arguments for the incompatibility of Thesis One and determinism are in fact answerable; these arguments are fallacious

> The seemingly unanswerable arguments for the incompatibility of Thesis One and indeterminism are in fact answerable; these arguments are fallacious

> The seemingly unanswerable arguments for Thesis Two are in fact answerable; these arguments are fallacious

> It is *not* evident that it is simply false that nothing is ever anyone's fault; and not only is it not evident, it's not even *true*: the apparent self-evidence of that thesis is illusory.

The Statement of the Problem

My statement of the problem is in the form of three interrelated questions:

[6] See Section 5.3 of *An Essay on Free Will* (Oxford: Clarendon Press, 1983) and Chapters 1 and 6 of the present volume.

[7] This may be a difficult exercise, but do your best not to attend to the question whether the statements I make in the course of laying out this problem are true or false; what you should be attending to is the fact that, in making these statements, I never use certain words and phrases, to wit: 'free', 'freely', 'freedom', 'could have done otherwise', and 'moral responsibility'.

Which of these four propositions is true? If any of the first three
is true, what are the fallacies in the arguments to which those
propositions allude? If the fourth proposition is true, what is the
nature of the illusion that has made it seem self-evident to me and
many other philosophers (and, indeed, to the great mass of humanity)
that many things that have happened in the course of human history
are someone's fault?

For reasons that I hope I have made clear, I decline to call this problem
'the problem of free will'. It will, however, be convenient to have a name
for it. I will call it the Culpability Problem – with the understanding that
this name is a mere tag whose purpose is to facilitate reference – a proper
name, if you will. The fact that *culpa* is the Latin word for 'fault' or 'blame'
should be regarded as a mere *aide-mémoire*. (I introduce a name for the
problem only at this late point in the chapter with the specific intention of
underscoring the fact that I ascribe no significance to the name I have chosen. And if anyone does find some reason to dislike this name, if anyone
regards it as tendentious or in any other way objectionable, I'll simply call
it something else – 'the Three Questions Problem' or 'Peter's Problem' or
'Arthur'.)[8] Note that the only philosophical technical term that occurs in
the statement of the Culpability Problem is 'determinism' – 'indeterminism' being merely the contradictory of 'determinism'.

I have given up on the Culpability Problem. It's too hard for me. But my
purpose in this paper is not to solve it or even to examine proposed solutions to it. It's to show that much philosophical work whose announced
subject is "the problem of free will" is simply irrelevant to the Culpability
Problem – not addressed to that problem at all. (I don't deny that this
work may be valuable for other reasons. After all, it's no objection to the
discipline of social psychology that its investigations and theories are of no
relevance to the problems of astrophysics.)

I do not mean to imply that *all* work that is specifically addressed to "the
problem of free will" is irrelevant to the Culpability Problem. My own work
is a case in point. The subject matter of, e.g., "The Incompatibility of Free
Will and Determinism" and *An Essay on Free Will* is the Culpability Problem,
although not under that name. The work on "free will" that is irrelevant to the
Culpability Problem is that which involves what I shall call *verbal essentialism*.[9]

---

[8] Reporter: "What do you call that haircut?"; George Harrison: "Arthur."

[9] Well, much of it certainly does. Perhaps there is work on "free will" that is irrelevant to the Culpability
Problem that does not involve verbal essentialism. I'll say this, at any rate: If some philosophical book
or essay that purports to address "the problem of free will" does involve verbal essentialism (in the
manner described below in the text), that is *sufficient* for its irrelevance to the Culpability Problem.

A piece of philosophical writing exhibits verbal essentialism if there is some philosophical term of art (either a word or phrase invented by philosophers – like 'actualism' and 'nowness' – or a dictionary-entry word that is used by philosophers in a special technical sense, like 'proposition' and 'validity') such that the thesis presented in that text could not be stated *without using that word or phrase*. I have, for example, recently accused Karen Bennett of falling prey to verbal essentialism – you will have guessed that I regard verbal essentialism as a Bad Thing, something one can properly be said to fall prey to – in her paper "Proxy 'Actualism'."[10] In that paper, Bennett presented certain criticisms of Alvin Plantinga's so-called actualism (in his philosophy of modality). In the introductory paragraph of my critique of Bennett's criticisms of Plantinga, I wrote,

> My conclusion will be that [Bennett's] criticisms fail, owing to the fact that they depend on the historical accident that the customary designation for Plantinga's position is "actualism" – that if this position had been given a name that did not contain 'actual' or any word formed from 'actual', the criticisms of the position that are presented in "Proxy 'Actualism'" could not even be stated.[11]

The works I mean to call attention to are like that, *mutatis mutandis*: you could not rewrite them in such a way as to eliminate the phrase 'free will' and the words 'freedom' and 'freely' from them – there would simply be nothing left; a translation of these works into 'free'-free language is impossible. (That would not be the case with, for example, *An Essay on Free Will* – which is essentially an essay on the Culpability Problem; nothing in its substantive content hangs on my choice of 'free will' as a term of art.)

It is time to turn to examples. I begin with Dan Dennett's latest thoughts on free will, those contained in the chapter on that topic in his recent book *Intuition Pumps and Other Tools for Thinking*.[12] But lest you think that my accusation of verbal essentialism is directed only at those philosophers who, like Dennett, take what might be called a "deflationary" position on "free will," let me assure you that I will also consider examples of philosophers (conveniently cited by Dennett) who speak favorably of things like "ultimate moral responsibility" and "absolute free will" and agents who are

---

[10] *Philosophical Studies* (2006): 263–294.

[11] "'Who Sees Not that All the Dispute is About a Word?': Some Thoughts on Bennett's 'Proxy "Actualism"'," *Hungarian Philosophical Review* 3 (2012): 69–81.

[12] New York: W. W. Norton, 2013.

"perfectly free to do otherwise." Those philosophers and Dennett, in my view, occupy two sides of the same coin – the same verbally essentialist coin.

One of Dennett's targets in that chapter is those scientists who contend that science has shown that free will is an illusion. He says of these scientists that they

> have typically been making a rookie mistake: confusing the manifest image [Dennett regards free will, like color and solidity, as a denizen of Sellars's "manifest image"] with what we might call the folk ideology of the manifest image. The folk ideology of color is, let's face it, bonkers; color just isn't what most people think it is, but that doesn't mean that the manifest world doesn't really have any colors; it means that colors – real colors – are quite different from what most folks think they are ... Similarly, free will isn't what some of the folk ideology of the manifest image proclaims it to be, a sort of magical isolation from causation.[13] ... I wholeheartedly agree with the scientific chorus that that sort of free will is an illusion, but that doesn't mean that free will is an illusion in any morally important sense. It's as real as colors ...

and, moreover, that they

> are making the mistake people make when they say that nothing is ever [colored],[14] not really. They are using an unreconstructed popular concept of free will, when they should be adjusting it first, the way they do with color ...

Now I am not convinced that science has shown us that color just isn't what most folks think it is. This is not because I think that what science has revealed about color shows us that color *is* what most folks think it is. It's rather that I'm not sure whether "most folks" think color is *anything*, bonkers or not – whether they have any particular views on what color is. I'm not sure whether there is a "folk ideology" of color. If there is such an ideology – I would ask – what is its propositional content? Dennett mentions the indisputable facts that electromagnetic radiation in the 390–700 nm range is not made of little colored things and that atoms have no colors, but I can't tell from the context of that remark whether he meant it to imply that the denials of these two propositions

---

[13] A very misleading phrase. See note 17.
[14] Dennett actually has 'solid' and not 'colored' here. I have substituted 'colored' for 'solid' in order that my scattered quotation should express a unified thought. Dennett had earlier used solidity and color as parallel examples of things that are *real* and yet not much like what we thought they were before science revealed their true nature.

were contained in the folk ideology of color. If he did, he would certainly be wrong, since this folk ideology of color, if it ever existed, must have antedated our knowledge of atoms in the modern chemical sense of the word and of electromagnetic radiation. (I don't deny that ordinary people often have *false general beliefs* about colors. My father, an art school graduate and a fine painter who knew all about how to mix pigments to obtain a desired color, firmly believed that green was a mixture of blue and yellow. And that's a general belief about color – at any rate, a general belief about three particular colors – that is just *not true*. There is a perfectly good sense in which orange is a mixture of red and yellow and purple is a mixture of red and blue, but green is not a mixture of blue and yellow in that sense or any other. My father's false belief couldn't be said to be bonkers, for it was based on a very extensive range of experience: there had been hundreds of occasions on which he had mixed a blue pigment and a yellow pigment, and every single time the resulting mixture was a green pigment. But that experience, extensive though it was, was deceptive: it was due to certain accidental physical properties of commercially available blue and yellow pigments. In my view, this wasn't a case of my father's having a false *theory* about color; he simply had a general belief about three colors – blue, yellow, and green – that was wrong.)

But let's suppose that Dennett is right: there *is* a folk ideology of color and scientific investigation shows that it's (almost?) entirely wrong; but we should not infer from the (almost) entire wrongness of the folk ideology that color is an illusion; color is real, but it's not what everyone used to think it was and most people still think it is.

But what, then, does it mean to say that color is real and why does Dennett think it is real in that sense? Dennett does not define 'real' and he does not exactly argue for the reality (in any sense) of color; what he says in defense of the reality of color is more along the lines of an appeal to common sense: "[Color] is not an illusion in the sense that matters: nobody thinks Sony is lying when it says that its color televisions really show the world of color or that Sherwin-Williams should be sued for fraud for selling us many different colors in the form of paint." I would myself offer something a little more theoretical in support of the reality of color – although what I would offer is certainly consistent with the point Dennett means those two examples to illustrate. I would say something along the following lines. Most of the statements we make in ordinary life that contain color-words ('The car that left the scene of the accident was a dark green Lexus'; 'Titanium dioxide is the most common white pigment'; 'The predominant color of Picasso's *La Vie* (1903, Cleveland Museum of Art) is blue') are *true*;[15] and if the sentences 'Color is an illusion' or 'Color is not real' mean anything at all (they certainly don't wear their meanings on their sleeves), they must mean something that implies that most of those statements are false.[16] But that's by the way.

Dennett's thesis, then, is that free will is like color (as he represents color). It's real enough, but it can't be what the folk ideology of free will says it is: there's no place for *that* in the scientific image (the image that stands in opposition to the manifest image). The "unreconstructed popular concept of free will" is inconsistent with what science has discovered about the nature of the beings (us) to whom it is supposed to apply.

I said a moment ago (in effect) that I was not sure whether there was any such thing as the *unreconstructed popular* concept of color – although I was willing to grant for the sake of argument that there was such a thing. However that may be, there is certainly such a thing as the concept of color. That is to say, there are such things as the meaning of the word 'colored' and the meanings of the words 'green' and 'brown' and 'mauve'. (Let nominalists understand that statement as they will: there has to be some sense in which it's true.) Here is why the case of the concept of color (even assuming that Dennett is right when he says that there is an unreconstructed popular concept of color and that nothing in the real world corresponds to it) is not parallel to the case of the concept of free will: there is no such thing as the concept of free will. And, of course, if there is no such thing as the concept of free will, there is no such thing as the unreconstructed popular concept of free will.

But I suppose I'm getting ahead of myself. Before I say anything more about the non-existence of the concept of free will, I should tell you what Dennett thinks the unreconstructed popular concept of free will is, and I should tell you what the scientific-image-friendly concept with which he means to replace it is. As to the former, he says (towards the end of the chapter):

> People care deeply about having free will, but they also seem to have misguided ideas about what free will is or could be (like their misguided ideas about color ...). Our decisions are not little miracles in the brain that violate the physics and chemistry that account for the rest of our bodies' processes, even if many folk think this must be what happens if our decisions

---

[15] Not all of them: people do make mistakes and tell lies.

[16] Not *all* of them. I suppose that 'The car that left the scene of the accident was *not* a dark green Lexus' could be true even if color were an illusion – but comparatively few of our real-life "color statements" are negative statements.

are to be truly free.[17] We can't conclude from this, however, that then we don't have free will, because free will in this bonkers sense is not the only concept of free will.

And he says this about the latter, early on in the chapter:

> The intuition pumps in this [chapter] are designed to wean you from [the folk ideology of] free will and get you to see a better concept, the concept of real free will, practical free will, the phenomenon in the manifest image that matters.

Unfortunately, Dennett never gets round to spelling out the precise content of either concept (maybe he can't be blamed for that in the case of the folk concept, supposing it to exist; maybe it *has* no precise content). He does tell us quite a bit about both concepts, however. For example, he quotes statements by various philosophers that are intended to illustrate the folk concept – such as this passage from Jerry Fodor's review of his book *Freedom Evolves*: "One wants to be what tradition has it that Eve was when she bit the apple. Perfectly free to do otherwise. So perfectly free, in fact, that even God couldn't tell which way she'd jump." And this passage, from Galen Strawson's review of the same book: "[Dennett] doesn't establish the kind of absolute free will and moral responsibility that most people want to believe in."

Dennett supposes that this "being perfectly free to do otherwise," this "absolute free will" are not philosophers' inventions but are components of the folk ideology of free will – that Fodor and Strawson have correctly (if rather sketchily) identified as what "one wants to be" and what "most people want to believe in." He seems to come down rather hard on Fodor's "even God couldn't tell which way she'd jump" idea – that is, he seems to suppose that absolute unpredictability, unpredictability even in principle, of (some?) human behavior is the essential core of the folk-ideological concept of absolute free will. And I think that he sees Strawson's well-known contention that to enjoy absolute free will one would have to be the sole and ultimate cause of one's actions as also being essential to the folk ideology. He wonders why anyone would want to be an in-principle-unpredictable

---

[17] Whatever "many folk" may think, this is not what philosophers who profess and call themselves 'incompatibilists' think. According to incompatibilism, if an agent decides to do A rather than B, then – if the agent was *able* to choose to do B – *neither* a decision to do A *nor* a decision to do B would have violated the laws of physics and chemistry. In Dennett's defense however, it should be noted that he elsewhere mentions an unnamed philosopher who "has frankly announced that a free choice is a 'little miracle'." As President-for-Life of the World Society of Incompatibilists, it is my unpleasant duty to inform that philosopher that if he or she is a member of the Society, he or she is hereby excommunicated for having made this heretical statement. (The heresy in question is sometimes called 'contra-causal freedom'.)

agent and the ultimate cause of one's actions, and why anyone would be attracted to the belief that we were agents of this sort. And well he might. I would too – at least if I were sure I understood what Fodor and Strawson were talking about. In my view, however, Fodor and Strawson are simply reproducing some ideas invented by philosophers and not reporting what "the man on the Clapham omnibus" wants to be or believes in the existence of. Or, better, not *ideas* invented by philosophers but words and phrases invented by philosophers – "a certain special, happy style of blinkering philosophical English."

In any case, he wants to replace the folk-ideological concept of free will with something else: a better candidate for the office "free will," something that is consistent with our present scientific knowledge, something that isn't bonkers, something that it would actually make sense to want to have oneself and to want to believe that one's fellow human agents had.

My only problem with this project is that there's no such office. Whatever the replacement he may have in mind may be, there's nothing for it to replace.

It's not entirely clear what the proposed otiose replacement is, although it certainly has these features:

> It involves a certain amount of unpredictability in practice, but not unpredictability in principle. (Like it or not, life occasionally requires us to compete with other inhabitants of the world, and organisms that are deficient in unpredictability tend not to pass their genes along to their descendants – think of a gazelle that always swerves left when it's being pursued by a lion. But since we're unlikely ever to be in competition with the Laplacian Reckoner, unpredictability in principle would enjoy no advantage over unpredictability in practice – unpredictability by the organisms with which we are actually in competition.)
>
> It involves certain kinds of "freedom from" – from coercion, from physical bondage, from illusion and hallucination …
>
> It is compatible with determinism.

Well, I'm happy to give Dennett the words 'free will'. Let him spell out the details of the concept he intends this phrase to denote as he wants. Possibly he would spell them out the way Liam Clegg does in his paper "Protean Free Will,"[18] a paper for which Dennett (in the chapter of *Intuition Pumps* that I've been examining) has expressed great admiration:

---

[18] Available on line at http://authors.library.caltech.edu/29887/

Consider an agent who faces an environment which includes sophisticated other agents with interests contrary to hers. Call the agent Mary, and call the other agents predators. One good way for Mary to avoid exploitation by predators, exploitation which may include death, is to engage in *protean behavior* ... That is, she may behave somewhat erratically so as to be unpredictable. As documented by Miller ... the protean strategy offers many clear advantages over the alternatives of concealment of intentions and active deception. While most notions of 'reason' prescribe a single optimal action in any situation, Mary's behavior must sometimes be locally suboptimal for the sake of unpredictability.

   Such local sub-optimality means that at some times t, there are multiple courses of action A_t available which are tied for the strategic optimum. Call the set of such courses of action Mary's strategy S_t. For the purpose of this discussion, no generality is lost in assuming that the optimal probability distribution over S_t is uniform, so that each A_t is equiprobable. Furthermore, while S_t is defined from a bird's-eye view, we may assume that Mary has evolved some reasonably good mechanism for approximating it in the real world. The elements of S_t depend on Mary's preferences, of course, but the strategic optimality of each course of action also includes the risk of exploitation by predators. This, in turn, depends on Mary's past actions and predators' resulting guesses about her next action. If Mary and her predators both use optimal mixed strategies ... each A_t should be equally optimal for Mary, and there should be no advantage to a representative predator of predicting that Mary will perform any given $A_t \in S_t$ rather than any other $A'_t \in S_t$. However, if a predator knew *or reasonably suspected* at time r, $r < t$, that Mary were going to perform A^*_t at time t, the predator could exploit this knowledge. A^*_t would therefore no longer be optimal for Mary, and would therefore not be an element of S_t when time t arrived. Call the ability to select an A^*_t from S_t and perform it such that A^*_t is still in S_t at time t 'protean free will' (PFW).

In any case, there's *some* concept Dennett wants to replace the supposed folk-ideological concept of free will with – and it seems to be *something* like Clegg's "protean free will." Let's suppose we have Dennett's concept before us. Whatever precisely it may be, I am, as I have said, happy to let him call it 'free will' – or for that matter, 'the one possible non-bonkers concept of free will' if that's what he wants to call it. And then let him and Fodor and Strawson – those guys on the other side of the verbally essentialist coin – fight over the words 'free will'. Let them fight over who's got free will *right* or over what free will *really is* (or really would be if it existed). Let Fodor and Strawson accuse Dennett of purveying (in Kant's words) *ein elender Behelf* – "a miserable substitute" for *true* free will.[19] Let Dennett reply that a belief in the phenomenon Fodor and Strawson want the words 'free will' to designate would be as bonkers as a belief in levitation (a comparison he uses at one point).

I think such a debate would be about an entirely meaningless issue. It's certainly about a meaningless issue if, as I suppose, there is no concept that goes by the name 'free will'. But suppose I'm wrong about that. It's at least not clear that the debate would be a meaningful one even in that case. Suppose that most people *do* believe or want to believe that what they do is in principle unpredictable and *do* believe that they are the sole causes of what they do; why would what Dennett offers as a substitute for what they want or believe in or want to believe in *be* a substitute – even a disappointing substitute – for *those* things? After all, supposing that what Fodor and Strawson say people want is non-existent, still, not just any existent thing counts as substitute for just any non-existent thing, if I may so express myself. ("I want to find the fountain of youth." "Oh, you're like Ponce De León. You want to find the unreconstructed, folk-ideological fountain of youth. That's bonkers. There's no such thing. But, fortunately, the fountain of youth exists; it just isn't what the folk think it is. It isn't a fountain that, when one drinks from it, one is magically restored to youth and then never ages. It's a regimen of diet and exercise that can extend the vigor of one's youth by as much as fifteen years.") The only thing that ties Dennett's substitute to the Fodor–Strawson original – whether that original is a philosopher's invention or an actual folk ideology – is that he calls it 'free will'. In his defense, I'll concede that he has as much right to call some concept of his devising 'free will' as Fodor has to say that a person whose behavior is not predictable even in principle is 'perfectly free to do otherwise' or as Strawson has to call the ability to create one's character *ex nihilo* 'absolute free will'. Since none of these terms – 'free will', 'perfectly free to do otherwise', 'absolute free will' – means anything in particular, they're available to be put to any use a writer wants to put them to.

But – again – suppose I'm wrong. Suppose the idea of a debate about "what free will really is" (or about "what free will should be" or about "the proper meaning of 'free will'") makes sense. Suppose, even, that such a debate would be a philosophically important debate. That meaningful and philosophically important debate, I contend, would be irrelevant to the Culpability Problem.

---

[19] *Critique of Practical Reason*, I, III, "Critical Examination of the Analytic of Pure Practical Reason." The famous phrase "a wretched *subterfuge*" is Abbott's mistranslation of this description.

CHAPTER 14

Ability

1 The "Classical" Understanding of the Problem of Free Will and Determinism

From the mid 1960s to the mid 1980s the problem of free will and determinism seemed to be a very straightforward problem. Easy to solve (and solved) according to some, difficult to solve (and unsolved) according to others, difficult to say anything new about according to most, but straightforward in the sense that everyone (that is, every analytical philosopher) knew what the problem *was* – everyone agreed, within very broad limits, about how the problem should be stated or posed. This is not to say that a philosopher writing in (say) 1968 would have set out the problem in exactly the same way as a philosopher writing in (say) 1982. Harry Frankfurt's essay "Alternate Possibilities and Moral Responsibility"[1] was responsible for an important change in the way the problem was formulated (a point to which I shall return).[2] But at any given moment in the classical era – as I shall call the mid 1960s to the mid 1980s – everyone accepted formulations of the problem that were more or less the same.

How did philosophers of the classical era see the problem of free will and determinism?

It was agreed, first of all, that the phrase 'free will' was not to be taken seriously. Everyone conceded that 'free will' had become something like a proper name: like 'the Holy Roman Empire', it was what something had once been called for what had then seemed to be a good reason and what it was now called for no better reason than that it had been called by that name for a very long time.

And everyone during the classical era agreed that this thing inappropriately called 'free will' was a sort of *n*-way power with respect to the future. Agents often deliberate between two or more courses of action, and to

---

[1] *Journal of Philosophy* 66 (1969): 829–839.
[2] "Difficult to say anything new about" – but not impossible, for in that essay Frankfurt *did*.

ascribe *free will* to a rational agent (everyone agreed) was to say that at least sometimes when that agent is trying to decide what to do, it is within that agent's power to do *each* of the things he or she is trying to decide between. Not *all*, mind you, but *each*. Suppose, for example, that Sally, who is in a sticky legal situation, is trying to decide whether to lie about where she had been on the night of March 11th or to tell the truth or to remain stubbornly silent. It may well be within her power to lie *and* within her power to tell the truth *and* within her power to remain silent – but it obviously could not be within her power to do all three (or any two) of those things. (Of course, she might vacillate – she might lie and then change her mind and tell the truth, for example. But in the end she is going to have to choose exactly one of the three options facing her.)

The concept of a course of action being "within one's power," it was universally held in the classical era, was to be explained by an appeal to one of the several meanings of the ordinary, everyday word 'can'. To say that Sally has the three-way power to lie or to tell the truth or to remain silent, for example, is to say simply that if she were to say these three things to herself

> I can lie
>
> I can tell the truth
>
> I can remain silent

all three statements would be true. And these statements (a philosopher of the classical era would have said) are verbal variants on

> I am able to lie
>
> I am able to tell the truth
>
> I am able to remain silent

and

> It is within my power to lie
>
> It is within my power to tell the truth
>
> It is within my power to remain silent.

It was generally recognized in the classical era that the concept expressed in such contexts as this by 'can' and 'able' and 'within one's power', while certainly in some sense a modal concept, the concept of a certain sort of possibility, is not the modal concept that goes by the name 'possibility' in modal logic. For no sense of 'it is possible that' are the statements

Sally can lie

Sally is able to lie

It is within Sally's power to lie

equivalent to the statement

It is possible that Sally will lie.[3]

They are not, for example, equivalent to 'It is physically possible that Sally will lie'. *Some* philosophers of the classical era, it is true, would have accepted the thesis that (e.g.) 'Sally is able to lie *only if* it is physically possible that Sally will lie' was a conceptual truth, but no one would have accepted the thesis that 'Sally is able to lie *if* it is physically possible that Sally will lie' was a conceptual truth.[4] The reason was simple enough. If it is physically possible that Sally will lie, that means that there is a "physically possible future of the world" (a future of the world permitted by the present state of the world and the laws of physics) in which Sally lies.[5] But from the fact that such a possible future exists, it does not follow that it is within Sally's power to ensure or see to it or bring it about that that possible future will be a future that actually comes to pass.

Suppose, for example, that I am locked in a room and that I am unable to unlock the door. I wish to leave the room – and I *shall* leave the room if something unlocks the door. As matters stand, however, the only "something" that can unlock the door is an indeterministic mechanism built into the door: there are physically possible futures in which the mechanism unlocks the door and there are physically possible futures in which it does not – and in some of those in which it does, I leave the room. But in the actual future[6] it is not going to unlock the door. (And therefore, I am unable to leave the room.)

[3] But some would have held that these three statements were equivalent to 'It is possible *for* Sally *to* lie'.

[4] Carl Ginet might be thought to be an exception to this generalization, but this would not be right. Ginet would certainly accept (and would have accepted during the classical period) the counterexample that I shall present in the next paragraph of the text.

[5] At any rate, that is one of the things one might mean by 'physical possibility'. There is another and weaker sense of the phrase: something is physically possible if it occurs in some world in which the laws are the same as those of the actual world (whether the past is the same as that of the actual world or not). That weaker sense obviously does not imply ability, for in the weaker sense it is physically possible that I, who am at the moment in North America, now be in Sydney.

[6] This argument presupposes that statements "about the future" all have truth-values – and that there is therefore exactly one "actual" future, to wit, the future such that a statement about the future is true if and only if it is true in or according to that future. In the example we are considering, it is undetermined by the laws of physics and the present state of things whether the mechanism will unlock the door; but the mechanism *will not* in fact unlock the door: that in fact *is* how the indeterministic evolution of the world is going to proceed.

Suppose we say that a sentential operator M is a *possibility operator* if, for some set of possible worlds S and any declarative sentence p, the sentence $\ulcorner M(p) \urcorner$ is true just in the case that p is true in some member of S.[7] Anthony Kenny showed (by an argument much more abstract than the argument of the preceding paragraph) that for no possibility operator M are sentences of the forms

X can ϕ

X is able to ϕ

It is within X's power to ϕ

equivalent to the corresponding sentence of the form

M $(X \, \phi s)$.[8]

The essential point of Kenny's argument may be stated as follows. Suppose that if one ϕs then one may or may not χ and one may or may not ψ, but if one ϕs one must either χ or ψ. (For example, if one throws a dart that hits the dartboard, one may or may not throw a dart that hits the left-hand side of the board and one may or may not throw a dart that hits the right-hand side of the board, but, if one throws a dart that hits the dartboard, one must either throw a dart that hits the left-hand side of the board or throw a dart that hits the right-hand side of the board. If one arrives in Chicago, one may or may not arrive on a Tuesday and one may or may not arrive on some other day of the week, but one must either arrive on a Tuesday or arrive on some other day of the week.)

Now for any possibility operator M, and any sentences p and q,

$\ulcorner M(p \vee q) \rightarrow .M(p) \vee M(q) \urcorner$

is a valid sentence (owing to the fact that, if S is the relevant set of worlds, $\ulcorner M(p) \urcorner$ is true if p is true in some member of S; and if a disjunction is true in some member of a set of worlds, one at least of its disjuncts must be true in that world). And, therefore, for no possibility operator M is

X is able to ϕ

equivalent to

$M(X\phi s)$.

---

[7] S might be, for example, the set of all worlds; or it might be the set of worlds in which the laws of nature are the same as those of the actual world; or it might be the set of worlds in which the laws *and* the present state of things are the same as they are in the actual world.

[8] See Anthony Kenny, *Will, Freedom and Power* (Oxford: Blackwell, 1975), pp. 137–140.

For if this equivalence holds, and if ϕ, χ and ψ are related in the way set out above, '$X\,\phi$s' is true in the same worlds as '$X\,\chi$s $\vee$ $X\,\psi$s' and

X is able to χ $\vee$ X is able to ψ

is therefore strictly implied by

X is able to ϕ.

But the latter may be true and the former false. For it may be true that I am able to throw a dart that will hit the dartboard but false that I am able to throw a dart that will hit the right-hand side of the board *and* false that I am able to throw a dart that will hit the left-hand side of the board. I may be able to ensure that I arrive in Chicago but have no choice whatever as to what day of the week I arrive in Chicago – the airlines being what they are these days.[9]

Finally, a word about the phrase (much used in the classical era) 'could have done otherwise'. Let us again consider Sally, who is deliberating about whether to lie or to tell the truth or to remain silent. Suppose that she *can* lie and *can* tell the truth and *can* remain silent. Suppose further that time passes and what she *does* do is lie. Then, since 'could have' is the present perfect tense of the modal auxiliary verb 'can', we can say in retrospect that she *could have* told the truth and *could have* lied and *could have* remained silent[10] – which, of course implies that she *could have done otherwise*. 'X could have done otherwise' is nothing more than a retrospective, present perfect "version" of the present tense statement 'X must choose among two

---

[9] Suppose someone insists that if I do something, then, before I did it, I must have been *able* to do it – that if, for example, I (who have no skill at manipulating playing cards) draw a card at random from a standard deck and it is the four of clubs, then it follows that, before I drew the card, I could have said truly, "I am able to draw the four of clubs." As we shall see in Section 2, there are many senses of 'able'. Let us say that any of them that has this feature is "minimal" (a more or less arbitrarily chosen word). Any sense of 'able' in which only a card-sharp or a stage magician is "able" to draw the four of clubs (apparently at random) from a standard deck is therefore not minimal. I will concede for the sake of avoiding a merely verbal dispute that there are minimal senses of 'able' (although I doubt whether there are). But I insist that if there are minimal senses of 'able', there are certainly non-minimal senses as well. All occurrences of 'able' in the remainder of Section 1 should be understood as having some non-minimal sense. (Similar remarks apply to 'can'.)

[10] The simple past tense of 'can' is 'could' ('I could speak French when I was a child, but I can't now'). But the simple past 'could' seems to be capable of expressing only the "skill" or "general" sense of ability (see note 29 below). It is therefore necessary to use the present perfect 'could have' to make statements about our past abilities with respect to, as one might say, particular occasions. Thus a woman might say 'I could have told my husband the truth yesterday' but not 'I could tell my husband the truth yesterday'. ('I could tell my husband the truth yesterday' would probably strike most speakers as a very puzzling statement, although one might make some sort of sense of it by assimilating it to such "longer-term" general-ability statements as 'I could tell my husband the truth about all my activities before I joined the CIA, but now I have to lie to him about practically everything'.)

or more alternatives and can (i.e., is able to, has it within her power to) choose each of them'.

If we call the preceding paragraphs – from 'The concept of a course of action …' to this point – "an account of ability," that account of ability is (more or less) the account of ability that was presented in the course Philosophy 301, The Problem of Free Will and Determinism (or whatever it might have been called), in the classical era.[11]

I have mentioned Frankfurt's remarkable essay "Alternate Possibilities and Moral Responsibility." The classical era may usefully be regarded as falling into two parts – before and after the publication of that essay. Or perhaps it would be more accurate to say "before and after the philosophers began to appreciate the power and significance of the arguments of 'Alternate Possibilities and Moral Responsibility'," and this did not happen till at least four or five years after the essay was published.

In the pre-Frankfurt years, so to call the part of the classical era before the arguments of Frankfurt's essay began to be widely known and appreciated, philosophers' understanding of "the problem of free will and determinism" can be described as follows. (So, at any rate, I contend.)

Suppose, first, that we say that 'determinism' is the thesis that the laws of nature (or the laws of physics) and the state of the physical world at any given moment determine the state of the physical world at any other moment. Then, in the pre-Frankfurt years, work on "the problem of free will and determinism" consisted almost entirely in attempts to provide and defend answers to the following two questions:[12]

Question 1 Is the existence of free will compatible with determinism?

Question 2 Is the existence of free will compatible with indeterminism?[13]

(Indeterminism, of course, is simply the logical contradictory of determinism.) These two questions were held to be important because everyone[14] accepted the thesis

Moral responsibility requires the existence of free will.

[11] Kenny's argument was published too late to have been known throughout the entire classical era, and was never as well known as it should have been. But the proposition that was to be its conclusion was well known and generally accepted throughout the classical era, owing to the influence of Richard Taylor's classic essay "I Can" (*Philosophical Review* 69 [1960]: 78–89).

[12] Or, perhaps, of these two questions and such further questions as might be raised by the various answers proposed for them.

[13] Actually, Question 2 needs to be expressed more carefully than this. The necessary qualifications will be stated later in the text (and in note 16).

[14] When I say that "everyone" – the universe of discourse being analytical philosophers who wrote on the problem of free will – accepted a certain view, I mean 'practically everyone' or 'more or less everyone' or 'pretty much everyone'.

Everyone agreed that moral responsibility was an important thing. And, therefore, everyone agreed that free will was an important thing – if only because it was necessary for moral responsibility. (Some philosophers thought that free will might be important for other reasons as well – it was, for example, commonly held to be a valuable thing in itself.) And, of course, if free will exists, it must be compatible with determinism or (inclusive) compatible with indeterminism. But there were important arguments for both the incompatibility of free will and determinism and the incompatibility of free will and indeterminism – hence, the importance of the two questions. It was commonly, if tacitly, held that if these two questions could be given satisfactory answers, the problem of free will and determinism could be regarded as solved – for those questions constituted the hard or philosophically interesting part of the problem of free will and determinism.

Most philosophers of the pre-Frankfurt years accepted one of the following two positions:

1. Determinism is true;[15] free will exists.

2. The existence of free will is incompatible with the truth of determinism; free will exists.

Position (1) was called (following William James) "soft determinism." Soft determinism immediately implies *compatibilism*, the thesis that the existence of free will is compatible with the truth of determinism. Position (2) was called 'libertarianism'. Its first component, the thesis that the existence of free will is incompatible with the truth of determinism, was called *incompatibilism*. Debates about the problem of free will and determinism in the pre-Frankfurt era, therefore, were largely debates about whether free will was compatible with determinism. (The soft-determinist defenders of compatibilism were far more numerous than the libertarian defenders of incompatibilism.) That is to say, the single most frequently addressed question in discussions of the free will problem was Question 1. But Question 2 was not neglected, owing to the fact that many, perhaps most, soft determinists accepted the following thesis (which is not logically implied by soft determinism):

The existence of free will is not only compatible with the truth of determinism, it is *incompatible* with the truth of *indeterminism* – or if

---

[15] Said with some sort of bow to quantum mechanics, something along the lines of 'Quantum mechanics apparently implies that some aspects of the "micro-world" are indeterministic; nevertheless, the "macro-world" is deterministic – or as nearly deterministic as makes no matter'.

not with the truth of indeterminism "in general," at any rate with the truth of the thesis that *human acts* are undetermined.[16] For if human acts were undetermined, they would be "bolts from the blue," events that were not grounded in the beliefs, values, or character of their agents, mere *intrusions* into the lives of their agents.

The position that James had called 'hard determinism',

> Determinism is true; the existence of free will is incompatible with its truth,

a position held by most of the eighteenth- and nineteenth-century materialists, was held by hardly any analytical philosopher in the pre-Frankfurt years, for in those years everyone believed in free will. One had to, you see, because free will was required for moral responsibility – and, in particular, moral responsibility for wrong-doing.[17] Obviously (everyone supposed) some people have behaved in ways in which they ought not to have behaved, and one cannot be responsible for having done something one ought not to have done if one was not able to do otherwise. If you had asked a philosopher of the pre-Frankfurt years why this was so, the response would have been something along the following lines.

Suppose you tell someone who has done X that he ought not to have done X. That statement presupposes that he ought to have done something other than X (let "doing nothing at all" be a special case of "doing something other than X"). You are in effect saying to him, "You ought to have done something other than X." But if you tell someone that he ought to have done something, by the very fact of making that assertion you

---

[16] This statement contains the qualification of Question 1 that was promised in note 13 above. Suppose that Sally, who had been deliberating between lying and telling the truth, lied at $t1$. Her lying at $t1$ was an undetermined act just in the case that there was a moment $t0$ shortly before $t1$ such that in some of the futures allowed by the state of the world at $t0$ and the laws of nature she lied *and* in some of those futures she did not lie. A definition of 'undetermined act' would be a generalization of this statement about Sally's act of lying. Let us say that an act that is not undetermined is determined. It follows from determinism that all human acts are determined. It does not follow from indeterminism that any human act is undetermined. If, for example, there is one particle in intergalactic space whose behavior is undetermined (and whose behavior affects nothing else) and if the behavior of everything else is fully determined, indeterminism is true and all human acts are determined.

[17] The eighteenth- and nineteenth-century materialists would have agreed. But those extremely "tough-minded" philosophers (to borrow another of James's pithy phrases) were willing to say that moral responsibility was as much an illusion as the free will whose existence it presupposed. (Some of them at any rate: those who, like Holbach, were incompatibilists – not, of course, a word any of them would have known. But some would have followed their seventeenth-century predecessor Thomas Hobbes and embraced compatibilism.)

commit yourself to accepting the thesis that he was *able* to do that thing. You can't, for example, tell King Canute that he ought to have halted the advance of the tides (and mean it) unless you believe that he was able to halt the advance of the tides. Hard determinism therefore implies that if a statement of the form 'You ought not to have done X' is addressed to someone who has done X, that statement *must* be false – or at least embody a false presupposition. Without committing ourselves to any controversial position on the semantics of moral judgments, we can say that hard determinism implies that any such statement will be a defective statement for the same reason (whatever it may be) as 'You ought to have halted the advance of the tides' would be a defective statement if it were addressed to Canute.

Enter Frankfurt. This is "the Principle of Alternate Possibilities"[18] – PAP for short – that was the topic of the essay of that name:

> A person is morally responsible for what he has done only if he could have done otherwise.

Frankfurt presented convincing counterexamples to this principle. The essential idea behind these counterexamples is the idea of an "offstage counterfactual manipulator." This is a typical "Frankfurt counterexample" to PAP:

Poisson has put arsenic in Dyer's tea, and this action caused her very soon afterwards to die of massive organ failure. Add to this case whatever *you* think is needed to make 'Poisson is morally responsible[19] for having poisoned Dyer' true: Poisson acted with the intention of causing her death, Poisson was sane and not of subnormal intelligence, Poisson was able to refrain from poisoning her, Poisson's poisoning her tea was undetermined … whatever you like. So: Poisson poisoned Dyer and is responsible for having done so. Now expand the story of Poisson and Dyer as follows. There was an evil genius, Manipula, who, for reasons of her own, in the days leading up to Dyer's death very much wanted Poisson to act on his intention to poison Dyer. Manipula could see, by looking into Poisson's soul, that he firmly intended to poison Dyer. And she could see that he had laid his plans very carefully. She therefore thought it almost certain that he would carry them out – almost certain, but not *perfectly* certain. Manipula was not the sort of evil genius to leave anything to chance, and she accordingly devised the following "contingency plan."

---

[18] Of course it ought to have been called 'the Principle of Alternative Possibilities'.
[19] In the sequel, 'responsible' will mean 'morally responsible'.

If Poisson shows any sign of wavering in his present determination to poison Dyer, I will – by direct manipulation of his brain – suppress all doubts and reservations, moral or practical, that may have crept into his mind, fill his mind with a sense of absolute certainly that his plan will succeed and that he will never be so much as suspected of poisoning Dyer. And, finally, I will strengthen his desire to poison her till it is irresistible.

Manipula had the power to do all the things she had (conditionally) decided to do. (And she was of such a nature that – unlike a human being – when she had made up her mind to do something, it was impossible for her to change it.) In the event, however, Poisson never "wavered": he went ahead and poisoned Dyer just as he had resolved to do, and Manipula's contingency plan never had to be put into effect. That is to say, she did *nothing* that affected Poisson in any way. It is evident, therefore, that what we have *added* to the "original" story of Poisson and Dyer does not remove, diminish, undermine, militate against – choose what verb you will – Poisson's responsibility for having poisoned Dyer. Therefore, since Poisson was responsible for that act in the original story, he was responsible for it in the expanded story, the story incorporating Manipula and her contingency plan.[20] But note: in the expanded story, Poisson was unable *not* to poison Dyer. Manipula's forming her contingency plan had the effect of "pinching off" all those possible futures (if there were any) that commenced shortly before the moment at which (in actuality) he poisoned Dyer and in which he changed his mind and did not poison her. *All* the possible futures that confronted Poisson as he slipped the packet of arsenic trioxide into his waistcoat pocket and set out for Dyer's house on that fatal day were futures in which he was going to poison her. Manipula's purely counterfactual plan, her *unacted-on* plan, has rendered non-existent all the "alternative possibilities" (alternative, that is, to his poisoning Dyer) that existed in the original story. PAP is therefore false – or at any rate, not a conceptual truth.

Most philosophers working on the problem of free will and determinism found Frankfurt's arguments convincing.[21] As a result, a third "general position" as regards the problem of free will and determinism emerged (in addition to soft determinism and libertarianism). Following John Martin

---

[20] Of course, if the contingency plan *had* been put into effect, then no doubt Poisson *would not* have been responsible for poisoning Dyer. But it wasn't. And he was.

[21] For my own views on the import of "Frankfurt counterexamples," see Chapters 1 and 6 of the present volume.

Fischer, we may call it "semi-compatibilism" (although this phrase was coined well after the close of the classical era):[22]

> Free will may or may not be compatible with determinism, but moral responsibility is compatible with determinism.

Semi-compatibilists, understandably, lost interest in Question 1 (and in Question 2). For, as I said above, 'These two questions had been held to be important because everyone had accepted the thesis "Moral responsibility requires the existence of free will."' And this was precisely the thesis that semi-compatibilists did not accept.

This must suffice for an account of how the problem of free will and determinism was understood in "the classical era." It is far from being a complete account. (I have, for example, said almost nothing about contemporary discussions of Question 2 – and nothing at all about the debates about "agent causation" that arose out of that discussion.) In my view, the classical era had it right.[23] The problem was correctly formulated, and philosophers discussing the problem of free will and determinism should focus on three questions: Question 1, Question 2, and

Do Frankfurt's arguments indeed show that ascriptions of moral responsibility do not imply the existence of free will (do not imply that human beings are sometimes able to act otherwise than they in fact do)?

Now suppose that, like me, you think that the answer to the third question is No: whatever the value of, whatever the import of, Frankfurt's arguments, whatever may be right about them, nevertheless, if no one is ever been able to do otherwise than he or she in fact does, then no one is ever morally responsible for anything.[24] Then you will believe, as I do, that Question 1 and Question 2 are the central questions of the problem of free will and determinism, and you will think that the problem of free will and determinism is an important problem (if for no other reason) because moral responsibility is important and moral responsibility is impossible if the ability to act otherwise than one does is incompatible both with one's actions being determined and with one's actions being undetermined.

---

[22] John Martin Fischer, *The Metaphysics of Free Will* (Oxford: Blackwell, 1994), p. 178ff.

[23] I am extremely skeptical about the value of almost all work done on the problem of free will and determinism (or the problem of moral responsibility and determinism) after the classical era. For my reasons for this, see Chapters 10 and 13 of the present volume.

[24] See Chapter 1 of the present volume. For a condensed version of the argument of this chapter, see Peter van Inwagen, *An Essay on Free Will* (Oxford: Clarendon Press, 1983), pp. 162–182.

And, if you believe these things, you will be interested in the question: What is ability – what is the meaning of the word 'able' in phrases like 'able to lie and able to tell the truth' and 'able to act otherwise' as these phrases were used in the discussions of the problem of free will and determinism in the classical era?

2 The Concept of Ability in the Classical Understanding of the Problem of Free Will and Determinism

The meaning of the word 'able' as this word was used in discussions of the problem of free will and determinism in the classical era, is, I believe, best explained in connection with a certain way in which promises can be defective. To specify the "way" I have in mind, it will be necessary to contrast it with other ways in which a promise can be defective. (And I hope that these examples will also make it clear what I mean by describing certain promises as 'defective'.) We shall examine some imaginary cases in which a promise is made and that promise is in one way or another defective.

A defective promise – case 1 Mr. Rich, the prominent industrialist, is about to have a delicate brain operation. His wife presses Dr. Sturgeon, the Chief of Surgery at St Luke's Hospital, to promise her that the operation will be performed by the most skilled brain surgeon on his staff. Sturgeon promises her this, knowing that if he did not make that promise she would have her husband's surgery performed in another hospital. And that is exactly what Sturgeon does not want, for he is both a man of the left and a strict utilitarian and believes that the overall utility of the world would be increased significantly if Rich, a powerful reactionary, were to die on the operating table. He further believes that if Rich remains at St Luke's, he can render that outcome reasonably probable – for he plans to assign the operation to a brain surgeon called Sharp whom he privately, and with some justification, believes to be a blundering incompetent. "If anyone can kill the bastard, it's old 'Notso' Sharp," Sturgeon says to himself.

This is a very straightforward kind of defective promise: Sturgeon promised to do something that he did not intend to do – that is, that he intended not to do. Following Mele, we may say such a promise is defective because it fails to be *sincere*[25] – or, more briefly, is *insincere*. And I suppose we also could say that a promise is insincere if the person making the promise has

---

[25] Alfred R. Mele, "Agents' Abilities," *Noûs* 37 (2003): 447–470; see p. 453.

not yet decided whether to keep it. (Suppose Sturgeon is *toying* with the idea of assigning the operation to the incompetent Sharp, but has certain moral qualms about doing this even when the patient is someone like Rich – he's not a strict utilitarian as he was in the first version of the story. He promises to assign his best surgeon to the operation in order to keep the "have Sharp do it" option open while he ponders the morality of the matter further.)

A defective promise – case 2 Mr. Rich is about to have an operation. The operation has very little chance of success – it's all but hopeless. His wife presses Dr. Sturgeon (who is to perform the operation) to assure her that the operation will be a success. (She doesn't know that the operation has little chance of success, for our story takes place in the bad old days when doctors never told patients bad news and never told the patients' relatives bad news till the patients were actually dead. Thank God those days are past!) Sturgeon has nothing against Mr. Rich, and would save him if he could, but he knows he can't[26] – or at any rate that his chances of doing so are very, very slim. Now Sturgeon hates emotional scenes, so he says, "I promise you, Mrs. Rich, that the operation will be a success and your husband will be completely restored to health."[27] (He intends to leave the hospital after the operation by a route that will enable him to avoid an encounter with Mr. Rich's widow.)

This is not a case of someone's promising to do something he or she intends not to do. And it's not a case of promising to do something that – one is aware – one might *later* decide not to do. It might well be called an insincere promise – there's certainly something insincere about it – but it's not insincere in the sense in which the promise in case 1 (or the variant on case 1 mentioned in the parenthesis) was insincere. Nevertheless, it seems clear that something is seriously wrong with Sturgeon's promise. It is, as I have said, defective. What is its defect? Does it lie simply in the fact that the person making the promise is unable to keep it (or almost certainly unable to keep it)? No, for there are non-defective promises that the person making the promise is unable to keep. For example:

> **A non-defective promise** Mr. Rich is about to have an operation. The operation has very little chance of success – it's all but

---

[26] Perhaps he "can" (and hence doesn't know that he can't) in what we earlier called a minimal sense of ability (see note 9 above). If, in the event, a medical "miracle" occurs and the operation is a success, then if Sturgeon had said beforehand, "I can [minimal sense] save the patient," he would have spoken truly.

[27] Or, if you like, "I promise to restore your husband to health." One might dispute about whether a "promise that" [something will be the case] is a promise in the same sense as the sense in which a "promise to" [do something] is a promise.

hopeless. But this fact has to do with some peculiarities of Mr. Rich's brain that are unknown to Dr. Sturgeon (who is to perform the operation); Sturgeon is certain (and given the evidence he has, justifiably certain) that the operation will be a simple and straightforward one, as simple and straightforward as the most routine appendectomy. Mrs. Rich presses Sturgeon to assure her that the operation will be a success. Sturgeon says, "I promise you, Mrs. Rich, that the operation will be a success and your husband will be completely restored to health." (He is shocked and chagrined when bizarre and unforeseeable complications – a consequence of Mr. Rich's aforementioned physiological peculiarities – transpire during the operation, and Mr. Rich dies on the table.)

Contrast that case with the following case:

A defective promise – case 3 Mr. Rich is about to have an operation. The operation will be a simple and straightforward one, as simple and straightforward as the most routine appendectomy – and, for that reason, it will be a success. But these facts are unknown to Dr. Sturgeon (who is to perform the operation); owing to some bizarre flaw in the evidence available to him, Sturgeon is certain (and given the evidence he has, justifiably certain) that the operation has very little chance of success – that it's all but hopeless. Mrs. Rich presses Sturgeon to assure her that the operation will be a success. Sturgeon has nothing against Mr. Rich, and would prefer to save him, but he firmly believes that he (almost certainly) can't. Now Sturgeon hates emotional scenes, so he says, "I promise you, Mrs. Rich, that the operation will be a success and your husband will be completely restored to health." (He intends to leave the hospital after the operation by a route that will enable him to avoid an encounter with Mrs. Rich – who, he now believes, will then almost certainly be Mr. Rich's widow.)

It seems evident from consideration of case 2 and "A non-defective promise" and case 3, that, although the first of the following two principles is false, the second is true.

(F)   A promise is necessarily defective if the person making the promise is unable to keep it

(T)   A promise is necessarily defective if the person making the promise believes that he or she is unable to keep it.

Now let us consider a variant on case 2:

> **A defective promise – case 2′** Mr. Rich is about to have a delicate brain operation. His wife presses Dr. Sturgeon (who is to perform the operation) to assure her that the operation will be a success. Sturgeon knows that the operation may succeed and that it may fail. The CT scans are inconclusive. Everything is going to depend on what Sturgeon finds when Mr. Rich's skull has been opened and he can visually examine the condition of things in the cranial pia mater. Sturgeon hopes the operation will be a success, but he really has no idea what its outcome will be. Now Sturgeon hates to be in the presence of anyone who is in emotional distress, so he says, "I promise you, Mrs. Rich, that the operation will be a success and your husband will be completely restored to health." (He intends to leave the hospital after the operation by a route that will enable him to avoid an encounter with Mrs. Rich if the operation is a failure.)

It seems clear that case 2′ is case of a defective promise. But it would not be right to say that, when Sturgeon makes the promise, he *believes* that he is unable to do what he is promising to do (that is, unable to bring about the outcome he has promised will occur). Rather, he doesn't know whether he is able to do what he is promising to do. That the promise in case 2′ is defective can be accounted for by the following principle:

(T′)   A promise is necessarily defective if the person making the promise does not believe that (does not have the belief that) he or she is able to keep it.

But in what sense of 'able'? Let us continue to assume (I by no means endorse this position) that there are minimal senses of 'able'. Sturgeon certainly does not have the belief that he is able to keep his promise in even a minimal sense. (He may well believe that *for all he knows* he is able to keep the promise in a minimal sense – after all, for all he knows, the operation will be a success. But to have that belief is not to have the belief that he *is* able [minimal sense] to keep the promise.) There are other senses of 'able',[28] but it would seem that there is *no* sense of 'able' in which Sturgeon believes that he is able to keep his promise. (Although it may well be that for *every* sense of 'able' x he believes that *for all he knows* he is able to keep the promise in sense x.)

[28] For a discussion of the many senses of 'able', see *An Essay on Free Will*, section 1.4 (pp. 8–13). Mele's "Agents' Abilities" presents a rival account – much more fine-grained than mine – of the senses of 'able'. I do not accept all the distinctions that Mele makes.

Let us say that if *x* and *y* are two senses of 'able', *x* is *stronger* than *y* just in the case that (i) if someone is able to do something in sense *x*, then, necessarily, that person is able to do that thing in sense *y*, and (ii) it is possible for there to be someone who is able to do something in sense *y* but is not able to do that thing in sense *x*. For example, a sense of 'able' in which only people with the skills of a card-sharp are able to deal themselves a flush in hearts is stronger than any minimal sense; there's a sense of 'able' in which Grigory Sokolov is able to play Chopin's Prelude in E Minor even when no piano is available to him,[29] and there's a stronger sense in which he's able to play that difficult work only when he has access to a piano; a loan officer who is "able" to approve the loan I've applied for because all she has to do to approve it is to sign her name on a certain piece of paper is not lying when she tells me she's unable to approve it: she has a stronger sense of 'able' in mind.[30] (Say that two senses of 'able', *x* and *y*, are *equivalent* if, necessarily, someone is able to do something in sense *x* if and only if that person is able to do that thing in sense *y*. Note that if two senses of 'able' are non-equivalent, it does not follow from our definition that one of them is stronger than the other.)

I will now define a certain sense of 'able' that, perhaps tendentiously, I will call the Relevant Sense.

> Someone is able in the Relevant Sense (is "able$_{RS}$") to do something just in the case that that person is able to do that thing in the *strongest* sense of 'able' such that, if one made a promise and did not believe that (did not have the belief that) one was able (in that sense) to keep that promise, that promise would be defective.[31]

I have said that in case 2′ "it would seem that there is *no* sense of 'able' in which Sturgeon believes that he is able to keep the promise." I contend that, for every sense of 'able' *x* in which Sturgeon fails to have the belief

---

[29] This is the "'skill" or "general" sense of ability' sense alluded to in note 10 above.

[30] One sense of '*x* is able to *Y*' is 'If *x* were to choose to *Y*, *x* would *Y*'. Call this the Conditional Sense. Let '**ABLE**' represent any sense of 'able' other than the Conditional Sense itself. 'If *x* were to choose to *Y*, *x* would *Y* – and *x* is **ABLE** to choose to *Y*' is a sense of 'able' that is stronger than the Conditional Sense. This is an adaptation of a point that frequently surfaced in discussions of compatibilism in the classical era, for in those days compatibilists often maintained that to have free will was simply to be able to have done otherwise than one did in the Conditional Sense of 'able'.

[31] But suppose that there are two senses of 'able' that satisfy the condition *vis-à-vis* promising laid down in the definition, that no stronger sense of 'able' does, and that neither sense is stronger than the other (perhaps the two senses are equivalent; or perhaps they are simply "incommensurable": they are not equivalent but neither is stronger than the other)? I'll cross that bridge if I come to it – that is, if someone presents a plausible example of two such senses. The definition presupposes that there *is* a strongest sense of 'able' that satisfies "the condition *vis-à-vis* promising." If there is no such sense, the definition will, of course, have to be revised.

that he is able in sense x to keep the promise he has made, one is the strongest: *if* Sturgeon is able to keep his promise in *that* sense, he is able to keep it in every other sense of 'able'. And – surely? – if that sense exists (and if minimal senses of 'able' exist) that sense is stronger than any minimal sense. The definition I have given may be described as a *functional specification* of the "Relevant Sense." It is natural to ask whether an *analytic definition* of the Relevant Sense can be given. (As 'undefeated justified true belief' was once supposed by some to be an analytic definition of 'knowledge'.) I am sorry to have to say that I have none to offer. (It is certainly implausible to suppose that such an analytic definition of 'able$_{RS}$' could be devised if there were no other, better understood sense of 'able' that could figure in its *definiens*.)

Now one might wonder whether I can *justifiably* believe that I am able (in *any* sense of 'able') to keep a promise I have made.[32] Suppose, for example, you ask me to give you a ride to work tomorrow morning and I say that I will (thereby promising to give you a ride to work tomorrow morning). How do I know that I am able to do that? (Perhaps it would be more natural to frame the question in the future tense: 'How do I know that I *shall* be able to do that?" If this is so, it strikes me as a mere matter of idiom. Since the modal auxiliary 'can' has no future tense, one is forced to use the present in the parallel case: "How do I know that I *can* do that?"; there doesn't seem to be anything logically odd about that question.) After all, my car (which has started right up every day for the last three years) *might* not start tomorrow. My hitherto reliable alarm clock *might* fail me. Despite my apparent good health, I *might* die in my sleep. Literally hundreds of things whose non-occurrence I'm not in a position to predict with certainty *might* happen to prevent me from keeping my promise to you. And if I don't know whether I am (or shall be) able to give you a ride to work tomorrow, this is presumably because I am not justified in believing that I am able to give you a ride to work tomorrow. The same point, of course, applies to any conceivable promise. And if I can't justifiably believe that I am able (in any sense) to do a certain thing, and I know that I can't justifiably believe that I have that ability, then I ought *not* to believe that I am able to do that thing. And, therefore, if there is a sense of 'able' such that a promise I make at t is defective if at t I do not have the belief that I am able to keep it, then either I ought never to make any promises (because doing so would require me to have a belief that is not justified) or all promises are defective (which would also seem to imply that I ought never to make any promises). But

---

[32] See section 4 (pp. 457–461) of Mele's "Agents' Abilities."

it's evident that (in normal circumstances) I violate none of my epistemic duties in promising to give you a ride to work tomorrow and it's evident that not all promises are defective.

This sort of argument, it seems to me, sets a very high standard for a belief's being justified. Anyone who adheres to this standard ought to say that I should never make any statement about the future. I should never say things like, "I'll see you in Chicago on Thursday" or "At our next meeting we'll discuss Thomson's Trolley Problem." (And of course I should never believe what others say when they make similar assertions about the future.) Well, I'll leave it to the epistemologists to sort this one out. Whatever the correct epistemological account of justified beliefs about the future (beliefs about the future of the simplest, most straightforward sort) should be, it is not very plausible to suppose that it will imply that my beliefs about what I'm going to be doing the day after tomorrow are necessarily unjustified.

So we have the Relevant Sense of ability. And what I am contending it is relevant to is, of course, the classical understanding of the problem of free will and determinism. That is to say, the classical understanding of the problem turns on a definition of free will that is something very much like the following:

> x has free will $=_{df}$ x must sometimes choose among two or more alternative courses of action and, on at least some of these occasions, x is able$_{RS}$ to choose each of them.

I say that the classical understanding of the problem of free will and determinism turns on this definition of free will (or on one very much like it) because it is in this sense of 'free will' that an agent's having free will is, or seems to be, incompatible with the agent's actions being *un*determined.[33] Disputes about the compatibility of free will and universal causal determinism in the classical era were much less sensitive to the precise meaning of 'able' that figured in the disputants' definitions of free will – for the usual arguments for the incompatibility of free will and determinism required only that free will be understood as involving a sense of 'able' (a) such that in that sense no agent is able

– to render false a necessary truth
– to render false a true proposition about the past
– to render false a law of nature,

---

[33] See Chapter 11 in this volume.

and (b) such that all instances of the following schema are valid if the word 'able' therein is understood in that sense:

> p and no one is or ever has been able to render the proposition that p false

> (If p then q) and no one is or ever has been able to render the proposition that if p then q false

> *hence,*

> q and no one is or ever has been able to render the proposition that q false.[34]

There seems to be *no* sense of 'able' such that any agent, natural or supernatural, is able to render false a necessary truth or a true proposition about the past (*pace* Descartes). And, whatever may be the case with supernatural agents, there seems to be no sense of 'able' in which a human being is able to render a law of nature false. (But see Lewis's "Are We Free to Break the Laws?"[35] for an argument that purports to show that this is not the case – or, more exactly, for the conclusion that if a sense of 'able' satisfies all the incompatibilists' *other* requirements, then, in *that* sense human beings are able to render laws of nature false.)[36]

[34] In "A Reconsideration of an Argument against Compatibilism," *Philosophical Topics* 24 (1996): 113–122, Thomas McKay and David Johnson have shown (in effect) that there are counterexamples to the validity of this schema (they are not particularly sensitive to the sense of 'able' involved) if 'x is unable to render p false' is understood as 'there is nothing x is able to do such that, if x did that thing, then p would be false'. These counterexamples, however, are not counterexamples to the validity of the schema if that phrase is understood as 'there is nothing x is able to do such that, if x did that thing, then p *might* be false'. The validity of the schema, understood in the latter sense, is sufficient for the apparent soundness of "the usual arguments for the incompatibility of free will and determinism."

[35] In David Lewis, *Philosophical Papers, Volume II* (Oxford University Press, 1987), pp. 291–298. The paper first appeared in *Theoria* 47 (1981): 113–121, and is available on line at www.andrewmbailey. com/dkl/Free_to_Break_the_Laws.pdf

[36] Interestingly enough, this argument had nothing to do with Lewis's Humean conception of laws. I have often heard philosophers express puzzlement that Lewis did not appeal to the Humean conception of laws in his defense of compatibilism. *I* am not puzzled. That a true universal proposition represents a "mere exceptionless regularity" hardly implies that human beings are able to render it false. Suppose, for example, that the most massive star is 260 times as massive as our sun. 'All stars have masses less than or equal to 260 solar masses' may well be a mere exceptionless regularity: it may well be that there could have been a star with a mass of 261 solar masses. But, no doubt, no human being is (or ever has been or ever will be) able to cause a counterinstance to this regularity to exist. I would suppose that, even if Lewis's Humean conception of laws is right, it would be an even more difficult task to produce a counterinstance to a *law* – in the sense in which it would be "even more difficult" for me to lift an object weighing 10,000 kilograms than it would be for me to lift an object weighing 1,000 kilograms. I am certain that these considerations are more or less those that Lewis would have adduced if he had been asked why he did not appeal to his Humean conception of laws in his defense of compatibilism.

There are obviously senses of 'able' such that if 'able' is understood in any of those senses (taking into account the point mentioned in note 34) the schema is invalid. The "skill" or "general" sense of ability and the Conditional Sense are two. Now obviously the "skill" sense of ability is not a sense that has much relevance to the problem of free will and determinism: no one would say that Grigory Sokolov now has a free choice about whether to play Chopin's Prelude in E Minor if he is now a castaway on a pianoless desert island, not even if he has the piece in his fingers, as pianists say. Nor would anyone say that it was "within his power" to play the Prelude in E Minor. There seem, moreover, to be arguments that prove decisively that free will requires more than the ability to do otherwise than one does in the Conditional Sense.[37]

Matters are otherwise when we turn to the question whether an undetermined act can be free. Suppose that our friend Alice is once more deliberating about whether to lie, to tell the truth, or to remain stubbornly silent. Suppose she is able$_{RS}$ to do each of these things. Then, if free will is incompatible with determinism, it is undetermined whether she will lie, will tell the truth, or will remain silent. It is a consequence of libertarianism that it is undermined which of these things she will do *and* that she is able$_{RS}$ to do each of them. For an examination of the difficulties that face this consequence of libertarianism, the reader is directed to Chapter 11 of this volume.

---

[37] It may be that in the closest possible worlds in which one chooses to X, one has abilities one does not have in actuality – and it may be that the ability to X is one of them. To take an extreme case, suppose that Alice is in a medically induced coma – but has no "long-term" motor disabilities. It may be that in all the possible worlds closest to the actual world in which she chooses to walk, she is conscious in the normal sort of way and, as an immediate consequence of her choice to walk, she walks. According to the usual understanding of counterfactual conditionals, it is true – true in the actual world – that if she chose to walk she would. But obviously she is unable to walk: she does not have a free choice about whether to walk; it is not within her power to walk. One could hardly imagine a clearer case of someone unable to walk than a person in a medically induced coma.

Index

If a chapter is devoted largely or entirely to a topic or a philosopher, and if that fact is evident from the title of the chapter, the index entry for that topic (that philosopher) does not contain references to the pages on which that chapter appears. For example, the entry 'Dennett, Daniel' contains no references to pages 49–59 – Chapter 4 – owing to the fact that the title of Chapter 4 is "Critical Study of Dennett's *Elbow Room*." For the same reason, the entry 'moral responsibility' contains no references to the pages on which Chapter 6, "Moral Responsibility, Determinism, and the Ability to Do Otherwise" appears.

There is no entry 'free will', although there is an entry '"free will"' and an entry 'free-will thesis, the'. There is no entry 'determinism' and no entry 'indeterminism'; there is instead a single entry 'determinism and indeterminism'. Similarly, there is a single entry 'compatibilism and incompatibilism'. In the entries 'free-will thesis, the', 'determinism and indeterminsim', 'compatibilism and incompatibilism', and 'moral responsibility', the pages cited have been kept to a carefully selected minimum, since there the book contains a very large number of passing references to those topics. Similar remarks apply to the entry 'Van Inwagen, Peter'. The names of editors of volumes in which cited essays appeared are not (as such) included in the index.